CW01183298

'YOUR FATHERS THE GHOSTS'

'YOUR FATHERS THE GHOSTS'

BUFFALO BILL'S WILD WEST IN SCOTLAND

TOM F. CUNNINGHAM

BLACK & WHITE PUBLISHING

First published 2007
by Black & White Publishing Ltd
99 Giles Street, Edinburgh EH6 6BZ

1 3 5 7 9 10 8 6 4 2   07 08 09 10 11

ISBN 13: 978 1 84502 117 7
ISBN 10: 1 84502 117 7

Copyright © Tom F. Cunningham 2007

The right of Tom F. Cunningham to be identified as the author of this work has been asserted by him in accordance with the Copyright, Designs and Patents Act 1988.

All rights reserved.
No part of this publication may be reproduced, stored in a retrieval system, or transmitted in any form, or by any means, electronic, mechanical, photocopying, recording or otherwise, without permission in writing from the publisher.

A CIP catalogue record for this book is available from the British Library.

Typeset by Ellipsis Books Limited, Glasgow
Printed and bound by MPG Books Ltd, Bodmin

The author has made every reasonable effort to contact all copyright holders. Any errors that may have occurred are inadvertent and anyone who, for any reason, has not been contacted is invited to write to the publishers so that a full acknowledgement may be made in subsequent editions of this work.

ACKNOWLEDGEMENTS

Pride of place has to go to Barry Dubber. A book on Buffalo Bill's Scottish venues was Barry's idea and, for a while, we were going to be co-authors. Sadly, it wasn't to be. Barry has been inspirational in locating some key images, by the exclusion of which this book would be very much diminished. Thomas Lindsay's 1904 Glasgow photographs were Barry's discovery and it was when he showed them to me that my imagination was first ignited. It's just too bad that the best one of the lot is unaccounted for.

In my first book, *The Diamond's Ace – Scotland and the Native Americans*, I acknowledged a select inner cadre of friends who had assisted me almost to the point of entitlement to co-author status. Of those five, it gives me no pleasure whatsoever to report that Rich Gralewski and Stanley Hunter have since gone to join the ghosts. However, Stanley's posthumous influence is all over this book. Richard Green is still very much with us and I sincerely hope that he will continue to aid and inspire me for years to come with his vast insight into Lakota culture.

I am greatly indebted to John Whelan of Liverpool for donating his extensive collection of newspaper cuttings. This single factor above all else has given me a far broader perspective on the English and Welsh venues on the 1891 tour than I could possibly have attained otherwise.

An indispensable role has been played over many years by the staff of the Buffalo Bill Historical Center at Cody, Wyoming, particularly Lynn Houze, the ever-enthusiastic curatorial assistant of the Buffalo Bill Museum. Grateful thanks are also due to the Garlow Memorial Fund for financial assistance.

Shelley Howe at the Buffalo Bill Grave and Museum in Golden, Colorado, has also proved to be an inestimable long-term contact.

To Iain MacLennan, by far the longest-standing friend listed here, gratitude is due for proofreading.

Thanks to Ray Foord for general encouragement and to the many, too numerous to mention specifically, who have contributed a myriad fragments to the overall picture.

A special thank you goes to Ronnie Scott for his role as facilitator.

But my biggest debt of gratitude is to Lucy and other members of my family for their continued understanding and support.

Scottish National Buffalo Bill Archive

While the present volume represents no more than a passing phase within a much larger context, the Scottish National Buffalo Bill Archive is intended as a permanent and ongoing project. The archive's objectives are to identify, recover and preserve as much as possible of the historical record relating to the visits of Buffalo Bill's Wild West to Scotland.

Anyone minded to extend my existing collection of photographs, documents and other materials, or to whom I can offer some assistance, is very welcome to contact me via the e-mail link at:

http://www.tnais.com/bbis/

This book is affectionately dedicated to the memory of
Thomas Paton Cunningham,
my uncle.

CONTENTS

	INTRODUCTION	xi
1	BUFFALO BILL'S WILD WEST COMES TO GLASGOW	1
2	HORSEMEN APPROACHING	14
3	FROM PINE RIDGE TO WHITEHILL	27
4	'VEXATIOUS DELAYS'	40
5	THE THEATRE OF WAR	54
6	INDIANS!	67
7	'THE WAVES OF SUCCESS ROLL ON'	80
8	NEW YEAR, 1892	95
9	INTERPRETERS AND MISSIONARIES	107
10	MEXICAN JOE, RUNNING WOLF AND THE NEW OLYMPIA	119
11	NEW DEPARTURES	132
12	PARTING SHOTS	145
13	THE INTERVENING YEARS	157
14	GRAND ENTRY, 1902–04	169
15	BUFFALO BILL'S SHOW, 1904	179
16	GALASHIELS AND THE INDIANS	192

17	INTO THE WEST OF SCOTLAND	205
18	EDINBURGH, FALKIRK AND FIFE	216
19	FORFARSHIRE AND ANGUS	231
20	THE NORTH-EAST	245
21	THE HIGHLANDS	258
22	PERTH, STIRLING AND THE BIRTH OF CINEMA	271
23	RENFREWSHIRE	282
24	AYRSHIRE	291
25	GALLOWAY, DUMFRIES AND THE GREAT TRAIN HOLD-UP	302
26	FALSE TRAILS	315
	BIBLIOGRAPHY	329
	INDEX	343

INTRODUCTION

I bring you word from your fathers the ghosts that they are now marching to join you, led by the Messiah who came once to live on earth with the white men, but was cast out and killed by them. I have seen the wonders of the spirit-land, and have talked with the ghosts. I traveled far and am sent back with a message to tell you to make ready for the coming of the Messiah and return of the ghosts in the spring.

Matò Wanachtàka (Kicking Bear), 1890[1]

Let me take you back to the beginning of an intensely personal journey.

Around 1969 – when I was twelve years old – something happened to me which, with the benefit of hindsight, was distinctly strange. I was in a car being driven down Duke Street, in the East End of Glasgow. I have no idea why we were there at all as this was a part of the city that my family never (otherwise) had reason to visit. The only other person I can positively recall being there was my late mother but, as she never learned to drive, I can only conclude that others were present too. My father and sister recall no more of the occasion than I do. None of the others who might have been there remains alive to offer clarification.

The only circumstance that makes that day memorable at all is that, during our eastward progression, my mother pointed suddenly and deliberately up a side street – Whitehill Street – in the direction of an imposing red sandstone building and announced, 'That's where I went to school!'

It was a grey winter's day and I have to confess that I gave an involuntary shudder. The charms of Dennistoun, particularly under such conditions, are more prospective than immediate. I didn't fancy going to school there at all nor, for that matter, did I particularly desire any kind of connection with the area. In short, as is so often the case during one's formative years, I had no suspicion of the vital significance which the association would assume for me, twenty-odd years further down the line.

Of course, my mother left out the best part of the story. If only she had told me that around eighty years previously, then still well within the living memory of some of the oldest inhabitants and by virtue of an odd twist in the historical continuum, the patch of waste ground lying just a little further beyond had been the abode of the legendary Buffalo Bill Cody, companies of cowboys and Mexicans and, best of all, a band of genuine Sioux Indians, there's no telling what impression this revelation would have made upon me.

Dennistoun Village

Fast-forwarding more than three decades, I had a letter published in *The Herald*, on the 4th of July 2003. On one of several pilgrimages to the former site of Buffalo Bill's 1891–92 winter season, I had become aware of a new housing development – 'Dennistoun Village' – which was under construction there. I argued that any new streets should be named after characters in the entourage or that, at the very least, some attempt should be made to commemorate the location's extraordinary past.

My reasoning obviously struck a chord with someone at Regency Homes for, on Friday, 17 November 2006, I was among those invited to attend the official unveiling of a statue and commemorative plaque. It was as vile a November day as can be imagined but the rain slackened off and that universally recognised sign of divine favour renewed – a rainbow – appeared for just long enough to permit the ritual to proceed in relative comfort.

The plaque's full inscription reads:

Colonel William F Cody
(Buffalo Bill)

Buffalo Bill brought his Wild West Show to Dennistoun, Glasgow in October 1891 and it opened on the 16th of November and closed on the 27th of February 1892.

The show played at the East End Exhibition Building off Duke Street as part of the great East End Industrial Exhibition set up to raise funds for the People's Palace.

He recruited several famous people to perform in his show including Annie Oakley, Kicking Bear, Short Bull, John Shangrau, Johnny Baker, Claude Lorraine Daly and George C Crager.

Presented to the people of Dennistoun by Regency Homes and unveiled by Mr Paul Martin MSP on 17 November 2006

Although I diplomatically made no reference to it when interviewed for both *Scotland Today* and *Reporting Scotland*, these statements are not wholly accurate. Buffalo Bill's Wild West was *not* a part of the East End Industrial Exhibition. That attraction had taken place the previous winter and the whole of the buildings in which it was given were specially renovated in the autumn of 1891 to accommodate Buffalo Bill's show.

Note also that John Shangrau and George C. Crager were *interpreters*, rather than performers.

The PR man for Regency Homes had asked me to nominate those

whom I thought should be honoured and the names listed here are in accordance with my advice. However, it's a pity that I wasn't asked in advance for my thoughts on the intended wording!

As regards the statue, the tribute to Lobey Dosser in Woodlands Road is the parallel that seemed to be on everyone's lips. (When did Buffalo Bill ever ride a bucking bronco?) Even its location is a bit suspect. The place where its stands wasn't part of the Wild West at all – it was the playground of the Whitehill School next door. Maybe they should have played safe and put up a statue to my mother instead.

Buffalo Bill was a man with an extraordinary capacity for generating myths, on both sides of the Atlantic, and this regrettable tendency shows no signs of abating, ninety years after his death. New misconceptions are still being generated and even set in cement, faster than I can lay them to rest!

Notes

1 James McLaughlin, *My Friend the Indian*, p. 185

1

BUFFALO BILL'S WILD WEST COMES TO GLASGOW

DRAMATIS PERSONAE

It was Monday, 26 October 1891, in the Scottish city of Glasgow, an afternoon, to all intents and purposes, like any other during the late Victorian age and one which, as far as the broad brushstrokes of history are concerned, has passed unnoticed.

Arriving from London, by means of the Midland Railway, three specially chartered trains steamed into Bellgrove Station in the city's East End, conveying the advance guard of what the *Glasgow Herald* was moved to pronounce 'the most extraordinary company that has ever visited the city'.[1] It included almost three hundred people, together with a full complement of one hundred and seventy-five animals – mostly horses but also including a team of mules and even a modest herd of American buffalo. Together these comprised the entourage and stock-in-trade of American frontier-legend-turned-showman, Colonel William F. 'Buffalo Bill' Cody. For this was the day on which Buffalo Bill's Wild West came to Glasgow – lock, stock and both barrels blazing.

Among the several props unloaded at Bellgrove were covered wagons and the Deadwood Stage. These vehicles formed part of the eerie procession that wended its way to the nearby East End Exhibition Buildings which, in those days, stood just off Whitehill Street, in the prosperous suburb of Dennistoun. The East End of Glasgow has witnessed a lot of odd things in its time but never anything quite like this.

The collection of around twenty shaggy, snorting, shambling buffalo numbered among the largest of the few viable herds still remaining in existence. Based upon what had been recorded at other venues,[2] it may be inferred that the horsemen formed a mounted cordon around the animals to keep them from bolting while herding them along the main thoroughfares. After all, it would never do for there to be a buffalo stampede in Duke Street!

But who exactly were these people? What was their story and what were the circumstances which brought them together and conspired to direct them to, of all places, Glasgow?

Buffalo Bill

William Frederick Cody was born on the 26th of February 1846, in Scott County, Iowa, near to the eastern bank of the Mississippi. Eight years later, his family were amongst the first migrants into Kansas Territory after it was thrown open to settlement. This initial westward momentum was sustained during the next decades of his life.

In the course of his extraordinary career, he would find occasion to try his hand at practically every occupation characteristic of frontier life, though with varying degrees of success. Cody's famous epithet was acquired after his employment in 1867 as a buffalo hunter. His job was to feed the small army of labourers engaged in the construction of the Kansas Pacific Railroad and he is conventionally reckoned to have killed 4,280 buffalo over a period of eighteen months.

Cody had earlier been a rider for the Pony Express and later became Chief of Scouts for the 5th US Cavalry during the years when the Indian wars on the Great Plains were at their zenith.

He rose to national celebrity status after highly sensationalised reports of his exploits appeared in the newspapers back east. His destiny was assured from 1869 onwards, when dime-novel writer Ned Buntline selected him as his real-life hero.

By the end of 1872, Buntline was writing, producing and appearing in a series of lurid melodramas, in which the hero of the dime novels, Buffalo Bill, was graphically brought to life. In December, Cody, with some initial reluctance, was persuaded to go east to make his debut upon the stage, starring as himself!

Over the next few years, Cody embraced the twin aspects of his career, scouting during the summer months and enacting his latest exploits for adoring eastern audiences in winter. It was during these crucial years that Cody underwent the metamorphosis from authentic frontiersman to public entertainer and semi-fictionalised character, whose principal stock-in-trade was his own legend. So seamless was this transition that it probably represented nothing more than the latest in a long series of Cody's semiconscious adaptations to the reality of flux inherent in a constantly shifting frontier.

As the wars against the Sioux and Cheyenne drew to an apparent conclusion during the mid 1870s, Bill concentrated upon his theatrical activities. The limitations of the stage became manifest and a bolder plan began to form. Buffalo Bill's Wild West toured from 1883 onwards. Authentic Indians supplanted down-at-heel Chicago actors and Sitting Bull himself was persuaded to tour with the show for one season, in 1885. In Montreal, Buffalo Bill and Sitting Bull famously posed together for a series of photographs at the studio of William Notman, a Scottish immigrant originally from Paisley.

In 1886, an indoor pageant, grandly titled *The Drama of Civilization* and based upon a narrative devised by Steele Mackaye, played for a full season in New York. This avoided the hardship and expense of endless travelling and held the further advantage that state-of-the-art scenic effects became feasible.

Buffalo Bill's Wild West began its first venture overseas on the 31st of March 1887, sailing to England from New York on board the SS *State of Nebraska*. The show raised a sensation in London, Birmingham, Manchester and Hull. There would be no appearances north of the border this time but Scotland would not be denied its part. Captain Andrew Gardiner Braes, a native of Linlithgow, served as captain of the *Nebraska* from 1881 until 1889 and thus to a Scotsman was accorded the honour of being the first to steer Buffalo Bill's Wild West across the storm-tossed Atlantic. The *Nebraska*, a Stateline Steamship Company vessel, had been launched on the Clyde in 1880. The charter contract, which presently forms part of the collection of the Maritime Museum at Irvine, reveals that, on the 24th of February 1887, the day on which Bill's business partner Nate Salsbury concluded with Austin Baldwin & Co, ship brokers of New York, for the *Nebraska* to conduct the company to London, the ship was plying its regular route between New York and Glasgow.

At least one other ripple of success was felt in Glasgow at this time. On the night of Thursday, 17 November 1887, a play entitled *Buffalo Bill – Or, Life in the Wild West* opened at the Theatre Royal, with H. J. Daulton in the title role. The drama was roundly slated by the 'Cantankerous Critic' in *Quiz* the following day, though he did concede that the audience seemed pleased enough with it.

The Wild West toured continental Europe during 1889–90 and, in Paris, the celebrated artist Rosa Bonheur presented Buffalo Bill with a magnificent portrait of himself, clad in buckskins and mounted upon a white horse.

Salsbury and Burke

Among those accompanying Colonel Cody to Glasgow were Nate Salsbury and his general manager, 'Major' John M. Burke. Salsbury had served the Union cause in the 1st Illinois throughout the Civil War and pursued a successful theatrical career from 1868 onwards. He subsequently teamed up with Cody to create Buffalo Bill's Wild West. Burke was a native of Washington DC and it is far from clear that he was actually entitled to the military rank habitually asserted by him. He had somehow acquired the epithet of 'Arizona John' despite apparently never having set foot in the State of that name. Aside from Colonel Cody's unofficial foster son, the sharpshooter

Johnnie Baker, Burke was the only associate to remain with Cody for the entire duration of his career. Burke was a one-man public relations machine and his boundless creative energies lay behind the show's copious (and frequently mendacious) press releases.

Lakota Apocalypse

> This is what I will do in the last days,
> God says:
> I will pour out my Spirit on everyone.
> Your sons and daughters will proclaim my message;
> your young men will see visions,
> and your old men will have dreams.[3]

Also arriving were scores of Indians. They were members of the famed Sioux nation or, as they called themselves, Lakota, a dialectical variation of Dakota, signifying 'friends' or 'allies'. They belonged to the Oglala and Brulé sub-tribes, from the Pine Ridge and Rosebud reservations respectively.

Uniquely in the annals of Wild West shows, Buffalo Bill's company during this season included Indians with prisoner-of-war status. The most prominent among this faction were Kicking Bear and his brother-in-law Short Bull. The pair had risen to notoriety during what the *Glasgow Herald* inaccurately termed 'the last Indian rebellion' of the previous winter.[4]

A cousin and close associate of that icon of Indian resistance, Crazy Horse, Kicking Bear was an exemplar of the Lakota martial tradition who had won great honour in the old-time wars against rival tribes. An Oglala by birth, he became a Minneconjou band chief through marriage to a niece of Chief Big Foot. He subsequently distinguished himself as a leading figure in the engagements with the US Cavalry at the Battles of Rosebud, Little Bighorn and Slim Buttes in the course of the 1876 campaign. Lakota resistance collapsed in 1877 and Kicking Bear languished restlessly in the obscurity and unremitting tedium of life on the Cheyenne River reservation for a term of twelve years thereafter. His face a habitual mask of sullen intransigence, Kicking Bear was marked as the obvious champion of traditional ways and as the most likely focus of future discontent.

Rumours of a new religion, appearing in far-off Nevada in the late 1880s and founded by a Paiute Indian named Wovaka, spread like wildfire among the demoralised inhabitants of the reservations. Patently a native adaptation of Christianity, it offered a message of deliverance and renewal to the despairing Indians as they struggled to come to terms with enforced assimilation to the dominant culture. In the autumn of 1889, Kicking Bear and Short Bull were among eleven emissaries sent by their respective tribal councils from the Lakota reservations as delegates to Wovoka and returned as converts.

With the first grass of the spring of 1891, the Messiah would come, having first manifested himself to the white men some two thousand years before. Now he was approaching from the west, at the head of an army of ghosts, the resurrected Indian dead. Some cataclysmic event – the details of which vary from one account to the next – would sweep the invaders beyond the seas whence they had come, leaving the Indians in undisturbed possession of an earthly paradise, restored to its pre-contact state of perfection.

Wovoka taught his disciples the rituals of the 'ghost dance', which, as well as hastening the advent of the Messiah, enabled believers to catch glimpses of the wonderful new land that was in preparation. Dancing themselves to the point of exhaustion, participants fell into trances. In this altered state of consciousness some received visions in which they conversed with long-dead friends and relatives, miraculously restored to life as it had been in days gone by.

Kicking Bear and Short Bull were therefore the foremost Lakota apostles of the ghost-dance movement. In the course of the tour of England and Wales preceding the Glasgow season, the Wild West show's publicity materials billed Short Bull as 'the "high priest" of the Messiah craze'.[5] As the origins of the cult were not yet properly understood, some reports actually claimed him as its founder.

Kicking Bear was generally designated 'the fighting chief of the ghost dancers'[6] but this is something of an oversimplification since he was also a prominent medicine man in his own right. Kicking Bear was the key figure whose vigorous proselytising activities proved decisive in establishing the cult on the Lakota reservations.

The summer of 1890 was a particularly traumatic one for the Lakota people. Hot, dry weather destroyed the crops and made a mockery of the government's efforts to recreate the Indians as sedentary farmers. This failure coincided with simmering resentment over the fraudulent land treaty of 1889 and with ration cuts that were intended to encourage self-reliance but which, in reality, reduced the people to destitution. Everywhere, the Indians – a nation in a state of revelation – abandoned material pursuits and danced in great chanting circles from morning to night in clandestine religious assemblies bearing more than a superficial spiritual affinity with the open-air conventicles of Scotland's Covenanters of more than two centuries previously.

One specifically Lakota refinement was the 'ghost shirt', a garment which supposedly rendered its wearer inviolate from bullets. The immediate inspiration for this came from Black Elk, a rising medicine man who had performed in England with Buffalo Bill in 1887–88.

Order at the agencies collapsed and tensions escalated as the authorities, apprehensive lest the incessant dancing heralded an imminent general outbreak, deployed the military to suppress the ghost-dance cult during the second half of November 1890. A substantial body of Indians, led by Kicking Bear and Short Bull, immediately fled the reservation and took refuge on the Stronghold, a natural fortress in the Badlands. The scene was set for a bizarre and tragic final postscript to the Indian wars which all sane commentators must have considered finally extinguished and this at a time when the frontier scarcely still existed.

By a curious dispensation of providence, Buffalo Bill Cody now fortuitously entered the scene. His tour of continental Europe had been cut short by accusations of systematic mistreatment of his

Indian charges. Returning to the United States with the entire Indian contingent, the allegations were investigated at Washington and shown to be unfounded. Rumours of war next hastened him to the scene of the disturbances in South Dakota.

The Wild West's publicity materials generally imply that Buffalo Bill and even his sidekick John M. Burke played an important part in the conflict. However, apart from one farcical mission to bring in his old friend Sitting Bull, aborted by political infighting, Cody's personal involvement did not extend beyond an essentially preventative role as brigadier general in the Nebraska National Guard.

Sitting Bull was no more than a peripheral player in the ghost-dance movement but it was feared that, if a figure of his status were to throw in his lot with the hostiles, a serious escalation would ensue. James McLaughlin was the agent at Standing Rock and, in consequence of his vindictive paranoia, a detachment of Indian reservation police was sent to arrest him. This resulted in a shoot-out in which the old chief was shot dead during the early hours of the 15th of December.

In the resulting panic, Big Foot's band of Minneconjou struck out for Pine Ridge and, amidst concerns that they intended to join the 'hostiles', they were intercepted by the 7th Cavalry at Wounded Knee. The outcome was the infamous slaughter of men, women and children which erupted on the morning of the 29th of December 1890.

Kicking Bear led the desultory skirmishing in the days which followed. By sheer force of numbers, however, the army ensured that the violence soon petered out. Kicking Bear's sullen submission to General Miles on the 15th of January 1891 effectively brought down the curtain on almost four centuries of Native American resistance.

On the evening of the 26th of January, General Miles boarded the train for Chicago at Rushville, taking twenty-seven hostages with him. By the 29th, they were in confinement at Fort Sheridan, Illinois, where Miles intended to keep them under his personal observation for a period of at least six months.

As well as leading figures from the recent disturbances, the party included old men, women and boys. Of these, twenty-three were later released into the custody and employment of Colonel Cody, on the strict condition that they travel as performing members of his Wild West show. From the original complement, seventeen remained when the show arrived in Glasgow.

Other leading figures among the Indians now arriving had viewed the ghost-dance cult with extreme scepticism and recognised the futility of continued resistance to the white man's civilisation. They had actively taken the part of the federal government against their more visionary and intractable fellow tribesmen, earning official recognition for their services in the capacity of army scouts. The most prominent of these were men returning from the 1889–1890 tour of Europe.

The powerful figure of Chief No Neck, the most notable of the 'friendly' faction, was no neophyte on the white man's road. He had thrown in his lot with the new order many years before and was already serving as an army scout during the decisive struggles of the 1870s. No Neck was shadowed almost everywhere he went by a waif of around six years of age, a little Indian boy who less than authentically appeared wearing a war bonnet. No Neck's little protégé, at least so the show's publicity materials claimed, had lain clinging to life in the midst of his slain relatives on the field of Wounded Knee before being discovered by a burial party sent from Pine Ridge agency three days later. The press releases billed him as:

"Little Johnny Burke No Neck," the sole survivor of the decisive battle of Wounded Knee.[7]

This status is impossible to square with the historical record and owes more to melodramatic sensationalism than hard fact. A fairly substantial minority of Big Foot's band is known to have fled from the scene of slaughter. Robert M. Utley lists five adults and two children as having been found by the burial detail on the 1st of January

1891.[8] No independent confirmation can be found that the boy was among them.

Major John M. Burke and No Neck jointly stood as the orphan's godfathers and their conjoined names he now bore. For No Neck, the adoption of the little orphan was a plain act of humanity but it may be surmised that, for 'Arizona John', the transaction was primarily a calculated publicity coup.

The Interpreters

Then there were the interpreters, John Shangrau and George C. Crager, for few of their Lakota charges were conversant in English. Each had his own story to tell and occupied a unique position on the bridge between two very different worlds. Shangrau, a mixed-blood, had been present in a similar role at Wounded Knee as a scout and interpreter for the US 7th Cavalry and, in Colonel Cody's employ, he retained special responsibility as 'In Charge of Hostile Indians', to quote the words of his Wild West calling card, preserved in the Wyoming State Archives.

Crager was a native of New York City, whose inconsiderable physical stature – *Eastern Bells* described him as 'dainty little Mr Crager'[9] – belied his extraordinary career record to date. He had been at various times a soldier – serving in the US Cavalry from 1876 to 1878, during which time he saw active service as a trumpeter, and enlisting again in 1880 – an Indian interpreter, an administrator and a journalist. In the latter capacity, Crager was present at Pine Ridge during the ghost-dance disturbances, as special correspondent for the *New York World*.

By his own account, he had left home at the tender age of thirteen. Irresistibly drawn by the fast-receding frontier, he drifted westward and fell in with, first, the Pawnee and, later, the Lakota. A natural linguist who additionally acquired a command of several European languages, he became proficient in Lakota. He was adopted by a Lakota chief called Two Strikes and found employment in various capacities as a government employee on the reservation.

He brought to Glasgow a prodigious collection of Indian artefacts, including at least one 'ghost shirt', of which much more would later be heard.

Cowboys and Mexicans

There were also detachments of authentic cowboys and Mexicans. Just maybe, the cowboys felt instantly at home on alighting on Bellgrove Street for, in days gone by when this thoroughfare was known as the Witch Loan, it had been the favoured and time-honoured route of cattle drovers crossing the meandering River Clyde at Dalmarnock ford. As a legacy, the trail's culmination now accommodated the local cattle market.

The Marksmen

Apart from Buffalo Bill himself, there were three other sharpshooters: Johnnie Baker, the 'Cowboy Kid'; the highly respected pistol and revolver shot Claude Lorraine Daly, a Pennsylvanian aged twenty-five; and, best of all, Annie Oakley. Almost continuously from 1885 until 1901, Annie Oakley was Buffalo Bill's leading lady and the foremost attraction with the show. But Annie, who was born Phoebe Anne Moses, in Darke County, Ohio, in 1860, has to be considered something of an impostor.

She was announced in the show as 'the lovely lass of the western plains, Little Sure Shot, the one and only Annie Oakley'[10] but, in truth, it would be another five years before she first ventured west of the Mississippi and even then it was as a performing member of the Wild West. Her famous epithet – *Watanya Ciclila*, when rendered in Lakota – had been conferred upon her by Chief Sitting Bull himself but it is doubtful whether she had ever had any significant contact with Indians before that time.

The Cowboy Band

The 'Cowboy Band' was led by William Sweeney, quondam bandmaster of the 5th Cavalry. For two of the band members, brothers Harry and David Livingston, the arrival was in the nature of a homecoming. Both had been born in Bridgeton, Glasgow, in 1865 and 1869 respectively. The Livingston family migrated to the United States in 1873 and settled in Connecticut. The entries against Harry and David's names in the 1891 Norwich City Directory noted them as 'in Europe' and gave their employer's name as 'Buffalo Bill'.

The Frontiersmen

The frontier was the defining element in the formative years of American history, with the corollary that the romantic figure of the frontiersman – a living contradiction since embodying the frontier itself and simultaneously the inevitability of its own demise – was elevated from the simple plane of folk hero to iconic status.

Practically the entire history of the frontier from 1734 onwards can be narrated in terms of the overlapping lives of Daniel Boone (1734–1820), Davy Crockett (1786–1836) and Buffalo Bill Cody himself (1846–1917). As the culminating figure in this movement, Cody's was the spirit presiding over the concluding phases of frontier history.

The lives of Boone and Crockett had long been celebrated in pulp literature and stage dramas. But, for all that Buffalo Bill merely drew together themes and ideas which had already entered into nascent existence as a series of disparate elements, it was left to him to forge and perfect the vision of a grand theatrical entertainment which, at the close of the nineteenth century and in the opening years of the twentieth, would comprehensively articulate the dominant themes in the emerging legend of the American West.

Buffalo Bill's Wild West took his vision to towns and cities the length and breadth of North America and beyond. Glasgow's turn had come.

Notes

1. 5 November 1891
2. *Leicester Advertiser*, 5 September 1891
3. *Good News Bible*, Acts, ch. 2, v. xvii
4. 6 November 1891
5. *Liverpool Daily Post*, 7 July 1891
6. *Birmingham Daily Post*, 8 September 1891
7. *The Argus* (Brighton), 12 October 1891
8. *The Last Days of the Sioux Nation*, p. 3
9. November 1891
10. Walter Havighurst, *Annie Oakley of the Wild West*, p. 93

2

HORSEMEN APPROACHING

INDIAN CHIEF AND COWBOY

The spring of 1891 brought no sign of the promised Messiah but deliverance, of a kind, did appear in the unlikely form of the Indians' old adversary, Buffalo Bill Cody. Most of the former hostiles held at Fort Sheridan were packed off to Europe as the leading attractions with the Wild West show, willingly accepting this course in preference to the alternative of indefinite imprisonment.

An undated article from an unidentified newspaper, preserved by the Colorado State Historical Society, supplies much of the missing detail.[1] The captives had become something of a political embarrassment, a veritable 'herd of white elephants'. The Indians were 'resigned' in attitude and Kicking Bear had proved the most 'morose and uncommunicative of them all'. But, when they beheld the familiar form of Colonel Cody, who arrived immediately upon obtaining the necessary authorisation from Secretary Noble of the Indian Department, the sullen expressions of the Indians instantly gave way to smiles of joy.

Kicking Bear, who had assumed – or, rather, retained – the leadership of the band of captives, was the first to come forward and shake Cody by the hand. He told him, 'For six weeks, I have been a dead man. Now that I see you, I am alive again.'

Buffalo Bill outlined his proposal to them and, after the Indians had briefly conferred, Kicking Bear advanced once more and said, 'I have advised them to go and they will go. I think I may go, too.'[2]

The deal was sealed by a subsequent visit from Major Burke. So attractive was the offer of travel in unknown lands, with a good salary, that most of the Indians accepted. Only four of the original twenty-seven declined. Takes the Shield Away, His Horse Voice, White Beaver and Little Horse, all apparently afflicted by that sickness of body and spirit so characteristic of the captive Indian, wished to remain in the United States. They were detained at Fort Sheridan until the end of April, at which time they were deemed no longer to present a significant threat to the nation's security. On the morning of the 30th, they were packed off home to Pine Ridge, under the charge of interpreter and scout Louis Shangrau, brother of John.

Europe

The remaining twenty-three were released on the 30th of March into the custody of Major Burke, accompanied by three interpreters, John Shangrau, George C. Crager and Jack Russell. Crager in particular was destined to emerge as a key figure as the 1891–92 tour of Europe unfolded. Russell, in contrast, is a shadowy character. He is known to have sailed to Europe but it is difficult to locate any mention of him after the first days of the tour in Germany and Belgium.

The hostages were conducted to Philadelphia and sailed with the rest of the company on the 1st of April for the Belgian seaport of Antwerp on board the SS *Switzerland*. About forty other Indians had enlisted as volunteers at Pine Ridge, several of whom had actively assisted the federal government during the late outbreak. Cody himself was not on board and is understood to have travelled separately on board the SS *Noordlund*.

Kicking Bear and Short Bull had journeyed with their associates far further west than any Lakota had ever done before, at the time of their pilgrimage into Nevada. Their encounter with the prophet

Wovoka must have seemed like a lifetime away as their peregrinations brought them east, as despairing or at least passive captives, into the distant heart of the white man's original domain beyond the stormy ocean, hitherto known to them only as the abode of the rising sun.

Two weeks later, on the 15th of April, the *Switzerland* cast anchor in the teeming Belgian port of Antwerp. A grand tour of the city included a visit to the cathedral, where Short Bull, Scatter, Revenge and others stood in rapt amazement before Rubens's grand masterpiece, *Descent from the Cross*. The substance of the meditations passing through their minds when confronted with this vivid depiction of the Messiah whose heralded return had so conspicuously failed to materialise, at so recent a date and in so painful a manner, can now only be a matter for unaided speculation.

The following day, a special train brought the party to Strasburg, from whence they made the further short transit to the Wild West encampment at Benfeld. Here, the show's equipment and a large part of its personnel had been left in the care of Nate Salsbury the previous autumn.

A few days of busy rehearsals followed and the Indians were introduced to their roles. To their obvious delight, they were each allocated a pony. Restored to a semblance of their former spirits, they threw themselves into the performances with a level of enthusiasm and alacrity that confounded all legitimate expectations.

A four-day engagement at Strasburg opened the 1891 season. Engagements at eight other cities followed before the German leg of the tour closed in the border town of Aachen on the 27th of May.

On the 26th, George Crager personally conducted Kicking Bear and a dozen of his companions on a visit to the tomb of Charlemagne at Aachen Cathedral. Short Bull would also have been present but, as if to underline the dangerous nature of the undertaking, he had unfortunately sustained an awkward fall in the opening performance at Aachen.

On the 28th, the show commenced a two-week residency in

Brussels, Belgium, and this was followed by a week in Antwerp, concluding on the 17th of June.

The undoubted highlight of the Belgian sojourn was the visit on the 2nd of June of the entire company in full costume to the site of the battlefield at Waterloo. Photographs were taken of large groups on the Lion Mound. Short Bull, his injured foot now recovered, was among those present on this occasion.

On the evening of Wednesday the 3rd, Colonel Cody attended a musical soirée hosted by the singer Madame Lemmens-Sherrington in Brussels. Among the 'turns' was Mrs Salsbury, who favoured the company by singing 'Within a Mile of Edinboro' Toun'.

The Wild West Show

The avowed intention was to give a representation of the various aspects of frontier life as it had existed during the preceding decades but that had now surely passed beyond recall.

Particular prominence was given to those episodes forming the subject matter of Buffalo Bill's personal career. The scenes depicted were re-enacted, insofar as was possible, by the very individuals who had taken part in the original incidents. These were men who – in some cases, only a few months previously – had risked their own lives and taken the lives of others in the course of the exploits now so graphically and faithfully recreated for the public's amusement and instruction.

Each performance opened with 'The Star Spangled Banner', stirringly rendered by the Cowboy Band and introducing a programme of seventeen items, consisting of: a 'Grand Processional Review'; a horse race between a cowboy, a Mexican and an Indian; a display of Annie Oakley's prodigious feats of shooting; a re-enactment of Buffalo Bill's legendary hand-to-hand duel with Chief Yellow Hand in July 1876 – the 'first scalp for Custer'; a display of the manner in which the US mail was carried westward in the days of the Pony Express; an assault on the emigrant train by Indians, with Buffalo Bill and his cowboys riding heroically to the rescue, guns blazing;

another shooting exhibition, this time by Johnnie Baker, the 'Celebrated Young American Marksman'; 'Cowboy Fun', consisting mostly of exploits with bucking broncos; a shooting exhibition with pistols and revolvers by Claude Lorraine Daly; another lively horse race, this time between a pair of frontier girls; the capture of the Deadwood Stage by Indians and its subsequent rescue by a party of cowboys; two Indian boys racing on bareback ponies; the 'Life Customs of the Indians'; a display of shooting by Buffalo Bill himself; the 'buffalo hunt', in which a mixed party of Indians, cowboys and Mexicans somewhat pathetically coursed Cody's herd around the arena; an attack upon a settler's cabin by Indians, who set it on fire, once again foiled through the timely intervention of Buffalo Bill and the cowboys, with the customary deafening and reckless expenditure of gunpowder; and, finally, a parting salute, during which the show ended much as it had begun with the Cowboy Band striking up a stirring rendition of 'God Save the Queen'.

Two of these items in particular require detailed attention.

Item 1, the 'Grand Processional Review', served to introduce the main groups of performers and the leading individual characters, each of whom was powerfully announced in turn by H. M. Clifford, the 'orator'.

The first party of mounted figures to burst upon the arena from behind the painted scenery were a dozen or so 'Arapahos', riding bareback on ponies as spirited as themselves. These Indians were headed by their 'chief', Plenty Wolves, a notable of the 'friendly' faction, who had seen service as a sergeant of Indian scouts for the US army during the previous winter. The Indians were spectacularly bedecked in eagle feathers and warpaint and they filled the air with war whoops and other strange cries but it must be stressed that the tribal affiliations attributed to them in this context were essentially fictitious.

Their headlong charge towards the main grandstand came to an abrupt halt and the 'Arapahos' lined up in front of the audience, their war-bonnet-clad chief to the fore. Next came the cowboys, in their familiar slouch hats and wide-fringed leggings, led by Jim

Mitchell. Then came the 'Brules', under Short Bull, and, hot on their heels, the 'Cut-off' tribe led by Kicking Bear. Kicking Bear's awesome reputation had clearly preceded him and created some general appreciation of his importance for the *Liverpool Daily Post* recorded that his entrance upon the scene was 'received with loud applause'.[3] The 'Cut-offs', incidentally, were a subdivision of the Oglalas and arose from a schism dating to around the year 1840 and persisting until 1871. Whether Kicking Bear held any real affiliation is not clear. They were followed by the Mexican vaqueros under Antonio Esquivel, also parading in flamboyant and characteristic attire. Lone Bull rode in at the head of the 'Cheyennes' with the 'Ogallala Sioux' under Black Heart following. Then came a group of ladies of the Far West. The Indian women rode slowly into the arena, their voices raised in a plaintive chant. The braves acclaimed their arrival on the scene with a resurgence of their shrill whoop.

Various individuals followed. The first of these were two sons of (apparently unidentified and quite possibly non-existent) Sioux chiefs. Next was John Nelson, a veteran of the frontier, originally from Virginia. According to the show's publicity material, it was Nelson who had acted as guide and interpreter to the Mormons under Brigham Young on their westward trek to Utah some decades previously. John's son, Jim, also known as Yellow Horse, was one of a family of children resulting from his union with a Lakota woman, and he travelled with the show as one of the Indians. The rearguard was brought up by Bone Necklace, an octogenarian once distinguished as a warrior among his people and now announced as 'the legendary historian of the Sioux'; No Neck; and Long Wolf, 'the medicine man of the Sioux'.

Two cowboys bore the flags of the United Kingdom and the United States into the arena.

The heroic figure of Buffalo Bill, mounted on a white charger and clad in his trademark buckskins, was the last of the riders to make his entrance. Raising his hat into the air, he received the wild applause of the performers and audience alike.

In Item 13, 'Life Customs of the Indians', the entire body of Indians moved camp and engaged in dances and other traditional activities. A ghost-dance song was included although here it was transplanted into a culturally inauthentic context. A confrontation with a rival 'tribe' of Indians provided a noisy and dramatic climax.

England and Wales

Sailing across the North Sea on board the steamship *Lincoln*, immediately upon the conclusion of the final performance in Antwerp, the company landed at Grimsby in the early hours of the 19th of June. The English and Welsh legs of the tour were commenced in Leeds on Saturday the 20th. From then until late October, the entourage would undertake a gruelling tour of thirteen provincial towns and cities, travelling in three specially chartered trains. There were a great many incidents and adventures along the way, but, for now, only those having a bearing upon the subsequent Scottish appearances are recounted.

Outdoor performances were given twice daily, with the evening shows illuminated by means of Wells oil and air lamps. An imposing street parade was given on the first Monday morning at each new venue.

The Wild West encampment was thrown open to public inspection prior to each performance. The tipis of the Indian village afforded their actual living accommodation. Fashioned from canvas, the exterior of each bore the name of its principal occupant, together with rudely drawn representations of battle scenes, animals and other totemic symbols. Following the traditional arrangement, each tipi housed an extended family group. During their leisure hours, the men would lounge on mattresses or else while away their free time playing cards and dominoes, as the women practised beadwork and other native handicrafts around the central fire.

Buffalo Bill issued a standing and open invitation to local owners to bring unmanageable steeds to the show, with a challenge to his cowboys to tame them, thus showing that no trickery was involved. This invitation was taken up at Liverpool, where a wild South

American horse was subdued by Harry Shanton, the cowboy personally selected for the task by Colonel Cody, and also at Nottingham.

At Manchester, on the evening of Friday the 31st of July, a benefit performance was given for the surviving local Balaclava veterans, seventeen of whom were in attendance. This appears to have been the very first occasion on which extraneous elements were translated into the show. Proceedings began with a display of mounted drill with lance and sword exercises by a detachment of the 12th Lancers and the regimental band played in alternation with the Cowboy Band. A company of 'miniature volunteers' – boys aged between six and ten years of age, complete with a miniature brass band – gave an exhibition drill. Later, the old heroes marched once around the arena, raising and waving their hats in acknowledgment of the rapturous applause from the spectators.

An engaging pictorial record of the occasion survives in the form of a group photograph. The veterans, proudly displaying their medals and some in uniform, are seen in company with Wild West personnel, including Colonel Cody, Major Burke, both interpreters and six of the Indians. The photograph was taken by R. Banks, a local studio photographer. A further photograph, also by Mr Banks, was probably taken on the same occasion. It depicts George C. Crager with his wife Julia and their two children seated at the opening of the tent in which the family was quartered and exhibiting selections from the interpreter's collection of Indian artefacts.

On the morning of the show's final day in Manchester, Saturday the 8th of August, Black Heart was married to Calls the Name, a sister of No Neck, at Saint Bride's Church, Stretford, in the presence of the entire company. John Shangrau, her nephew, officiated as interpreter and best man and also as a witness. The happy couple and Shangrau all signed the register with 'X' marks.

Tragedy took a hand at Sheffield where, in the course of a performance, Paul Eagle Star met with the accident that was to claim his life. Riding out of the arena at the end of the opening review, his horse slipped and slid on its forefeet, trapping the rider's foot under its body. His companions, without once slacking rein, swooped down, gathered up the stricken Indian and bore him out of the arena. On removal to the local infirmary, Eagle Star was found to have sustained a compound dislocation of his right ankle.

At Stoke, George C. Crager gave an interview, published in the *Staffordshire Sentinel*.[4] He detailed his exceptional personal career to date and exhibited his Wild West relics, whose individual histories were suggestive of nothing short of simony on a medieval scale. These included: a peace pipe fashioned from catlinite; the actual pistol with which Bob Ford had shot Jesse James dead three years before; an eagle feather worn by Sitting Bull on the day he died; moccasins that had also belonged to Sitting Bull; and the leggings Chief Spotted Tail had been wearing when he was assassinated by Crow Dog on the Ponka agency.

The morbid theme was sustained by a number of arrows allegedly retrieved from Wounded Knee. Crager was also stated to have a number of ghost shirts in his possession, souvenirs of the recent disturbances. One of these had also been exhibited to journalists at Sheffield.

Meanwhile, at Sheffield Infirmary, Paul Eagle Star had suffered a serious reverse. Lockjaw set in and, on Saturday the 22nd of August, the injured foot was amputated as the final futile hope of saving his life. The lockjaw became worse and this, in combination with the shock of the operation, proved fatal. George Crager was present at Eagle Star's bedside when the end came, early on the morning of Monday the 24th.

When the news reached the Wild West at Nottingham, the entire company sank into a profound depression. So loud were the dirges and lamentations of the Indian women, as they perambulated the encampment that night, that a false rumour swept through the district that some form of outbreak was imminent.

An inquest took place in the boardroom of Sheffield Infirmary on the following morning, in the presence of Kicking Bear, Black Heart, Lone Bull and Bull Stands Behind, a cousin of the deceased, all in traditional costume. The jury returned a verdict of 'accidental death'. The deceased was next conducted by train to London and taken for burial at West Brompton cemetery, in the same plot as Surrounded, an Indian who had died in 1887 during the show's visit to Manchester.

The *Leicester Daily Mercury* published a letter from one J. Eagle, protesting at the manner in which a party of Indians, while taking an evening stroll along Brandon Street, had been subjected to 'the jostling, hooting, and insulting remarks' of a crowd of local young men and women.[5]

Cody was supposed to keep his Indians out of the way of temptation, especially where alcohol was involved. The reality of the situation, however, is reflected by an anecdote appearing in the *Birmingham Daily Mail*:

> When Buffalo Bill's Indians go on the 'spree' they are not always profitable customers. They say to the barman, 'Beer quart.' They then say 'Beer – more quart.' After awhile (*sic*) the barman says, 'money for beer.' And they reply with a sad smile and a shake of the head, 'no money,' and with the air of intense self-absorption walk away.[6]

The type of liaison that the Indian men were likely strike up with local girls is indicated in an unidentified newspaper cutting preserved in the *Crager Scrapbook*.[7] After the conclusion of the evening's entertainment, a brave could frequently be found on the streets with some ostentatiously dressed young lady by his side or else in one of the hostelries enjoying the society of a female admirer. A barmaid in a local hotel received love letters, written in somewhat defective English. One unnamed young Indian was so smitten that he took up residence with the object of his affection. The arrangement was not to prove a permanent one for two representatives of the Wild West followed and removed the absconding Indian to Bristol. As the account sadly concludes, 'the girl he left behind him' showed the strength of her affections by deciding to remain in Aston.

One of the largest buffaloes fell ill and died at Birmingham and was consigned to a taxidermist.

Shortly after arrival in Cardiff, Major Burke and Mr Salsbury departed the scene, with Burke going to Bristol and Salsbury to Glasgow to make the necessary preliminary arrangements at these future venues. Back in May, a winter season in London had been in contemplation but, at some intermediate stage, this was changed in favour of Glasgow.

On the morning of Sunday the 27th of September, Buffalo Bill hastened to Temple Mead Railway Station, Bristol, at the express request of his friend and famous contemporary, the classical actor Henry (later Sir Henry) Irving so that their respective visits to the city might at least briefly coincide. Accompanying him, as he bid Irving a fond farewell, were Short Bull, Lone Bull, No Neck and Johnny Burke No Neck. All shook hands with the actor as they wished one another 'good luck'.

The White Lily Company

Groundbreaking research by Alan Gallop reveals that, around this time, the entourage split into two.[8] Sherman Canfield, one of the stage managers, was hired out to the actress Viola Clemmons, along with some performing horses and twelve Indians, led by Black Heart, for the epic production of *Onita, the White Lily*, which toured English and Welsh theatres from the 24th of September until the 31st of December. From September onwards, therefore, Cody's Indian contingent was substantially diminished.

Disaster loomed in Brighton during the early hours of Sunday the 11th of October, when it was only with great difficulty that Major Burke succeeded in finding a local contractor willing and able to undertake the removal of the show's equipage from the station to the exhibition grounds. This haphazard transportation method contrasts neatly with the later British tours, when removals would be taken care of by a large and permanent staff of labourers under the show's direct employment.

Brighton will, however, chiefly be remembered for the dreadful storms that erupted on Tuesday the 13th of October, bringing a night of fear and discomfort in the Wild West encampment. The *Sussex Daily News* offered the following commentary:

> The gale is spoken of as the worst that Colonel Cody and his followers have experienced since their return to this country. It disturbed the equanimity of the Indians to a marked degree. Throughout the night they were to be heard singing in their own language pleading with their messiah for the wind to cease.[9]

On Thursday the 22nd of October, a party of eight Indians, accompanied by Major Burke and Mr Crager, was taken into London by train from Croydon for a visit to St Paul's Cathedral and Westminster Abbey. These were Kicking Bear, Short Bull, Lone Bull, No Neck, Coming Grunt, White Cloud, High Bear and young Johnny Burke No Neck. The Indians were attired in their highly colourful and conspicuous traditional costumes and wondering crowds followed in the wake of their every move.

The excursion was probably an elaborate publicity stunt, designed to entice paying customers to the show. But this was not the only motive for, as the account appearing in *The Herald* chillingly concluded:

> The Indian is a close observer, and those who have travelled can hardly avoid knowing and telling those who have any doubt upon the subject that the white man has the power, if he cared to exercise it, of blotting the red man off the Continent of America.[10]

It was Buffalo Bill's conscious policy to overawe his Indian charges with evidences of the white man's superior military, numerical, industrial and even spiritual might. At Sheffield, the Indians were conducted around a cutlery works; at Stoke, the premises of Minton's pottery; at Birmingham, the gun works; and, at Portsmouth, the naval dockyard, all to impress upon them the futility of further rebellion. It was an old trick and had routinely been used to intimidate previously or potentially hostile tribes, going back to colonial times. In the present context, it appears to have been intended to demonstrate to the federal authorities, upon whose goodwill Cody depended for a continuing supply of Indians, that his show was useful to the cause of assimilation.

The final performance in Croydon took place on the evening of Saturday the 24th and, on the following day, Sunday the 25th, the entourage departed on its long northward journey to Glasgow.

Buffalo Bill himself remained in London and would follow shortly after. Croydon was the last outdoor venue of the tour. The entire travelling plant, including the portable grandstand, was disposed of by auction sale at the Wild West grounds on Wednesday the 28th.

Notes

1 *Cody Scrapbook*, p. 13
2 Ibid.
3 7 July 1891
4 20 August 1891
5 5 September 1891
6 12 September 1891
7 Buffalo Bill Historical Center
8 *Buffalo Bill's British Wild West*, pp. 179–83
9 15 October 1891
10 25 October 1891

3

FROM PINE RIDGE TO WHITEHILL

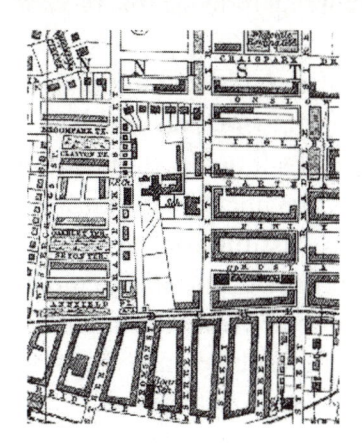

Glasgow in 1891

Glasgow, as Buffalo Bill Cody found it in the late autumn of 1891, was no overnight boom town but a vibrant industrial community with thirteen and a half centuries of history already to its credit.

The city was originally an obscure settlement in Strathclyde, the ancient kingdom of the Britons, and traditionally traces its genesis to the monastery established by the semi-mythical personage of Saint Mungo around the year AD 540. It is probable, however, that a village on the banks of the Molendinar Burn, its name approximating to the modern form of 'Glasgow', was already in existence at this time.

Over the next thousand years, Glasgow gradually consolidated its status as an important ecclesiastical and mercantile centre. Located during its early history entirely on the north side of the River Clyde, its original centre stood at the crossroads formed at the intersection of the High Street by Rottenrow to the west and the Drygate to the east. Glasgow Cross was subsequently established at its present site, the focal point marked by the convergence of the High Street, Gallowgate, Saltmarket, and Trongate.

A cathedral was established in the city, around the year 1124, as was the second university in Scotland, in 1451. It stood on the eastern side of the High Street until 1870, when it was relocated to Gilmorehill. The students established torchlight processions as a regular event at the time of the removal and the tradition is still observed on an occasional basis – most recently to mark the university's 550th anniversary in 2001.

Glasgow was elevated to the status of an archbishopric in January 1492 at the outset of the same year in which Columbus undertook his first voyage of discovery to the Americas – as if in unconscious acknowledgement of the extent to which the city's future greatness was bound up in transatlantic commerce.

During the mid sixteenth century, Glaswegians warmly embraced the wave of spiritual renewal known to history as the Reformation. Papal authority was formally abolished by the Scots Parliament in 1560 and Glasgow, indeed practically all of Scotland, became firmly Protestant. In a New World context, the demarcation of Europe into mutually hostile Catholic and Protestant sections manifested itself in discord between previously friendly governments and unleashed an age of violent, unbridled competition between the nations for the acquisition of colonies in the Americas.

It was with the Act and Treaty of Union of 1707 that Glasgow truly came into its own. Political incorporation with England was greeted with popular disquiet, manifesting itself in serious rioting and civil upheaval but it soon proved to be the key to enhancement and prosperity. The Union opened up to the merchants of Glasgow the prospect of trade with England's North American colonies and ensured the rise of the city's pre-eminence in the tobacco trade, thus laying the foundation for an immense reservoir of personal and municipal wealth, still reflected in the 'Merchant City' architecture surviving from this period. The city expanded westwards, into the vicinity of George Square, and many of the street names in this quarter – such as Virginia Street and Glassford Street – commemorate these times.

Spectacularly successful transatlantic intercourse also came in the form of sugar and molasses and, shameful to admit, the slave trade too. These West Indian connections are preserved in the names of

Jamaica Street and Saint Vincent Street. The resulting accumulation of prodigious reserves of capital would serve to fund the ensuing programme of investment and growth, while Glasgow's evolution as a primary industrial centre advanced.

The outbreak of the American War of Independence in 1775 brought a fatal disruption to the previously assured prosperity of the 'Tobacco Lords' and, in the aftermath, local enterprise diversified into textiles, steam locomotion, and shipbuilding, together with a multitude of lesser undertakings as the nineteenth century wore on and the process of economic and social transformation, now known as the Industrial Revolution, got underway.

In Glasgow, no less than in America's Deep South, cotton was, for a time, king. It supplanted the native linen industry and a cottage industry appeared in which a myriad handloom weavers within a forty-mile radius laboured to supply the apparently insatiable demand for the new textile. With the invention of the power loom in 1804, cotton mills no longer depended upon the immediate proximity of fast flowing streams and the industry, with its numerous workers, was soon concentrated within the city, entailing a rapid process of urbanisation.

The cotton industry acted as a stimulus for the simultaneous expansion of the coal and steel industries. The ready availability of these primary commodities in turn led to the creation of industrial canals and, from 1825 onwards, a network of railway lines. As was the case in the American West, the establishment of the rail network was preceded by stagecoaches, which had connected Glasgow with a variety of other locations since 1763.

The Glasgow and Greenock railway line was opened for passenger traffic in 1840. Queen Street Station was constructed by the Edinburgh and Glasgow Railway Company in 1842 and completely rebuilt around 1880. The Caledonian Railway Company opened Buchanan Street Station to passenger traffic in 1849. Central Station followed in 1879 and was extended in 1906. St Enoch's Station and Hotel, belonging to the Glasgow and South Western Railway Company, date to 1880.

Clydeside's famed shipbuilding industry, which would flourish well into the twentieth century, was a further natural fulfilment of Glasgow's economic potential. It became particularly important after 1841 with the development of steam propulsion, and the adoption of iron as a construction material. Glaswegians were among the original partners of the Cunard Company, whose ship *Britannia* first sailed from Liverpool to Boston in 1840. A regular direct service between Glasgow and New York was in place by 1850 and would continue to operate until the Second World War. The Allan Line also ran regular sailings from Glasgow to Montreal, New York, Boston and Philadelphia around the time of Buffalo Bill's first visit to the city.

The Clyde was originally a wide, meandering and shallow river. Glasgow was therefore denied the status of primary port for several centuries and goods had to be transported by land to and from Greenock and Port Glasgow. Ambitious but impracticable plans for the artificial enhancement of the Clyde's navigability by narrowing and deepening its course were advanced as early as 1456. Measures to carry this major civic preoccupation into practical effect were taken from 1769 onwards but it was not until 1886 that the project finally came to fruition. In the same year that the US federal government took the last surrender of the Apache war leader Geronimo, Glasgow completed its gradual conquest of the Clyde.

By the 1840s, the cleanliness and architectural elegance that had previously attracted admiring comments from such visiting luminaries as Defoe had degenerated into the filthy, overcrowded and disease-ridden slums which were to become Glasgow's unenviable trademark.

Employment opportunities in the opening decades of the nineteenth century proved insufficient to provide for all those who crowded into the city from every quarter and soldiers returning from the Napoleonic wars swelled the ranks of the standing unemployed. Violent fluctuations in the trade cycle brought about severe disruptions and hardship and the revolutionary tensions convulsing the whole of Western Europe in 1848 came close to exacting a radical toll in Glasgow. Somehow, the city's native genius prevailed and the evil hour passed but the long-standing tradition of 'Red Clydeside' was nonetheless firmly established.

The first major demographic change came with the mass influx of Irish immigrants from the 1840s onwards. Presbyterianism was, by this time, established as a primary defining element in the Scottish national character and a general sense of resentment inevitably attended the influx of these predominantly Roman Catholic newcomers – particularly since their arrival undercut the economic position of the Scots labouring class. The resulting mutual antagonism is a declining force today but survives as a standing tribal confrontation still overshadowing all subsequently arising ethnic tensions.

In 1891, there was a small Jewish community of rather less than one thousand souls – the first corpse to be buried in the Necropolis when it opened in 1832 was that of a Jew, Joseph Levi – but the better part of Jewish settlement in Scotland still lay in the future. Since the Jews were comparatively very few in number and their chosen professions did not involve direct competition with the native population, their assimilation, in stark and happy contrast with the pattern generally established elsewhere, was effected without any significant measure of friction. In 1891, the Italians, with their distinctive ice-cream parlours, were another recent addition to the local ethnic mix. The city had long been cosmopolitan in outlook but this was only beginning to be reflected in the composition of its inhabitants.

Over the course of the nineteenth century, Glasgow's population multiplied almost ten times over, from around 77,000 in 1800 to approximately three-quarters of a million at the close of the century. In the census returns of 1891, the figure stood at 565,714, or 656,185 if the areas to be added when the city boundaries were enlarged in November of that year are included. Population levels not dissimilar to those of the early twenty-first century were achieved within a much smaller area by means of a far greater concentration. Large numbers of families were still being shoehorned into single-room tenement flats.

The more prosperous classes joined a steady westward expansion firstly to the streets surrounding Blythswood Square and later to the vicinity of Great Western Road. The poorer sections of the population were left to the old and decaying neighbourhood around the High Street and to the ancient suburb of the Calton or else banished to the slums of the industrial hinterland emerging further to the east. Even this unprecedented territorial expansion far beyond the original city limits proved insufficient and the vertical solution generated the evolution of the tenement block. By the close of the nineteenth century, architecture in the 'second city of empire' had come to assume the distinctive and peculiar identity which remains familiar to us today.

However, in 1891, much of the present urban sprawl of Greater Glasgow had yet to come into existence. The new and affluent suburb of Dennistoun was about as far as the East End extended. It bears the name of a dynasty whose wealth was largely founded upon the lucrative North American trade. The district, established upon his family estate, was the creation of Sir Alexander Dennistoun, who, from 1861 onwards, developed it on a definite plan.

Several of the streets in Sir Alexander's model suburb were named after his various relatives by marriage, a prime instance being Oakley Terrace, lying to the immediate west of the old exhibition grounds. The ready presumption that this must have been a tribute to Annie is effectively excluded by the fact that it predates the visit of the Wild West by three clear decades. In 1861, just a year after Annie's birth, it was one of first streets to be laid out upon Dennistoun's foundation. It was actually named after Georgina Oakley, Sir Alexander's daughter-in-law.

Meanwhile, Ibrox Park, home of Rangers Football Club, marked the effective south-western boundary of the conurbation while, to the north, the old villages of Possil and Springburn still retained their ancient isolation. The latter of these, however, was undergoing an accelerated development, stimulated by the North British Railway Company's works at nearby Cowlairs.

Barlinnie Prison stood as a cluster of buildings beyond the city boundaries to the north-east, and had been built during the years 1880–86 in response to prison congestion. Duke Street Prison, a short distance to the right of the foot of John Knox Street, was also known as the North Prison, in contradistinction to the South Prison, otherwise the Burgh Prison at Glasgow Green, which had been closed in 1862. After public executions ceased in 1865, Duke Street was Glasgow's place of execution until 1928, when it was succeeded in this capacity by Barlinnie. Duke Street Prison finally closed in 1955 and was demolished in 1958.

During November 1891, a matter of days before the Wild West show opened its doors to the public, the city boundaries were expanded to absorb the previously separate 'police burghs' of Govanhill, Crosshill, Pollokshields East and West, Hillhead and Maryhill. Calton, Anderston and the Gorbals had already been added in 1846 but the third major boundary extension, involving Govan, Partick and Pollokshaws, would not follow until 1912.

This chaotic and uncontrolled growth in the city's population, with the dire social and economic consequences which accompanied it, was to some extent mitigated through the enlightened and energetic rule of the local authority, which controlled the city's infrastructure by means of a wide-ranging system of public works and amenities. The ancient Town Council would remain in place until 1895, when all municipal functions passed to the newly created Glasgow Corporation.

The general prevalence of cholera and typhus in the mid nineteenth century made the availability of a clean and reliable water supply an imperative. A revolutionary system for drawing fifty million gallons from the waters of Loch Katrine each day was officially opened by Queen Victoria on the 14th of October 1859. From that time on, these former scourges dramatically declined.

Work had already begun on a projected suburban underground railway system during 1891 but this would not open for business until December 1896.

Various boats and ferries, including river buses called Cluthas, plied the stinking waters of the Clyde. Aside from these and the city railway lines, local public transportation was effected principally by the tramcars, which ran from August 1872 until September 1962. They had been preceded by horse-drawn omnibuses, introduced to Glasgow in 1845. The tramcars were operated at first by the Glasgow Tramway and Omnibus Company and were exclusively horse-drawn at the time of Buffalo Bill's first visit. When the company's lease expired in 1894, the service was taken over by the Council. The horses were phased out between 1898 and 1902 and the trams were powered by electricity thereafter.

Gas street lighting had been introduced as early as 1817 and was under the control of the Town Council by 1869. Electricity in 1891 was limited to a few specific buildings such as St Enoch's station, the first establishment to be lit by electricity in Glasgow. The Town Council was empowered to operate a public electricity supply in 1890 but this was not brought into effect until early 1893. It was in the same year that the first electric street lighting was introduced but the yellow glare of the gas lamps would continue to predominate for some time to come. The new source of power received a gradual public acceptance and was in general domestic use by 1913.

A telephone exchange was in existence during this period. With only a limited number of subscribers, it was at that time in the hands of a private company. The service would be operated by the Glasgow Corporation from 1900 until 1907.

In 1891, the City Improvement Trust was engaged in the perennial problem of slum clearance, having begun a programme of building tenement blocks in the Saltmarket and elsewhere in 1888.

Glasgow, as Buffalo Bill found it, was a city in a state of transition, with the direction of events dictated by essentially the same dynamic of rapid progress and technological change as held sway in his homeland. It had one foot in the distant past and one already confidently planted in the twentieth century. The only certainty was the inevitability of impending change.

The noble Molendinar, which had presided over a procession of historical change spanning many centuries, was effectively reduced to the status of a covered and festering sewer, discharging all manner of filthy effluent into the contaminated and lifeless waters of the River Clyde. The *Glasgow Evening News* carried a graphic commentary upon this sad decline:

> The Molendinar gurgled into the Clyde to-day, and the people passing knew of the fact a couple of hundred yards off. There was no mistake about the scents – there were three separate and distinct odours, and they were thick, solid, and lasting.[1]

Even within living memory, salmon had been common, to the extent that it was a staple of the Glaswegian diet, and, during the 1840s, boys had fished for flounders at the Broomielaw. But, by the time the final decade of the nineteenth century was underway, these aquatic life forms were, as far as the once-pure waters of the Clyde were concerned, as effectively consigned to historical oblivion as the American buffalo.

Preparations

You can just about imagine folk's reactions, on Thursday the 3rd of September 1891, to the rumours reverberating and ricocheting around the bars, workplaces and playgrounds of Glasgow. For, on that day, a quite momentous announcement was made through the 'Gossip and Grumbles' column of the *Evening Times*: 'Buffalo Bill, with his entire show, is coming to the East-End Exhibition buildings, which are to be altered at no distant date.'

There was, at the time, no permanent structure in Glasgow of sufficient size to accommodate the show but, as luck would have it, the complex of buildings which had housed the previous winter's East End Industrial Exhibition – a fund-raiser for the proposed 'People's Palace' on Glasgow Green, which eventually opened in 1898 – had not yet been demolished. Lew Parker, the contracting agent, acting as an advance party for the management of the Wild West, secured the lease. The permission requisite for the conversions was granted by the Dean of Guild Court, also on the 3rd of September, without objection.

An intensive publicity campaign, directed by Charles P. Watson of St Vincent Street, was soon underway and, by the middle of October, Glaswegians found Buffalo Bill's features staring down at them from a good proportion of the city's public houses. Pamphlets were delivered door to door and posters, depicting such delights as cowboys, Indians, buffaloes and mustangs, soon made their ubiquitous appearance on hoardings. Saturation press coverage was no local phenomenon but extended to one hundred and twenty-seven papers the length and breadth of Scotland.

The Indians were an exotic presence in the East End from the day of their arrival and were reported by the *Glasgow Evening News* as 'already casting an air of romance and gaudy horse blankets over the East End'.[2]

Meanwhile, a cowboy, while taking a wander down Duke Street just as one of the schools was coming out, was assailed by the youngsters with cries of, 'Get your hair cut!'

By the end of the month, Dr Fortune of Townhead was hotly tipped for appointment as the Wild West's medical officer.[3]

On the Frontier

When the first news broke that Buffalo Bill was coming, there must have been plenty who awaited further details with baited breath and as many again who just couldn't wait for the show to open. As luck would have it, they didn't have to for an advance party of around twenty Sioux Indians was already on its way.

At 10.40 in the evening of Sunday the 6th of September, these Indians rode the iron horse into the Central Station as the leading attraction with 'Hardie and Von Leer's Great American Company', for a week's engagement at the Royal Princess's Theatre, in Gorbals Street, from Monday the 7th until Saturday the 12th. As the front-page adverts proclaimed throughout the week, they were to perform in a dramatic extravaganza entitled *On the Frontier*.

This 'military melodrama',[4] as it was termed, was highly derivative of the theatrical genre pioneered by Buffalo Bill himself and also bore close affinities to the White Lily production with which Viola Clemmons was preparing to go on tour. The White Lily Company advertised:

> Only full-blooded Sioux Indians in this country excepting those held by Col. W. F. Cody ('Buffalo Bill') as Prisoners of War.[5]

This was probably intended as a direct swipe at the Great American Company although the malediction might well have included Mexican Joe Shelley in its ambit as well.[6]

According to the promotional materials dutifully reproduced by the *Evening Times* on the 7th of September 1891, the Glasgow performances of *On the Frontier* were its British debut. Subsequent appearances are known at Greenwich, Cardiff and Brighton, in connection with which a daily street procession was advertised.[7]

In substance, the production was built around a distillation of practically every cliché spawned over the course of four centuries of Indian warfare. It was advertised as portraying the realities of frontier life through an adaptation of two of James Fenimore Cooper's novels – although exactly which was not specified. The stock characters of this genre were already as well established as in pantomime and Yiddish theatre and, over the course of the next few decades, the genre would evolve into the Western movie. Among the cast of fifty, there numbered the 'good guy' – James M. Hardie as the hero, a scout by the name of Jack Osborne – and the 'bad guy'. There was also the inevitable Pocahontas figure, the 'Indian princess', here going under the name of 'Blue Flower' and interpreted by Sara B. Von Leer who, by all accounts, was an effective and popular heroine. An additional twist to the plot was that Blue Flower – and one is irresistibly led to suspect that she doubled as the romantic interest – was in reality a white maiden who years before had been stolen away and raised by her Indian captors.

Mr Hardie was claimed as a native of Edinburgh, who had emigrated to the 'Far West' in his earliest years and – in a parallel with Buffalo Bill – was stated to have first made his way in life as a rider with the Pony Express. Miss Leer, it seems, possessed similar transatlantic credentials; she was born in Alabama, though her grandmother was 'Mrs Mary Duff, a famous English actress'.[8]

Even by the standards of 1891, the plot was 'on not unfamiliar lines',[9] and made much of the enmity between Jack and his adversary, Bill Morley, played here by Charles Harley. Mr Hardie's manly figure and fine baritone voice did full justice to his heroic role, while Mr Harley, a Victorian stage villain in the finest tradition, was hissed off the stage at the conclusion of every act. The play's climax came in the final scene with 'a highly sensational bowie knife encounter',[10] from which, it appears reasonably safe to assume, Jack emerged as victor.

Welcome light relief was provided by singing and dancing from two of the actresses and the comic eccentricities of W. H. Leary and Peter H. Gardiner, stated to be 'the funniest seen for a long time'. Of the Native American contingent, the same review offered the further assessment that:

> The piece is made all the more realistic by the appearance in all their native warpaint of a band of real Sioux Indians, who from time to time give graphic representations of the terrible nature of their mode of warfare.[11]

It was opined that several of the scenes were 'brilliant spectacular achievements', with that entitled 'The Surprise' being singled out as the most effective. This tableau depicted the by-now infamous Custer massacre although, of necessity, it must have been an even more scaled-down version than that which would shortly form the centrepiece of Buffalo Bill's show.

The next scene introduced the ghost dance, of which so much had been heard the previous winter and, within the play's limited historical perspectives, artistic licence operated to compress the Custer battle and the ghost dance cult of fully fourteen years later into a single historical episode.

The Royal Princess's Theatre had been built during the 1870s and became famous more as a music hall than as a legitimate theatre. It is credited as the home of modern pantomime and was sold in 1945 to become the Citizens' Theatre, under which name it remains, albeit in a more modern building, a familiar part of the city landscape.

Notes

1. 11 November 1891
2. 27 October 1891
3. *Evening Times*, 29 October 1891
4. *Evening Times*, 7 September 1891
5. Quoted by Alan Gallop in *Buffalo Bill's British Wild West*, p. 180
6. See Chapter 10, infra
7. E.g. in the *Sussex Daily News*, 19 October 1891
8. *Evening Times*, 7 September 1891
9. *Evening Times*, 8 September 1891
10. Ibid.
11. Ibid.

4

'VEXATIOUS DELAYS'

The Deadwood Coach

The grand opening of the Wild West show in Glasgow was originally scheduled for Monday the 9th of November. Work on the conversions had begun around the beginning of October but, 'to ensure perfection in this stupendous production',[1] it had to be postponed to Thursday the 12th. Five hundred carpenters laboured throughout the night in the hope of meeting this latest deadline but to no avail. Up until the 11th, the opening was still being advertised for the 12th but, when the great day dawned, Glaswegians were once again disappointed by an apology appearing on the front page of the *Evening Times* and elsewhere:

BUFFALO BILL'S WILD WEST CO.
TO THE PUBLIC

The Management of Buffalo Bill's Wild West sincerely regret to announce another Postponement.
 Having been under great expense for over two weeks, ready to fulfil, to the letter, their public promises, circumstances beyond their control (relative to the building, which should have been handed over to them November 2) has (*sic*) been the delay, and the

Management, therefore, throw themselves on the indulgence of the Scottish Public, with the assurance that it is in the interests of their future patrons' comfort, and that MONDAY, NOVEMBER 16, will be positively the INAUGURAL EXHIBITION.

Those who have already purchased Tickets can have them transferred to Monday, or any other Evening, or have money refunded, on application to Messrs Paterson, Sons and Co., 152 Buchanan Street, Glasgow.

Trusting that any annoyance necessarily created will be excused, owing to the Magnitude of the Enterprise.

We remain, yours respectfully,
CODY & SALSBURY

However, during the three weeks elapsing between the Wild West's arrival and the show's eventual opening, there was plenty in Glasgow for Buffalo Bill and his entourage to be going on with. Although the successive delays must have been costly and inconvenient at the time, the performers were at least afforded ample leisure in which to accustom themselves to their new surroundings. The process of acculturation involved was mutual and, before very long, the local people had pretty much become used to the strangers in their midst.

The Wild West Establishment

The East End Exhibition Buildings, which in those days stood in a 'thick grove',[2] were completely gutted and rebuilt. On the afternoon of Thursday the 5th of November, the conversions were formally unveiled to a substantial gathering of pressmen, who were accorded the additional privilege of meeting and shaking hands with the most prominent members of the Indian contingent.

The range of buildings which, during the previous winter's East End Industrial Exhibition had been divided into the 'Grand Hall', a series of avenues and the Fine Art Galleries, was now united under one handsome arched roof, raised by twenty-one feet to fifty feet in height. The structure was supported by girders which, in turn, rested upon steel columns thirty-one feet high. The main girder, which extended sideways across the arena, was 140 feet in length and twelve feet deep, with a carrying weight in the region of 400 tons. It naturally invited comparison with the Forth and Tay Bridges and was only exceeded in length by one roof girder in Scotland. That was to be found in Glasgow's Central Station and it measured 216 feet. The great virtue of this arrangement was that it obviated the need for pillars so that a clear and unobstructed view was assured from all parts of the house. The total cost of the steel work, undertaken by Messrs Somervail and Co., of the Dalmuir Iron Works, near Glasgow, was estimated at £2,000.

The building was thus converted into an amphitheatre, capable of comfortably accommodating a seated capacity crowd of 7,000. The arena, occupying its eastern portion, measured 210 feet deep by 150 feet long and was surrounded on three sides by the seating arrangements. Twenty-five boxes, each five feet square, were placed directly facing the amphitheatre and, to the left and right, the seats rose from the floor in galleries.

The back end of the arena was dominated by a curtained proscenium, seventy feet wide and thirty-two high, and with a semi-circular background, so arranged as to give the impression of immense distance, and illuminated from behind.

Realistic scenery, consisting of a painted backdrop, was created by local scene-painter William Glover, whose work was then well known. He had very recently won praise for his scenic accessories at the Edinburgh Police Bazaar. The scenery used in the show consisted of a series of seven panoramic pictures, each one 200 feet long by thirty-five high and mounted on a cyclorama by means of huge drums. Most of these were the creations of the late Matt Morgan and dated to the show's 1886 indoor winter season in New York. Mr Glover's contribution was the backdrop which would accompany the 'Pilgrim Fathers' sequence.

The principal entrances lay under the arena seating, measuring twenty-eight feet in breadth, with ten exits available to meet the eventuality of a crush.

A ten-foot tunnel was excavated, leading into the arena. Mounted warriors passed through this to launch a surprise flanking attack during one of the scenes.

The entire process of refurbishment was carried out under the direction of architect James Chalmers, of 101 St Vincent Street, Glasgow.

Lighting was entirely by gas, with the full pressure of the Duke Street main being called into service. Five handsome coronas lit the arena and there were five ranges of gas battens on the stage. The proscenium was illuminated by means of prismatic calciums and limelight effects. The interior of the building was painted white and the ground was covered with a white substance, in order to give the greatest possible effect to the lighting.

Ventilation, rendered all the more necessary by the vast quantity of gunpowder expended, was provided by means of a series of powerful Blackman air propellers fixed up in the roof close to the stage and powered by a six horsepower dynamo. Heating was by means of steam pipes passing around the building.

These arrangements were hardly impressive by modern standards but, at the time, the arena was widely advertised, with some justification, as the 'the Grandest Amphitheatre in Europe'.[3]

And, towering above all else, there was a shelf near the roof for those unsung heroes, the two limelight men, who, once the performances finally got underway, would perch precariously for hours on end, with their legs dangling, like a pair of 'doos' on a girder in St Enoch's Station.

One of the finishing touches was a covered driveway, twenty feet wide, enabling patrons to be dropped off at the door, saving them the walk along the lengthy avenue leading from Duke Street. This was still in the course of construction and would remain so for a while to come.

Living accommodation was provided in the former Boys' House of Refuge, adjoining the main building to the immediate south. This cruciform structure contained nine rooms, among whose occupants were Colonel Cody, George C. Crager and Annie Oakley, as well as three 'wards' or dormitories and an office.

Of Colonel Cody's personal quarters, the *Scottish Leader* reported that 'his private room is furnished in luxurious style, and interest attaching to it is enhanced by the display of curious relics and pictures'.[4]

Miss Oakley adorned her room with skins and curios and, according to the *Glasgow Evening News*, it was 'the prettiest little parlour that ever you did spy'.[5]

This building also housed the dining room, a poster room and a scene-painting room, where the journalists discovered Mr Glover hard at work.

The other permanent structures in the complex, otherwise known as the old Reformatory Buildings, were shown on the original plans – archived at the city's Mitchell Library[6] – as adapted to the show's requirements. These were: a chapel; workshops to be used as stables, located but a few paces to the rear of the main building; and a buffalo house, lying directly across the wall from the playground of Whitehill Public School.

Fire at the Welcome Wigwam

Buffalo Bill's sister, Helen Cody Wetmore, recounts the story of a misfortune befalling her brother, in chapter twenty-eight of *Last of the Great Scouts*:

> While Will was away at the seat of war, his beautiful home in North Platte, 'Welcome Wigwam,' burned to the ground. The little city is not equipped with much of a fire department, but a volunteer brigade held the flames in check long enough to save almost the entire contents of the house, among which were many valuable and costly souvenirs that could never be replaced. Will received a telegram announcing that his house was ablaze, and his reply was characteristic: 'Save Rosa Bonheur's picture, and the house may go to blazes.'[7]

The 'picture' was of course Cody's portrait executed by Madame Bonheur in Paris in 1889. In context, the phrase 'seat of war' refers to Cody's involvement in the ghost dance outbreak and so indicates a date in the winter of 1890–91. It is therefore at the least mildly puzzling to discover what is apparently the same incident – identical in points of essential detail – reported in the *Glasgow Evening News* of the 6th of November 1891, i.e. almost a year later:

> Buffalo Bill's ranche-house in Nebraska burned to the ground the day before yesterday. This is said to mean the loss of about £10,000, but B. William eats his clam chowder with the old appetite, and says it can't be helped.

The story was also covered by *The Scottish Leader* on the same date and the time reference here is to an interview which had been conducted on the previous day:

> It should be mentioned that Colonel Cody received on the previous night a telegram announcing that his house at North Platte, Nebraska, had been burned to the ground. The Colonel was only disturbed because of the probability of some of his valuable relics having shared the fate of his house.

According to a careful reading of *both* Glasgow clippings, the fire must be taken to have occurred on the 4th of November 1891, while Cody was in Glasgow, Scotland, and *not* in South Dakota.

While there are a few possible explanations for the discrepancy, the most likely one is that Helen Cody Wetmore has simply got her dates wrong. Although generally accepted as a primary source, her book is riddled with inaccuracies and serious errors of detail. It therefore seems clear that this oft-repeated story possesses a Scottish dimension that has hitherto generally been missed.

The honourable exception on this occasion is Robert A. Carter who, in his book *Buffalo Bill Cody – The Man Behind the Legend*, gives the date of the calamity as November 1891.[8] Noting and dismissing Mrs Wetmore's position on the subject, he concludes,

'The *Tribune* gives the year of the fire as 1891, which is undoubtedly correct.'

It is significant that Carter has clearly made this deduction without reference to the Glasgow sources and apparently unaware that the show was then in Scotland. This correspondence may, therefore, be taken as conclusively settling the matter.

On the evening of Friday the 6th of November, the Glasgow Athenaeum Dramatic Club gave a complimentary supper for Henry Irving. Irving's private secretary, Bram Stoker – to whom I shall return – and Colonel Cody also graced the assembled company.

Buffalo Bill at Ibrox

Soccer enthusiasts may care to note that on Saturday the 7th of November, Buffalo Bill 'and party'[9] took in a fitba' match at Ibrox. The occasion was a Glasgow Cup tie between Rangers and Queen's Park. The game had been rearranged from the previous week. On Thursday the 29th of October, a thick blanket of fog descended, enveloping both the city and its suburbs. By Saturday the 31st, the fog was denser than ever and materially impeded river traffic along the Clyde. At high noon, such was the unwonted darkness both inside and out that the gaslights were lit.

These conditions naturally played havoc with the football programme for the day. The match between Rangers and Queen's Park was postponed while Celtic's home tie against a long-defunct Springburn-based club called the Northern got underway but had to be abandoned. Both of these games were rescheduled for the 7th of November. The game at Ibrox was played before a near-capacity crowd of 12,000. This, it should be noted, was the original Ibrox Park, occupied by the club between 1887 and 1899. The sites of the old and new grounds overlap but the first one was marginally further to the north and to the east so that the traditional 'Rangers end' was then very much closer to the Copeland Road and covered the present site of Harrison Drive.

By all accounts, Rangers had the better of the encounter, to the extent that play was somewhat one-sided, but, owing to a combination of excellent defending by Queen's, bad luck and an inability to finish, the home side failed to score.

Buffalo Bill certainly picked the game to be at for, according to *The Scottish Leader*,[10] it was 'one of the most extraordinary games ever witnessed in a cup tie competition'. The journalist was obviously a bluenose himself for he recorded that 'the Rangers were, unfortunately, beaten by 3 goals to nil'. His assessment, whether impartial or otherwise, was that, 'The Queens were completely overmatched. In the open Rangers simply toyed with their opponents.'

Rangers hit the post six times and a striker called McPherson somehow contrived to miss from almost literally under the bar. In the face of such dismal 'shooting', the point that the forwards could have learned a thing or two from the expert marksmen of the Wild West was not lost on Colonel Cody!

The price of admission was just sixpence – though ladies were allowed in free. A seat in the stand cost an extra shilling. The total takings came to around £340, deemed by the *Scottish Sport* a very tidy sum for a Glasgow Cup tie.[11]

Such was the absence of the mutual sectarian hatred which would in later decades come to poison relations between the respective sets of Celtic and Rangers supporters, that T. Dunbar, of the Celtic Reserve, turned out for the Ibrox club that afternoon.

Queen's Park were already two up – the opener was hotly disputed as it looked offside – when Buffalo Bill and his entourage arrived. This may be taken as a deliberate ploy on Cody's part. If he had arrived at ten minutes to kick-off like everyone else, he would have gone unnoticed by the majority of the spectators. Most likely the real object was not to watch the game but to be seen by large numbers of people. This was a standard exercise in self-publicity, known as 'grandstanding', intended to advertise Cody's own show which would open shortly.

Maybe Cody, like many a visiting football manager since, was also concerned to check out the opposition. Almost certainly, he would have been particularly anxious to gauge the effect that the

'YOUR FATHERS THE GHOSTS'

football programme might be expected to have on his Saturday matinee performances.

As matters turned out, Buffalo Bill needn't have worried because football matches proved to be more of a help than a hindrance. Enthusiasts coming to Glasgow from the country districts for a game on a Saturday afternoon often decided to make a day of it and turned out in droves for the Wild West in the evening.

The visitors received a warm reception as they meandered up in front of the grandstand. Some wit in the crowd, referring to the Colonel's flowing locks, cried out, 'Get your hair cut!' Cody was described as wearing 'a white sombrero and a very large patronising smile'.[12] He appeared to be very happy with himself and with the occasion. The party failed to find seats in the stand and Mr Lawson, the club secretary, hurriedly accommodated them in the reserved seats at the front of the pavilion – this was presumably as far as 'corporate hospitality' had evolved.

Buffalo Bill was certainly in fine company on the pavilion veranda that day. The other dignitaries enjoying the same point of vantage were Bailies Ure Primrose and Guthrie (the former of whom, as Sir John Ure Primrose, was Lord Provost at the time of the show's return in 1904), as well as Alexander Stewart, Conservative candidate for the Hutchesontown Division.

Another notable of the time, whom Buffalo Bill met that day, was W. A. Donnelly, a local artist who did illustrations for various local papers and sporting publications.

The *Scottish Referee* recorded that, 'He was the most picturesque personality on the ground, and as he made the acquaintance in front of the pavilion with Artist Donnelly, of the "Graphic," the two offered a fine picture to the enterprising photographer.'[13] It is implied that 'the enterprising photographer' actually took advantage of this opportunity but, if this is indeed the case, the result is not otherwise known.

The *Graphic*, incidentally, was a London-based illustrated newspaper. It is to be regretted, however, that Mr Donnelly does not appear to have created a record of the occasion. Whether he was overawed or simply 'off duty' is not apparent.

'VEXATIOUS DELAYS'

At half time, Buffalo Bill was presented to both teams and was very much taken by the 'blue shirts'. He confessed that he did not know much about the 'show', as he persisted in calling the game, but invited the Rangers players to visit his.

However, he did not quite hit it off with the Queen's Park side, who, for some unaccountable reason, received him rather coldly. In mitigation, maybe the 'Spiders' were just short of breath. At any rate, they must have recovered their manners, as well as their sense of occasion, because they accepted Colonel Cody's subsequent invitation to attend the evening show on Christmas Eve.

In the end, Queen's Park ran out 3–0 winners. In those days, Queen's Park, the first-ever Scottish football club, was very much the side to beat – not that many did. *The Bailie for Wednesday, September 23rd, 1891* had referred to them as 'the premier club' but, in truth, by the time that Buffalo Bill saw them, their glory years were already behind them. The club's position of assured pre-eminence in the Scottish game during the first phase of its existence fell casualty to the club's implacable and perennial hostility towards professionalism and, initially, to their refusal even to accept league status. The championship in the Scottish Football League's inaugural season, 1890–91, had been shared by Rangers and Dumbarton. Queen's Park won the Scottish Cup for the tenth and final time in 1893 – the same year that the Scottish game turned professional – and have never lifted a major honour since.

Celtic meanwhile, overturned a two-goal deficit to beat the Northern by three goals to two.

The Glasgow Cup had been instituted four years previously, in 1887. For a time, it was probably the most vibrant and keenly contested trophy in the land. In season 1891–92, no fewer than twenty clubs took part. Among the clubs who competed at the quarter-final stage, alongside others marked down for future greatness, were Cambuslang, Linthouse, and Whitefield. Celtic emerged as eventual winners, beating Clyde 7–1 in the final, played at Cathkin Park on the 12th of December 1891.

At the Theatre

On Monday the 9th, following the success of *On the Frontier* just two months previously, the Royal Princess's Theatre saw some real cowboys – this time not on stage, but in the audience. Of the drama, *Crimes of Paris*, presented by Charles Melville and Company, the Wild West visitors were highly demonstrative in their appreciation. Buffalo Bill expressed his own enjoyment from the comfort of a private box. This was just two days after Cody's visit to Ibrox so he clearly intended to take full advantage of the entertainment on offer, before settling down to his more accustomed role as entertainer.

Mounting Excitement

For some time past, serious concerns had been expressed concerning the conduct of the tramway company's trace-boys, as evidenced by an article appearing in *Quiz* on the 5th of September 1890. The columnist had recently witnessed a gentleman being knocked over in Renfield Street, through the recklessness of a trace-boy, and recorded that an old lady had been rendered unconscious in the same manner not long before. He proposed that the company should introduce a standing rule requiring that the boys should lead, rather than ride, the horses back to the stance in Renfield Street or, at the very least, proceed by way of Hope Street, where the traffic was not so great.

However, an item appearing in the 'Lorgnette' column in the *Glasgow Evening News* admonished that there was serious potential for the antics of the trace-boys, under the dubious inspiration of Buffalo Bill, to get seriously out of hand.[14] For now – before the show had even opened its doors – they were no longer content merely to ride on the horses' backs but were using them to stage impromptu bucking-bronco exhibitions in the streets.

The columnist's considered advice to the trace-boys was that they should make personal application to Colonel Cody: 'He is a benevolent individual, I understand, and might be induced to take a limited staff of apprentice cowboys, incipient scouts, and suckling lariat throwers.'

On the 14th, the same column alerted the public to the hazards posed by schoolboys armed with lassos improvised from school slate boards and bits of string, with the alarming prospect of the playground being transformed into an amateur Wild West.

And, in the meantime, cowboy hats, of bespoke quality, went on sale at £3 10/- a time.[15] If the fashion ever caught on, it failed to stand the test of time.

A rider in the guise of Buffalo Bill – one among the first of many impersonators who would follow – put in an appearance at the Edinburgh Police Bazaar, in the course of the week ending Saturday the 14th of November. The growing enthusiasm, however, evidently did not extend to ecclesiastical quarters. Matters arising from the visit of Buffalo Bill came before the Glasgow United Presbyterian Presbytery on the 10th of November. The Rev. Dr Alexander Oliver called the meeting's attention to the odious form of Sabbath desecration that had arisen in consequence of the arrival in their midst of Buffalo Bill.

The Scotsman takes up the story:

> He was not there to advertise that man, but to protest against workmen being employed on Sabbath in getting up a place to accommodate him and his buffaloes. (Laughter.) He could assure the Presbytery that it had grieved the hearts of Christian people in the locality to have the Sabbath outraged in this particular way. It was agreed that the report of the Committee on Sabbath Sanctification should be delayed till next meeting.[16]

On Friday the 13th, Buffalo Bill was back at the theatre again. The *Glasgow Evening News* of the following day reported that, 'Buffalo Bill is already an institution in our midst. He was at the Theatre Royal last night, and was hailed uproariously by the "gods".' The programme on this occasion was a Carl Rosa Company production, *The Daughter of the Regiment*, with opera by Donizetti.

Buffalo Bill in George Square

It was not long before the city came to experience one of Colonel Cody's legendary acts of generosity. In the *Glasgow Evening News*, a correspondent to the 'Lorgnette' columnist recounted an incident which he had witnessed on the previous evening:

> I was making my usual purchase last night of a halfpenny worth of 'News' from an old lady who supplies evening papers to the lieges at a corner of George Square. A smart little girl, with bare feet and not over well 'put on,' was assisting her in her usual calling, when a distinguished looking gentleman, with a somewhat outré appearance, came forward, and after investing in a variety of papers, began to take notice of the juvenile newsagent. Pointing to her shoeless feet, which evidently attracted his attention on the cold night, he asked the old woman what it would cost to get a pair of shoes for the child, and then handed her the amount she named. He paid for his papers, gave the old lady a sixpence for herself, handed a silver coin to another poor body in the neighbourhood, and then went off with a smile on his face, that showed he felt pleased at being able thus unostentatiously to do a kindly action. On inquiring who the gentleman was, the old woman replied – 'Sure that's Buffalo Bill, an' he has bought his papers from me the last two nights. God bless him.'[17]

CODY AND BURKE AT THE GLASGOW ART CLUB

The Glasgow Art Club was founded in 1867 and boasts Buffalo Bill and Oscar Wilde among its famous visitors. In 1891, the club occupied a rented townhouse at 151, Bath Street; the present premises at number 185 were purchased in 1892. The first volume of the club's 'Special Guest Books', on the thirty-second and thirty-third pages respectively, contains entries relative to the introduction of Major Burke and Colonel Cody on Friday, 13 November 1891. The rules of the club permitted the extension of all privileges of membership, for a period not exceeding two weeks, to 'artists or special visitors from a distance'. No other entry relating to any member of the Wild West entourage appears in the club's books and so there is no surviving evidence to indicate that Burke and Cody were particularly active in the exercise of their membership.

On the evening of Sunday the 15th of November, the eve of the grand opening, Colonel Cody dined with Mr Irving once again, in Edinburgh on this occasion. As if in celestial acknowledgement of the momentous events about to commence below, a lunar eclipse began at 10.34 that night.

Notes

1 *Evening Times*, 11 November 1891
2 Lew Parker, *Odd People I Have Met*, pp. 82–83
3 See, for example, the *Evening Times*, 16 November 1891
4 5 November 1891
5 27 November 1891
6 1891, Dean of Guild file 1/1570, Mitchell Library, Glasgow
7 p. 266
8 p. 364
9 *Scottish Sport*, 10 November 1891
10 9 November 1891
11 10 November 1891
12 *Scottish Referee*, 9 November 1891. Note incidentally that the term 'sombrero' appears on a number of occasions and that the context appears to require a reference to the conventional cowboy hat, as opposed to the more flamboyant Mexican headgear.
13 Ibid.
14 6 November 1891
15 c.f. *Glasgow Evening News*, 14 November 1891
16 11 November 1891
17 Same date

5

THE THEATRE OF WAR

Miss Annie Oakley
The "Little Sure Shot"

Fathers, mothers, aunts and cousins,
Come in couples, come in dozens;
Bring your lads – lads bring your lasses;
Come by cars, or trains or buses –
Come on! East and pay your footing,
And see Miss Annie Oakley shooting.[1]

The whole of Monday the 16th of November was spent in rehearsals and, at eight o'clock in the evening, Buffalo Bill's Wild West was finally unveiled to almost 6,000 spectators who had crowded along Duke Street from an early hour. Lord Provost John Muir and almost all of the city magistrates graced the occasion with their presence and took up places of honour.

By a singular coincidence, a meeting was held by the Glasgow School Board on the very same evening, for the official opening of the new Whitehill Public School next door. A general invitation was extended to parents and other interested parties, this rival attraction commencing at seven-thirty, just half an hour earlier than the Wild West show.

Memories of this momentous conjunction of local events

inevitably became confused over the years, giving rise to a curious local legend. In 1973, James Black and Hamish Whyte, in the unpublished manuscript, *Dennistoun – a Brief History*, reported that rumours still persisted 'that Buffalo Bill presided at the opening of Whitehill School'.[2]

Proceedings were marred by some irksome moments of waiting between scenes but the audience took these in good part, readily accepting that the delays were necessarily incidental to the opening of such a gigantic undertaking. In consequence, the performance dragged on until after eleven o'clock but interest never seemed to flag.

The entertainment was a revival of *The Drama of Civilization*, the historical pageant staged at previous winter seasons in New York and Manchester. Although broadly similar in content, it was nevertheless radically restructured from the outdoor version of the show witnessed at the English and Welsh venues earlier in 1891. The spectacle was now enhanced with what were widely advertised to be 'the grandest and largest scenic effects ever produced'.[3] The *Evening Citizen* deemed the production to be 'not so much a triumph of art as a triumph of realism'.[4]

While no attempt had been made to arrange the seventeen outdoor items in chronological sequence, the performance now took the form of a narrative of conquest in six tableaux or episodes. The message of racial and cultural supremacy, although always implicit, was now made overt. This was in no sense the forerunner of *Dances with Wolves* – the elemental forces of nature, wild beasts, and savage tribes were encountered as so many obstacles to be overcome by the intrepid settlers in turn.

The episodes were interspersed with four separate exhibitions of marksmanship and one of horsemanship. These were essentially digressions from the narrative and are properly considered as dramatic interludes for which scenery was not deployed.

The Opening Review
The show was preceded by an overture from the Cowboy Band, lasting about half an hour and now incorporating a selection of

Scots airs. A stirring rendition of 'The Star Spangled Banner' announced that the programme would shortly commence. The musicians continued to discourse throughout the evening.

H. M. Clifford, the orator, took up his position on a sort of pulpit and introduced the various groups of performers and individual celebrities in the opening review. Since many of the principal characters from earlier in the season had already departed, this must have been considerably modified. It is to be regretted that no detailed account of this part of the show in Glasgow appears to exist. Whether Kicking Bear reprised his position as the chief of the Cut-offs is therefore unknown.

Once again, Buffalo Bill on a white horse was the last to appear and he was received with great enthusiasm. He raised his hat in a general salute and was compelled to bow his acknowledgements several times before the audience finally permitted the show to proceed. Cody then led the horsemen in an orderly departure from the arena.

The orator continued to announce each item in turn, in a voice of such power and distinctness that it was heard on all sides.

The Indian in his Aboriginal State

The first episode depicted the 'Primeval Forest of America before its discovery by the White Man'.[5] This sequence begins at 'midnight' and the first actors to appear are 'Wild Animals in their Native Lairs'.

Lewis Parker, the stage manager, in his book *Odd People I Have Met*, notes the use of 'real animals, bears, elk, deer, etc.'[6] Deer were also promised in the show's standard advertisement – for example, in the *Evening Times* of the 16th of November 1891. These creatures had taken no part in the tour. Where they were obtained from remains a mystery as Glasgow had no zoo at this time.[7]

Next to appear was the 'Indian as he was before the Discovery'.[8] Sunrise followed and, although of course this effect was easily accomplished by means of lighting in an indoor arena, it would have been unthinkable out of doors. A friendly meeting of two tribes ensued, in the course of which a 'Grand Council' in sign language took place, with instances of Indian oratory, and concluding with the 'Feather and Omaha or War Dances', to the accompaniment of drumming and chanting by the women. 'Six move round a ring as if one, while others dance in the most unskilled manner possible.'[9]

Several of the details fuel the suspicion that little concession was made to historical authenticity for these were clearly representatives of the stereotypical Plains culture – which, in the time depicted, had not yet emerged – transplanted somewhere in the eastern woodlands though, mercifully, *sans* the horse which, even Buffalo Bill conceded, had yet to be introduced to the Americas.

Although this sequence had not featured in the touring version of the show, it was a patent adaptation of 'Life Customs of the Indians', already familiar from the outdoor venues.

First Contact

In the second episode, first contact with the white settlers was symbolised by a re-enactment of the landing of the Pilgrim Fathers in 1620. They alighted from the *Mayflower* upon Plymouth Rock, in that part of the eastern seaboard thereafter known as 'New England'.

Annie Oakley

The first break in the narrative took the form of an exhibition of shooting from the legendary Annie Oakley. For *Eastern Bells*, she was 'the crowning charm of the whole show, as is nightly testified by the ringing cheers which greet her appearance.'[10]

Night after night, Annie held audiences spellbound with her prodigious dexterity, as she shot at clay pigeons and glass balls. On the rare occasions when she missed her target, she would stamp her foot in mock rage. On scoring a hit, she would give a kick of delight as a wave of enthusiastic and generous applause resounded in the packed arena around her. Among the other remarkable feats of marksmanship accomplished by her in the course of her act, Annie shattered ten glass balls thrown successively into the air, in as many seconds, changing her rifle ten times in the process. One of her specialities was to fire over her shoulder, aiming backwards with the aid of a mirror.

The Immigrant Train

Passing lightly over more than two centuries of United States history and diplomatically omitting all mention of such morbid themes as the French and Indian Wars, the Revolution, the removal of the eastern tribes to Indian Territory, black slavery and the War Between the States, the entire sweep of western expansion was neatly compressed into a single tableau.

That virtually all of the major conventions familiar in the modern western movie genre were established in advance by Buffalo Bill is particularly true of episode three, a depiction of the tribulations of a wagon train in its progress across the western plains.

Against a backdrop of the wilderness in the scorching noonday sun, Buffalo Bill, the hunter, came upon an oasis centred upon a drinking pool, with the buffalo herd grazing around it. He demonstrated his characteristic method of hunting these animals. While most Euro-American hunters shot with long-range rifles from a safe distance, Buffalo Bill rode into the midst of the herd, in the traditional manner of the Indians, heading off the leader and driving the animals in a tight circle.

A 'German Emigrant Train', under the escort of scouts and cowboys, next happened upon the scene. A band of marauding Indians attacked but they were repulsed by the defenders.

An element of comedy was injected by Jule Keen, who doubled as the show's treasurer, in the role of 'the Dutchman'. As the *Paisley & Renfrewshire Gazette* recorded: 'Jule Keen manfully fires his horse pistol into the air, and, after the fight is over, assumes a smiling air of "Alone I repulsed the Indians," in a manner that convulses the audience.'[11]

After the campfires were lit, a group of riders danced a Horseback Quadrille and there was singing from the Arlberger troupe of Tyrolean vocalists. This quartet has to be considered one of the very first extraneous elements successfully transplanted into the show and they made their debut in Glasgow. No mention of them can be found in connection with the English or Welsh venues. They were much appreciated and encores were regularly demanded.

As supper concluded, the campfires grew dim and the wagon folk retired for the night. But such was the unremitting peril of the life of the emigrant train there would be no happy ending. A prairie fire was simulated, through the ingenious deployment of a series of gas jets, and a stampede of terrified animals ensued, in all its violence and attendant horrors. A light appeared on the horizon and grew into a flame, spreading as it came ever closer. The alarm was sounded and the wagon train was overtaken by destruction.

Lew Parker supplies some useful detail concerning this sequence:

[T]he grass rows used in the prairie fire were graded from twenty-six feet high in the rear to three feet in front, giving the appearance of immense distance. The fire scene was most realistic. At that time we had no electric devices to help us out. I devised a steam curtain some distance in front of the burning grass and we forced the elk, buffalo and bears across the stage behind the steam effect, which gave the appearance of the animals going through a mountain of fire and smoke.[12]

Claude Lorraine Daly

In the second dramatic interlude, Claude Lorraine Daly gave an exhibition of pistol and revolver shooting.

Daly was additionally renowned for his impressive physique, and a somewhat unusual line drawing appeared in the *Evening Times*, illustrating 'the wonderful muscular development of his biceps and chest, the result of long and continuous training'.[13]

One of Daly's target cards is preserved in the collection of Glasgow's Mitchell Library. On one side appears a set of concentric circles, with a bullet hole breaking the innermost ring. Above this roundel are printed the lines:

> Claude Lorraine Daly,
> Buffalo Bill's Wild West.

Below it:

> The World's Greatest Pistol Shot.

On the reverse appears a handwritten inscription, dated December 1891:

> This target card was shot at with a revolver at 20 yards in our presence and handed to me by C. L. Daly a few minutes afterwards.

This message is authenticated with the signature 'W. L. Reid' and the address of the subscriber is given as 7, Royal Crescent, Glasgow. It was also from the private collection of W. L. Reid MD that the Mitchell Library acquired its copy of the show's official programme.

Cowboys' Fun

This ever-popular item in the Wild West programme, which made for a lively quarter of an hour, was, in common with the various displays of marksmanship, a deviation from the main programme but may have been intended as an introduction to the fourth episode, which was set on a cattle ranch.

The cowboys engaged in various acts of horsemanship, swooping down while at full gallop to gather objects from the ground and lassoing and riding a score or so of bucking horses. It was asserted in the programme that:

These Horses are not Trained, they are Wild, Unbroken Animals.

For reasons that are not entirely clear, the characteristic reaction to this sequence was one of intense mirth and gales of laughter resounded from all quarters of the arena.

The Cattle Ranche

The fourth episode, representing the next phase of settlement, gave an idyllic depiction of 'The New Home in the Wild West', with characterisations of the 'Pioneer Farmer' and 'Scenes and Incidents of Ranche Life in America'. The work of the dairy farmer and the ploughing of the fields were both represented and ingenious use of the scenery was made to simulate the changing of the seasons. The coming of autumn brought the harvest and the ingathering of the grain.

But once again, these happy and industrious scenes were but the tranquil prelude to the destructive violence of an Indian attack. Buffalo Bill's men effected a heroic and timely rescue and put the marauders to flight.

Master Johnnie Baker

In a further display of marksmanship, 'Master Johnnie Baker', billed as the 'Celebrated Young American Marksman', shot from almost every physical posture conceivable, standing on his head included.

Custer's Last Stand

The fifth episode was the undoubted high point of the entire show – a dramatic re-enactment of the events culminating in the Custer massacre. It has to be stressed, however, that this version was heavily fictionalised and fell far short of historical objectivity. In 1876, Buffalo Bill was the 5th Cavalry's chief of scouts and undoubtedly had an involvement in the wider campaign. However, he certainly did not take so direct a part in this particular engagement as was suggested in the show.

The Custer fight had not been on the touring programme. As the battle sequence, it supplanted the duel with Yellow Hand. Almost certainly, the same uniforms and props were used in both. However, the Custer massacre was by far the more spectacular of the two; the sequence in which Buffalo Bill fought with Yellow Hand had only lasted a couple of minutes.

The first of the three scenes was set in a military stockade. Buffalo Bill rode in to announce that a village of hostile Indians had been discovered. 'Boots and Saddles' was sounded and the troops departed. Buffalo Bill, meanwhile, was sent to summon reinforcements.

Scene two took place in a rocky canyon somewhere in the Little Bighorn Mountains and was entirely devoted to the musical drill of the doomed soldiers, no doubt serving to heighten the sense of tragedy in what would shortly follow.

Scene three took us to Sitting Bull's camp on the Little Bighorn River. The 7th Cavalry charged into the camp and fell headlong into a carefully laid ambush. Cody's logic is difficult to follow here. The soldiers were clearly the aggressors – they were attacking the Indians – but somehow the official programme contrived to portray 'brave General Custer and his entire command' as the victims and the slaughter of the entire company as the 'reddest page of savage history', conclusive evidence of the devious and underhand treachery of the hostiles. The Indians were, of course, only defending themselves against invasion and, if Custer in his ineptitude had grossly underestimated the strength of the enemy, with predictably fatal consequences, that was hardly the fault of his intended victims. Notice, of course, that, although much was made of the supposed atrocity, no mention was made of the recent carnage at Wounded Knee.

In the minds of contemporary British audiences, this scene was calculated to evoke parallels with of the fall of Gordon at Khartoum, just a few years previously in January 1885 – a true Victorian melodrama indeed.

It is, however, interesting to note that, back in 1876, when the *Glasgow Herald* printed telegrams from Washington, breaking the news of the reverse, on the 6th, 8th and 10th of July, the emerging picture presented was balanced and factual by comparison with the deliberately concocted fabrication that was the 'Triumph of the Bill' version of events. Mentions of war dances and perfidious savages lurking in ambush were conspicuous by their absence and the emphasis was placed squarely upon the role of Custer as the author of his own – and his command's – misfortunes. The contemporaneous press coverage, therefore, was far closer to the unromantic reality than to the tragic account purveyed to his audiences by Buffalo Bill.

The news relayed on the 10th is unobjectionable with regard to accuracy:

> It seems that General Custer owes his defeat and death to his own foolhardiness. He was sent by General Terry on a reconnoitring expedition, but as soon as he struck the Indian trail he followed up without communicating with the main body, and having divided his force, he fell a comparatively easy prey to the warlike Sioux, who are said to be thoroughly well equipped both as regards arms and horses.

Shortly after the last man, Custer himself, had fallen and the Indians had departed, Cody rode in at the head of the reinforcements he had (fictitiously) been dispatched to summon. A spotlight fell upon him as he doffed his hat and surveyed the field of slaughter. Behind him, the words 'Too Late!' were projected on to the cyclorama.

Darkness closed upon the scene, sparing the audience the absurd spectacle of the mangled corpses rising and walking away.

The reintroduction of the Custer battle into the Wild West programme was significant. The *Leeds Daily News*, uneasy that the Indians did 'not appear to have any other function in life than to be defeated',[14] had floated the idea that it might be more sporting to allow the Indians to win once in a while. It was reasoned that: 'Too much defeat of the Red Men is apt to become monotonous.'

And Heaven forfend that the impression be created that the course of westward expansion had been a mere one-way procession. The epic of the progress of civilisation demanded a martyr and, just as God had provided a sacrificial ram for Abraham, a victim was given in the form of George Armstrong Custer.

'Custer's Last Stand' even today remains a true *dies atra* in the history of the United States; it was the 9/11 of its age. With due theatrical timing, news of the reverse broke in the east right on cue to ruin the Republic's centennial celebrations on the 4th of July 1876.

But there is a Scottish dimension to the story, which has hitherto gone widely unnoticed for George Armstrong Custer may well have been one of our own. 'Armstrong' certainly indicates family connections with the frontier element that had its origins in the borderlands of Scotland.

Moreover, recent scholarship conducted by the Custer Society of Great Britain has advanced clear evidence that the surname 'Custer' was not after all derived from the Germanic *Koster*, as has hitherto been supposed, but is probably rooted in the common Orcadian surname 'Cursiter', pronounced locally as 'Custer'. A feature in *The Scotsman* discloses evidence that Custer had been made aware of this theory prior to his untimely death.[15]

Shooting by Buffalo Bill

In the fourth and final exhibition of shooting, Buffalo Bill himself rode around the arena and fired a repeating rifle at glass balls thrown into the air by an attendant who rode by his side. He also gave a demonstration in which he cracked a bullwhip.

The Mining Camp in the Black Hills

The sixth and final episode was set in and around a mining camp named Deadwood City. This lawless settlement had sprung up in the Black Hills following the discovery of gold in 1874, about the same time the region was stolen from the Lakota, who held it sacred.

Once again, this episode was divided into three scenes. In the first, a Pony Express rider rode up to the 'Wild West' saloon. This must be considered as something of a historical anomaly, since the Pony Express had gone out of business in 1861. After a game between a trio of card players seated outside had erupted into a pistol duel, resulting in the death of one of the protagonists, the Deadwood Stage arrived, bringing with it a party of artistes for the local theatre. After a variety of characteristic amusements had been introduced, the coach departed once more.

In the second scene, the Indians made an attack upon the Deadwood Stage, and were repulsed by Buffalo Bill's scouts and cowboys.

The third and concluding scene returned to Deadwood City, as it was destroyed by a cyclone. The blast of air, travelling at fifty-six miles an hour, was generated by means of the Blackman air propellers and Stockport gas engine. The result was a general devastation. The performers in the cyclone's path had difficulty in keeping their feet and several hats in the audience were blown away.

Subtle imagery was at work – the subliminal message was that every new phase in the evolution of the West was itself predestined to destruction, as cataclysmic forces beyond human reckoning laboured to maintain a never-ending state of flux. It is difficult to know what to make of the thinking behind this sequence. The final phase in the development of civilisation depicted was not very impressive and nature had the final ironic word.

The performance concluded as it had begun and a grand equestrian salute from Colonel Cody and the entire company was met with deafening applause.

The Cowboy Band struck up 'God Save the Queen' and the evening's entertainment was over.

Not half an hour later, a newsboy, at the door of the Gaiety Theatre in Sauchiehall Street, was heard to make the startling announcement:

'Evening Paper. Arrest of Buffalo Bill!'
'What for?' inquired a concerned passer-by.
'Tae get his hair cut,' was the reply.[16]

Notes

1 *Eastern Bells*, December 1891
2 Mitchell Library, Glasgow
3 e.g. in the *Evening Times*, 16 November 1891
4 17 November 1891
5 Official programme
6 p. 84
7 Parker probably had the New York season in mind. See Havighurst, *Annie Oakley of the Wild West*, p. 89.
8 The *Govan Press*, 28 November 1891, implies that the following sequence formed part of Episode 1 although it is hard to see where exactly it fitted in. There may be an element of confusion with the opening review: 'Here the spectators, we might say, are startled with a rush of Red Indians, who bear down on the central part with great speed and a whooping cry. They divide and pass out by side exits almost before the spectators have recovered their equilibrium.'
9 *Govan Press*, 28 November 1891
10 December 1891
11 21 November 1891
12 1891 *Odd People I Have Met*, p. 84. Note, however, that the *Glasgow Herald* of 17 November 1891 makes mention only of buffaloes and horses.
13 26 December 1891
14 25 June 1891
15 23 June 2001
16 'Gossip and Grumbles' column, *Evening Times*, 17 November 1891

6

INDIANS!

An Incident of Buffalo Bill's Visit. Green Shirt— "Ah, him brave man inside. Heap brave man." —Funny Folks.

'None but the Brave Deserve the Fair.'
(Scene – Room in a public-house, near Bridgeton Cross. Time – Saturday night. Dramatis personae – Two working men.)
First – Hae ye been tae the Wild West Show yet, Tam?
Tam – Na, man, a've nae great thocht of gaun ether. The wife's feared I wid com' hame scalpit.
First – Auch; thur's nae fear o' that. The injuns are as tame as rabbits. D'ye ken a saw yin o' thum in his full war pent, blanket an' a', airm an' airm, in Duke Street, the ither nicht, efter the performance, wi' as bonnie a white lassie as ever ye clappit e'en on. Ay, she wis a regular beauty; dressed up tae the nines tae, wi' her yellow hair hingin' frae below a nate wee hat. Man a' just fare envied the redskin.[1]

The story of Annie Oakley is very well documented but that of an even less likely Wild West heroine, also named Annie, is less so.

In 1891, Annie Edgar was a girl of sixteen who worked in her father's confectionery baker's shop at 108, Duke Street and her story comes down to us from her grandson, the late Robert Porterfield.

In later years, Annie would recall the various colourful characters who came into the shop but it was the visits of Buffalo Bill's Lakota Indians that held pride of place in her storytelling. They spoke little English and would stand at the window pointing to the items they wished to buy, before entering the shop to complete their transactions.[2]

Annie was afraid of the Indians and, when she saw them coming, she would call her father or her brother through from the bakehouse at the rear of the premises to come and serve them. It seems that Annie was far from alone in her apprehensions for she later recounted that local people would cross the street in order to avoid them. It may be that this nervousness was, to some extent, justified for Annie knew them to be frequently drunk. At such times, the Indians could get badly out of hand – an impression substantially corroborated by other contemporary accounts – and she even recalled incidences of pistols being discharged in the street, though presumably only blank cartridges from the show were fired.

By Annie's account, the Indians were 'huge men', towering above her sweetheart, whom she later married, and he stood six foot four inches tall. The Lakota are known as a tall race but this particular can be discounted as an exaggeration, serving as an indicator of the extent to which the timorous little shop assistant held her Indian visitors in mortal dread.

However, Annie enjoyed many opportunities to inspect the exotic strangers at a safe distance, in the course of their stirring performances in the Wild West arena. For her father received complimentary tickets in return for displaying publicity posters in his shop window.

It has to be conceded that memories handed down through the generations require to be treated with much the same prudent caution as that with which the young Annie Edgar regarded the Indians. Such accounts are very frequently confused and almost as often patently false.

However, this particular story has the ring of truth about it and several essential details are substantiated by the postal and census records. Reading the relevant entries, it is fascinating to watch the characters come to life.

Thomas Edgar – a 'pastry baker' according to the 1891 Post Office Glasgow Directory – was then aged forty-three. He and his wife Mary, in common with many Glaswegians of the period, had both migrated into the city from rural parts of Scotland. Thomas had been born in Stranraer, while Mary was a native of Argyllshire.

His shop, the site of which is now a private car park, stood next to the Great Eastern Hotel. The postal directory confirms the address and supplies the additional information that the family resided next door, up a close at number 110. The Great Eastern Hotel – which from 1907 until recently served as a hostel for homeless men – then, as now, was number 100.

The four children – Annie and her three brothers – were born in Glasgow. Young Thomas was just nine years of age, while two older brothers, David, aged twenty, and Neil, nineteen, were, like their father, described on the census returns as bakers. No doubt it was these two bigger lads who, on numerous occasions, heard and responded to their little sister's alarmed shout of, 'The Indians are coming!'

Annie herself appears in the census record as fifteen years old in April 1891 and her occupation is entered as 'shop girl'.

There can be no doubt at all that Annie's experiences were anything other than representative and that many more East-End shop girls had similar dealings with the Wild West visitors, now almost all sadly lost in the mists of time. At least one is known to have struck up a somewhat less tentative rapport with a Lakota man.[3] There is however no indication that Annie was ever the object of any romantic overtures from the Indians and this, no doubt, was a source of great consolation to her – others were not so fortunate!

From Sheena Crook come the recollections of her mother, who was born in 1881 and attended Whitehill Public School. One of the Indians was in the habit of sitting on the school wall and distracting the girl pupils at their lessons by shining a mirror into the classroom – weather permitting, it is presumed.

Dennistoun's status as one of the most affluent suburban districts of Glasgow is reflected by the circumstance that, as confirmed by the census records, a high proportion of the tenement households included maidservants, who lived in and were paid two or three shillings a week. Mrs Crook's mother also recalled that one little servant girl excited the amorous attentions of a Lakota brave, who, on at least one occasion, frightened the life out of her by pursuing her up Whitehill Street!

Scalps

Another memory is disclosed by the Whitehill diamond jubilee school magazine: 'And Red Indians stroll along Duke Street in their leisure hours looking at the shops and especially at a barber's window showing wigs which they mistake, greatly admiring, for scalps.'

This anecdote resurfaced in Jack House's 'Ask Jack' column in the *Evening Times*.[4] He offered the further clarification that the Indians thought that the barber must surely be a very great warrior to have taken so many scalps. It appears probable that Mr House took the item in the school magazine as his source.

This incident might actually have taken place but, personally, I doubt it. The question is unlikely ever to be settled either way but my own instinct is that the only 'foundation' for the story is the allegedly humorous cartoon appearing in the *Evening Times* on the 5th of December 1891.

How Many?

The question inevitably arises of just how many Indians there were in the company.

Unfortunately, this inquiry cannot be reduced to a precise science – firstly, since a comparison of the primary sources discloses discrepancies and, secondly, because figures given in contemporary press releases fluctuate wildly and are prone to exaggeration. During the English leg of the tour, seventy, seventy-five and eighty were the most popular figures quoted but it is futile to look for consistency.

The *Birmingham and Aston Chronicle* of the 12th of September

1891 stated that they were 'some eighty in number'. In contrast, the *Birmingham Weekly Mercury* for precisely the same date categorically asserted: 'There are fifty-two Indians in the present company.' The *Birmingham Daily Post* of the 5th had favoured the intermediate figure of sixty-five.

That there had originally been twenty-three hostages in the company – twenty men and three women – is not open to question. However, the position regarding those additionally enlisted at Pine Ridge is somewhat less clear.

A communication sent by the acting agent at Pine Ridge to the Commissioner of Indian Affairs, dated the 26th of March 1891, contains what bears to be 'a complete list of all the Indians taken from this Agency by Messers (*sic*) Cody & Salsbury'. Listed are the names of forty-two Indians – thirty-six adult males, including the half-breed Jim Nelson, also known as Yellow Horse, the son of veteran performer John Nelson and his Lakota wife; one little boy; and five women. This source also discloses the Indians' rate of remuneration. $25 per month was the going rate for an adult male and $10 for a woman. The leading attractions – Kicking Bear, Short Bull and Plenty Wolves, also known as Yankton Charlie – each received $50, while No Neck received $55 for himself and his adopted son.

The passenger list for the SS *Switzerland* departing from Philadelphia on the 1st of April is problematic since it is not identical to the agent's list. Medicine Bird, 'No Neck, Adopted son, from the Wounded Knee battle field', Shot At, and Mrs Long Wolf are all attested on the agent's list but are missing from the passenger list. However, it is likely that at least one error has been made since Johnny Burke No Neck's participation in the 1891–92 season is not open to doubt. There is a mysterious entry for 'John Shangren' – in addition to 'Mr John Shangren' – which is probably a mistaken reference to the boy.

The resulting total of between sixty-two and sixty-five approximates to the figure of sixty-three which is given in the *Grimsby News* as having arrived from Antwerp on board the *Lincoln* for the start of the English leg of the tour.[5]

Nine Indians are known to have been returned to the United States on the grounds of ill health and Paul Eagle Star had died at Sheffield by the date on which the figure of fifty-two was advanced, circumstances which tend to enhance its credibility. Further, it is unlikely that the management of the Wild West would have understated the figures. However, account also has to be taken of the replacements referred to in the *Staffordshire Sentinel*: 'Our climate does not altogether suit the Indian, and since the present tour began, ten have been sent home invalided but their places have been filled with fresh arrivals.'[6]

This statement has to be read in conjunction with a similar pronouncement subsequently appearing in the *Birmingham Daily Post*, according to which 'nine have been suffered to return, ill of chest complaints contracted in our changeable climate'.[7]

Documentary records exist, in the form of affidavits, as well as correspondence passing between Colonel Cody and the Indian agencies, which enable us to positively identify those nine Indians. Among them were some very prominent members of the party.

From the original company, both Horn Point Eagle and Sorrel Horse were allowed to leave towards the end of June and had safely returned to Pine Ridge by the 4th of August. Scatter, who was one of the principal figures in the late hostilities, lasted only until the 13th of July.[8] An elderly Brulé chief named Standing Bear departed during August, suffering from lung problems. Run Along Side Of represented another of the August departures. These five all numbered among the 'hostile' contingent.

Long Wolf, Bone Necklace and Crow Cane arrived back at Pine Ridge on the 21st of August. Long Wolf and Bone Necklace had previously been highlighted in the opening review and Crow Cane was one of the female hostages so that only seventeen of the twenty-three 'hostiles' originally participating in the tour now remained. Plenty Wolves was another of the principal attractions who had departed the scene, returning to Pine Ridge on the 4th of September.

The replacements, if they existed at all, are harder to identify. Nothing appears to be known about them. However, a measure of confirmation emerges from a somewhat remonstrative letter addressed to Colonel Cody at Nottingham, from Acting US Indian Agent Penney at Pine Ridge:

> It is reported here that your agent has, within the last two weeks, sneaked off about 10 Indians to be taken to your show. If this is true, it will very much injure the standing and reputation of your company with the Indian Department, and among a large class of people who are your well-wishers. Your agent, to who (*sic*) you referred as about to visit Pine Ridge, in one of your recent letters, did not come here, but I am told he came as far as Rushville, received these Indians surreptitiously and returned immediately with them to England, without notification to the Agent, or the Indian Department. I do not vouch for the truth of these reports, but give them to you for what they may be worth.[9]

It would appear on this evidence that the number of Indians absent from the reservations remained stable at around sixty-three. They were variously reported in the Glasgow newspapers as sixty and sixty-five but these figures were probably exaggerated. It will be recalled that a dozen Indians had been hired out to Viola Clemmons and this would have reduced the Indian contingent to around fifty. A further complication however is that High Bear, not accounted for on the *Switzerland* passenger list, is known to have been with the entourage from the early stages of the tour. Bear Growls, who is not otherwise known, received a mention in the *Nottingham Daily Express*.[10]

In summary, the best estimate is that there were between forty and just above fifty Indians who made it as far as Glasgow.

The Legend of Nav Bow

In connection with Buffalo Bill's tours, stories abound of Indians said to have come to Great Britain with the Wild West show and stayed behind. Glasgow, needless to say, is no exception. One curious piece of local folklore, which appears to have established itself in certain quarters as hard fact, concerns a party of Lakota Indians who are reputed to have settled there and established themselves as scrap merchants in the East End. This tradition is referred to in a letter from Joseph Mitchell to the *Scots Magazine* of May 1997.[11] Mr Mitchell, who was born and bred in the Calton, proposed a family of the surname Kiani as likely candidates.

The more usual epicentre of the story however is one David Bow or 'Nav' as he was generally known. His epithet is understood to be an abbreviation of 'Navajo' and his living descendents recall that he was of dark complexion. The surname Bow can be taken as providing evidence for the theory or else as indicating the manner in which such an odd notion found its way into common currency.

The theme has found its way into print on various other occasions – for example in Charles McDonald's *Old Parkhead*.[12]

It also surfaced in the *Evening Times*' 'Mr Glasgow' column.[13] This feature contained the interesting statement that the Indians in Cody's show were Navajos, a piece of misinformation undoubtedly prompted by the nickname of the above-mentioned Mr Bow.

Barrie Cox, of the Glasgow-based British North American Indian Association (BNAIA), was quoted as follows:

> Apparently, when Cody was ready to leave Glasgow the Navajos decided that they weren't going back to the reservation. They defected and set up as scrap merchants at Vinegar Hill, which was just off Gallowgate. It's a fascinating tale but I want to find out if it's based on fact.

By November, the BNAIA's futile quest had spread to the United States, inspiring an article in the *New Mexico Magazine* for that month, under the arresting title 'Group searches for lost Navajos in Scotland'.

The picture of David 'Nav' Bow's family history, as it emerges from the registers of birth, death and marriage, is sadly incomplete but there is sufficient information to enable a fairly definite (negative) conclusion to be reached.

No record of Nav's birth can be found in Scotland, England or Wales. Such a document, if it existed, could have been taken as resolving the matter once and for all. It appears likely that, in the final decade of the nineteenth century or else the first years of the twentieth, the Bow family came to Glasgow from somewhere outside of Scotland – the only question is from where.

He is variously designated as a 'scrap merchant, deceased', a 'general dealer' and a 'general hawker' and, from his marriage (1907) and death (1958) certificates, it emerges that he was born at some time between 1883 and 1886.

There is no trace of him or his father Michael in either the 1891 or 1901 census records for Glasgow. Perhaps, when the 1911 census is made available, it will prove to be of greater assistance.

The record discloses that the family has had a lengthy association with the East End, specifically Camlachie, and links to the old Vinegar Hill showground are clearly attested.

Beyond the unresolved mystery surrounding Nav Bow's place of birth, there is nothing in the record to suggest that his family were of Native American origin. In fact, this possibility is effectively excluded by the fact that his mother's maiden name was McDiarmid. This and his paternal grandmother's maiden name, Cusack, tend to suggest Ireland and not the western wilderness of North America as the family's most likely point of origin. None of the names of Indians known from passenger lists to have visited Scotland with Buffalo Bill even approximate to Bow.

I have little doubt that David 'Nav' Bow, the swarthy East-End scrap merchant, was a highly colourful character in his time. I am quite sure that he was worthy of the curious and enduring legend that has attached itself to his progeny. But the romantic notion that 'Nav' Bow was a Native American is no more than a romantic piece of urban mythology, a painted and embellished fiction which should be forever laid to rest.

The *Glasgow Evening News*' 'Lorgnette' column discloses the only known contemporary source suggesting that an Indian from the show ever even contemplated settling in Glasgow:

Dennistoun is just now ringing with the intelligence of a little comedy being enacted in its midst. The tale is one of true love, and the leading actor is one of the 'Wild West' Indians. The red man has conceived a violent passion, which fills him from top-knot to moccasin fringe, for a prepossessing young lady in a shop near the show, and he looks in during his leisure hours on the pretence of wanting to buy things, but really to enforce his suit, which he does with as much doggedness as he would follow the trail of the now very rare buffalo. In his earnestness he offers to carry the white squaw with him back to the wild and woolly West there to rule the domestic affairs in his wigwam, or alternatively to settle down in Glasgow and be a good if rather yellow husband. The awkward thing, however, is that the red man's arrival at the shop is the signal for the neighbours to gather round, and the progress of the courtship is watched by a little crowd which generally extends out to the street.[14]

The sequel, sadly, is not known but one doubts that the romance ran its course. An Indian who attempted to stay behind in Birmingham under similar circumstances was promptly rounded up by Wild West officials. The legal basis in either Scotland or England for coercing an Indian to remain with the show is unclear but, considering the weighty obligation under which the federal government placed Colonel Cody to ensure the safe return of his charges to their reservations, I would conclude that the chances were rather against a defection.

There is not merely an absence of evidence but an evidence of absence and, in the final analysis, the legend of 'the Indian who stayed behind' is like the Loch Ness Monster – no one can prove it but no one can quite make it go away either.

Living Quarters

There is also an oft-repeated – and probably apocryphal – tradition of an Indian encampment at Vinegar Hill. As is so often the case, the most interesting stories are the ones which cannot be authenticated. Typically, as was generally the case with Cody's career, the story of the Wild West's stay in Glasgow has been attended by its fair share of myth and legend and the two are difficult, at times impossible, to separate.

Given the logic and the spirit of the times, it would hardly be surprising if someone reasoned that this disreputable fairground surrounded by noxious enterprises was the ideal location for the only Indian 'reservation' ever sited in Glasgow. A tradition persists among Glasgow's show people of tipis having been erected there.

The story has proved impossible to locate in any primary source. It does make its way into print every so often, a prime example being *Old Parkhead* by Charles McDonald. McDonald[15] also cites a local tradition that Cody and members of his entourage frequented the Coffin bar in Whitevale Street. Carol Foreman repeated it in *Did You Know?*, stating that the Indians 'lodged with local residents or stayed in a camp erected at Vinegar Hill'.[16] The former statement seems to rely upon hearsay and cannot be verified.

The legend of Vinegar Hill was recounted in 'When the Wild West came to the East-End' by Brian Swanson, in *The Daily Express*: 'A special camp for the performers was set up at Vinegarhill – where the Parkhead Forge Shopping Centre is now located.'[17]

A possible explanation might be that the tipis belonged not to Buffalo Bill's company but to one of the many rival shows which were little more than pale imitations of the original and that, in subsequent retelling, the story became associated with Buffalo Bill's Wild West, as that was by far the most famous.

In the many documented anecdotes concerning sightings of Indians in the East End in the press and other contemporary sources, the clear focus is Duke Street, in the environs of the showgrounds. Not one has yet been identified in which Vinegar Hill or its immediate vicinity provides the epicentre.

Properly considered, the story does not have the ring of truth.

A broad distinction has to be borne in mind between the summer (outdoor) and winter (indoor) versions of the show. Glasgow, of course, fell into the latter category. Camping out in the East End would have held little charm, even for the fierce Lakota. The damp British climate did not agree with the Indians, as we have seen. It is one of the perennially recurring themes of Native American history that, however perfectly adapted and hardy the members of any given tribe proved upon their native soil, they would drop like flies from hitherto unknown ailments whenever they were transplanted somewhere else. Glasgow was certainly no exception and indoor accommodation would have been an absolute necessity.

The weight of available evidence, already considered in Chapter 5, supra, unambiguously establishes that the entire cast, Indians included, was accommodated in the former Boys' House of Refuge immediately adjacent to the main exhibition building. This fact is further confirmed by the addresses entered in the prison registers relative to Charging Thunder's period of incarceration and on John Shangrau's marriage certificate. These are 'East End Exhibition' and 'East End Exhibition Glasgow' respectively.[18]

It will be recalled that a well-publicised tipi village had been part of the show during the preceding summer tour of England and Wales. This was identical in concept to the encampment that would later form so prominent a feature on the 1904 tour. It provided the Indians' accommodation and members of the public were encouraged to inspect it. It was invariably on the same site as the show itself but it should be observed that Vinegar Hill lay at some distance from the exhibition buildings.

A further aspect of the indoor/outdoor dichotomy is that, while the Wild West's traditional pre-performance street parade took place at the English venues on the morning of the first Monday in town, I have been unable to locate even a single credible reference in relation to Glasgow. Carol Foreman states, 'Each day before the performance the whole entourage, cowboys, indians (*sic*) in full regalia, horses, stagecoaches, covered wagons, sharpshooters and musicians paraded through the streets.'[19] However, there appears to be an element of confusion here with the opening review, which took place in the arena.

Against such a background, it is hardly surprising if recollections of long-past events handed down by our grandparents are fallible and confused and, in the absence of even a shred of concrete contemporary evidence, the Indian encampment at Vinegar Hill has to be dismissed as no more than a seductive piece of urban mythology.

Notes

1 *The Bailie for Wednesday, December 9th, 1891*
2 A similar procedure was described in the *Croydon Advertiser*, 31 October 1891
3 See p. 75 infra
4 21 January 1981
5 19th June 1891
6 17th August 1891
7 5th September 1891
8 The *Glasgow Herald*, 6 November 1891, and other sources imply that Scatter was present in Glasgow but this is incorrect.
9 22 August 1891
10 26 August 1891
11 p. 547
12 p. 37
13 7 February 1990
14 15 February 1892
15 p. 37. See also *Parkhead People's Press*, Issue Three, 1989.
16 p. 14
17 14 July 1998
18 Both of these stories are considered in depth infra.
19 *Did You Know?*, p. 14

7

'THE WAVES OF SUCCESS ROLL ON'

On the 25th of November, the *Evening Times* reported on the excellent progress that had been accomplished. Everything in the show by now went without the slightest hitch and the final bow was taken 'exactly as ten o'clock was ringing out from the steeples in Dennistoun'.

Audiences were held spellbound and the *Glasgow Evening News* of the 24th of November explained the general absence of applause as anxiety not to miss the slightest word or gesture. That same evening, the audience were convulsed with mirth when a cockerel and two hens invaded the arena, just as the Indians were about to attack the sleeping wagon train, and the male bird announced his presence with a shrill 'cock-a-doodle-doo'. 'Some time elapsed ere the fowls were captured by a grinning "buck," who apparently enjoyed the unexpected fun as much as the audience did.'[1]

The Bailie for Wednesday, December 2nd, 1891 remarked:

> Buffalo Bill's great show continues to draw vast crowds day and night. The interest, if anything, is increasing to see real life as it is in the land of the setting sun. The prairie on fire and the battle scene is (*sic*) highly realistic. The shooting feats with gun and revolver are marvellous, and bring out well-merited applause.

The students, on the night of the torchlight procession, visited the 'Wild West,' and gave Colonel Cody a warm reception. He was much gratified with their visit.[2]

As *Eastern Bells* for December 1891 recorded:

The band is under the direction of Mr Sweeney, a gentleman of modest and unassuming character. It is only within the last few days that Mr Sweeney has been prevailed upon to give some of his exquisite solos on the cornet, but these have been so enthusiastically received that he dare not now leave it out of the programme.

For some reason, the show proved especially popular with the Roman Catholic clergy, who attended the opening weeks in considerable numbers.

Meanwhile, the tunnel leading to Duke Street was finally in place but the whitewash on the walls was not yet dry and displayed an alarming tendency to come away in quantities on people's coats.

Rail Excursions to the Wild West

Thirteen years later, on the 1904 tour, the show would appear in a total of twenty-nine different Scottish towns and cities. Thus practically the whole of the Scottish population was able to attend by taking a short train journey at most. But, back in 1891–92, it was a different story and intending spectators had to undertake the pilgrimage to Glasgow. However, the saturation press coverage was calculated to generate an enormous demand and people travelled to Dennistoun from all across Scotland.

Special excursions were run from different places after reductions in fares had been negotiated with the various railway companies. As the *Evening Times* announced on the 5th of November 1891:

To induce dwellers in all parts of Scotland to visit the Wild West Show, the North British, Glasgow and South-Western, and Caledonian Railway Companies are to provide special facilities in the form of cheap excursions to Glasgow from Edinburgh, Perth, Dundee, and other centres of population.

On the 21st of November, the first Saturday of the season, the Wild West show attracted a capacity crowd at both the matinee and evening performances, so that a total of 14,000 persons attended the exhibition on that day alone. As *The Scottish Leader* recorded, 'Of that number a great many were country people, some of whom had travelled from Inverness and Dumfries.'[3]

It may be assumed that those two towns were selected for specific mention since they represented opposing extremities of north and south. The management was obliged to refuse admittance to hundreds who clamoured at the gates for three-quarters of an hour before the evening show commenced.

From Saturday the 28th of November onwards, the starting time was brought forward to seven-thirty so that those with trains to catch could comfortably watch the show in its entirety. Trains departed Bellgrove at eighteen minutes past ten, with connections at Saint Enoch's for suburban towns.

The matinee performances in particular went from strength to strength and, on the afternoon of Monday the 7th of December, a special performance was given for the convenience of excursionists from Edinburgh, Carlisle and intermediate towns, starting at two thirty in the afternoon. The Caledonian Railway Company brought a total of almost 3,000 patrons at greatly reduced fares. This was a clear mark of enterprise, calculated to attract people who would not have risked facing the usual Wednesday afternoon or Saturday crowds. Ample time was allowed before the last returning trains departed.

On Wednesday the 9th, an excursion was run from Bo'ness, and, on Saturday the 12th, there were special trains from Edinburgh and all border towns at heavily discounted rates.

A closing assessment of the success of these arrangements was provided by *The Scottish Leader*, in its review of the final show:

Some disappointment has been felt at the exhibition having been confined to Glasgow, but its immensity and the number of persons engaged made this an absolute necessity. Special cheap railway fares, however, from all parts of Scotland, have placed it within the reach of everyone, and the public have not been slow to take advantage of them. The consequence is that the show has been as well patronised as if it had been on tour throughout the country.[4]

Return tickets to Bellgrove were also issued on Saturdays for the price of a single, from towns within a thirty-mile radius, with the exception of Greenock and Helensburgh since the ordinary fares to and from these towns were already at the minimum rate. Bellgrove Station, just five minutes' walk from the showgrounds, also proved highly convenient for visitors coming from Hamilton, Airdrie, Coatbridge and other towns on the low-level line.

For those travelling from closer at hand, a concession, which had proved satisfactory during the previous year's exhibition, was revived and the fare for a tramcar ride to the gates from the St Vincent Place terminus was capped at one penny.

Patrick Robertson, Deceased

For one poor soul, the agony of anticipation was too much to bear for, shortly before the performance commenced on Friday the 27th of November, a man in the audience suddenly expired. He was named by the *Scottish Leader*[5] as Patrick Robertson, a groom in the employment of Mr Jack, of Gayfield Square, Edinburgh. His widow, Margaret White or Robertson, of 3, Catherine Street, Edinburgh, identified the body.

Bram Stoker

Later that same evening, Colonel Cody once again found himself in the company of Henry Irving and Bram Stoker. The occasion, a banquet given by the Pen and Pencil Club in honour of Mr Irving, then appearing at the Lyceum, was held in the picture gallery of the Fine Art Institute in Sauchiehall Street. One hundred and thirty-seven members and guests attended. Irving and Stoker were no strangers to the Club, having dined with them on at least one previous occasion, during September 1887.

Mr Stoker proposed a toast to the prosperity of 'the City of Glasgow' and J. B. Howard, in toasting 'the Guests', proposed the health of Colonel Cody.

Replying, Cody was fulsome in his praises of Irving, on account of the kind assistance and powerful influence which the actor had exerted on his behalf.

Though, as the *Evening Times* commented, 'The company, however, could not refrain from laughing heartily as the Colonel naively described this generous interest as of a kind seldom shown to "a rival entertainer".'[6]

A record of the occasion was preserved in a line drawing in the *Quiz Supplement,*[7] in which Irving, Stoker and Cody were all among the gentlemen depicted. Other notables present were Sheriff Spens, of whom more will presently be heard, who proposed the toast to 'Literature & Art' and Harry Furniss, a theatrical impresario.

Cody's acquaintance with Stoker dated at least to the 1887 London season. Stoker lived in the shadow of Irving, who employed him as an amanuensis, but was an important figure in his own right and is chiefly remembered today as the author of the horror classic *Dracula*, first published in 1897.

In 1891, Stoker was in the process of gathering notes for his famous novel and, although the Wild West is a less than obvious source, its crucial influence is not to be overlooked. One of the characters, a Texan named Quincy Morris, was apparently based on Buffalo Bill himself. Consider also that, in the original work, the vampire was killed not with a stake through the heart but with a Bowie knife.

The conjecture that, in naming the character of Renfield, Stoker drew his inspiration from the city centre street of that name is not lightly to be dismissed.

'THE WAVES OF SUCCESS ROLL ON'

Annie Oakley

In addition to her scheduled appearances in the arena, Annie fraternised liberally with the shooting clubs of Glasgow and shot at the Darnley range. She also remained active on the competitive circuit and participated in various challenge shooting matches, as well as private exhibitions. On the 2nd of December, she overcame a certain R. W. Bilds, shooting twenty live pigeons out of twenty-five to her opponent's seventeen.

Frank E. Butler, Annie's husband and manager, accompanied her to Glasgow and had a letter published in 'The Voice of the People' column in the *Glasgow Evening News*, also on the 2nd of December, responding to certain detractors who had used the column to express doubts that the shooting feats at the Wild West were all that they were represented to be.[8]

Annie was thirty-one years of age when she came to Glasgow. She stood just five feet one in height and, from a distance, her slender figure gave her a girlish appearance. It is part of her legend that adolescent boys watching her perform regularly became infatuated with her, only to have their romantic illusions shattered like targets when informed that she was already married. Halliday Sutherland, in his book *A Time to Keep*,[9] tells a somewhat fanciful story in which he claims to have been similarly disappointed in love. Could it be that he was the boy, befriended by Annie, whose touching story was related in the *Glasgow Evening News* on the 7th of December 1891? Probably not since it emerges that Halliday was only nine years old!

An undated letter from 'Rob Roy' of Glasgow to the editor of the *Shooting Times* records a performance given for a group of friends.[10] In the course of this display, Annie shot at various sixpenny and shilling pieces, which had been thrown into the air, using a .320 Winchester rifle and she extinguished a cigarette smoked by an attendant fully thirty feet away. She next split a photograph of herself, held aloft by Frank Butler at the same distance. This feat she accomplished at the first attempt. Annie rounded off the display by shooting ten out of twelve live pigeons, at a distance of fifteen yards, using a French .32 bore pistol.

A great sigh of collective relief must have resounded around George Square when 'Little Sure Shot' finally left town!

The Galloway Dinner

On the 4th of December, John Galloway gave a complimentary dinner at his restaurant at 115, West Nile Street for the Indians, who attended in their native finery, their faces painted mostly in red and yellow. The chiefs Kicking Bear, Short Bull, No Neck and Lone Bull, all clad in bone breastplates, were among those present, as were the interpreters Crager and Shangrau. The four chiefs made speeches, in honour of their host, with Mr Crager interpreting. No Neck was especially extravagant in his praises. He pronounced that Mr Galloway must be the son of the man for whom Christmas was celebrated and concluded that, if the Indians could not find a way to repay him for his kindness, then God surely would. Musical selections including a war song from the Indians followed and a number of toasts were proposed. The proceedings ended with a general rendition of 'Auld Lang Syne', which was particularly enjoyed by all. Mr and Mrs Galloway personally waited upon their guests and, at the conclusion, presented each with a bottle of ketchup, with a magnum apiece for the chiefs.

Central Station Hotel

In the *Evening Times*' 'Gossip and Grumbles' column, there appears the intriguing and tantalising solitary line 'Colonel Cody resides at the Central Station Hotel'.[11] He may indeed have lived there for a part of his time in Glasgow although no other record is known. The establishment had been opened by the Caledonian Railway Company in December 1882. A letter, dated the 31st of December and addressed by Colonel Cody to Messrs Watson and Wilson, on Grand Hotel, Charing Cross headed notepaper, might indicate a sojourn at that establishment also.

Day Trip to Edinburgh

Tuesday the 15th of December 1891 marked the first anniversary of the death of Sitting Bull at the hands of Standing Rock reservation police but, whether or not Colonel Cody was appropriately sensible of the occasion, he chose to mark it with a sightseeing trip to Edinburgh. He visited the Castle and the Palace of Holyroodhouse, where the Queen's representative gave him a tour of the private apartments, including the Throne Room. Buffalo Bill even put in an appearance at the First Division of the Inner House of the Court of Session, where he 'attracted considerable attention among the members of the bar and the public'.[12] Buffalo Bill's overall assessment of Auld Reekie was:

> By Jove, ain't she a beauty. There is not, I make bold to say, even on my limited acquaintance with her charms, any city in the world like your capital. I was overwhelmed with the spectacle from the Calton Hill, and must treat myself to another view before leaving Scotland.[13]

Grand Hotel, Charing Cross

On the 22nd of December, a luncheon was given in honour of Colonel Cody by the '1390 Club' at the Grand Hotel (telephone number Glasgow 69). The hotel was demolished to make way for major redevelopment during the 1970s but it used to stand on the present location of the Clydesdale Bank on the corner of Sauchiehall and North Streets. On the evidence of *The Scottish Leader*, the significance of the imposing sounding date '1390' was mysterious even at the time and particularly in the light of the tongue-in-cheek nature of the wording of the menu and invitation, it is respectfully proposed that it should be taken as a hybrid of '1314' and '1690'.[14] It was apparently intended as an ad hoc designation for yet another permutation of the elite social set that Cody moved in and which included such luminaries as the ubiquitous Henry Irving and J. L. Toole, the

Mayor of Manchester. The secretary was William Guilford, manager of the Grand Hotel.

After the meal, a number of toasts were proposed, in the course of which 'Colonel Cody remarked that he had never been more kindly or hospitably received than during his visit to Glasgow'.[15]

The party next descended the stairs to the great hall for a 'private séance', where a number of the city's leading ladies and gentlemen had assembled by invitation, and were entertained by the Cowboy Band, which played a selection of airs. The Indians next entered in full costume and, after a display of native dances, they sang the hymn 'Nearer My God to Thee' in Lakota. In the course of an interview, Colonel Cody expressed a strong desire to visit the Highlands and to return to Scotland 'in a more favourable season'.[16]

A line drawing appearing in the *Evening Times* reveals that Johnny Burke No Neck was among those present that afternoon and that contributions were also received from a piper and Flint Frame, a popular local comedian.[17]

At the conclusion, a short address was delivered by an unidentified chief in Lakota, of which a translation was given.

Shopping Excursions

Throughout the Glasgow sojourn, Indians in crimson blankets were a familiar sight walking the public thoroughfares in Dennistoun and the city centre, even if locals never did quite grow accustomed to such encounters, which were routinely reported in the press.

On the 14th of December, two Indians were witnessed returning to the Wild West after a shopping trip, each with a small parcel in one hand and a toy balloon in the other.

These may or may not have been the same two Indian ladies who, according to *The Bailie for Wednesday, December 23rd*, 1891, spent twenty shillings apiece in the medical stores on Renfield Street, on perfume and other toilet requisites.

Christmas at the Wild West

During the Christmas season of 1891–92, Glasgow found itself, as ever, the entertainment capital of Scotland, with the Wild West show most definitely the foremost of its myriad attractions. From Christmas Day until Saturday the 9th of January inclusive, two performances were given daily and the people of Glasgow and visitors to the city turned out in even greater crowds than before.

Colonel Cody's benevolence towards children was legendary and Glasgow proved no exception. At a special performance on the afternoon of Christmas Eve, Buffalo Bill entertained 8,000 of the city's schoolchildren, having sent out 5,000 tickets to Robert Gray of the School Board in advance. Mr Gray had them distributed to children attending seven of the Board Schools. The balance of the audience was drawn from the inmates of the Chapelton, Mossbank, Maryhill, Rose Street, Green Street and Rottenrow Industrial Schools. A large number of the teachers also attended and the sight of thousands of children marching along Duke Street in an excited but orderly fashion drew much public attention.

The children's matinee was a roaring success. The children's enthusiasm proved contagious and the performance was carried on with even more spirit than usual. As the horseman bearing the Stars and Stripes rode into the arena, the 8,000 children packing the hall to capacity spontaneously launched into an enthusiastic rendition of 'Yankee Doodle'. Mightily touched by this fitting homage to his nation's flag, Buffalo Bill declared, 'Wall, I'm darned, if I ever did see children with more snap in them!'[18]

That occasion was graced by several members of the School Board and also, once more, by the Lord Provost himself. A curious misconception concerning this gentleman's badge and chain of office was swift to take hold for the notion somehow became current that they had been presented to him by Buffalo Bill, as a medal for riding a bucking bronco!

There can be no doubting that the whole occasion passed off successfully and in the highest of spirits for:

At the close of the bucking horse episode the Lord Provost rose and called for cheers for Colonel Cody and his partner, and the response was a ringing cheer such as it may safely be said our civic chief never raised before. His Lordship was also cheered on leaving the show. The whole arrangements were carried out without hitch or incident.[19]

There were undoubtedly other occasions when Glasgow weans were the objects of Buffalo Bill's generosity for the *Evening Times* of the 30th of December 1891 relayed that Colonel Cody had, thus far, entertained 12,000 of the city's children for free and was ready to play host to the same number again as soon as the Christmas rush was past. The *Glasgow Evening News* of the 29th of January 1892 reported that the boys of St Mary's Roman Catholic School had been treated to a free show and that 'one-half of them have resolved to be cowboys or nothing'.

That Christmas in Glasgow, Annie Oakley famously sent out Christmas cards to friends back in the States and to newer acquaintances in Great Britain. The motif depicted a pair of contrasting scenes, juxtaposing Christmas in the degenerate east with the hospitable west. In the one, a Western girl waves gaily to a party of visitors arriving at her cabin in a sledge while, in the other, a man of substance turns a family of orphans from his door. One of these cards landed on the desk of the *Evening Times*' 'Gossip and Grumbles' columnist, as reported on the 25th of December.

According to Walter Havighurst, in a chapter entitled 'Christmas Card from Scotland', this was the first personalised Christmas card ever printed. He states that the card was of Annie's own design and that she had copies made by a local printer. The design also incorporated a picture of Annie herself, accompanied by the rhyme:

> I've built me a bridge of the kindest thoughts
> Over the ocean so wide,
> And all good wishes keep rushing across
> From this to the other side.[20]

At least two photographs exist of Annie splendidly bedecked in a tartan outfit, complete with feathered bonnet. According to Havighurst,[21] it was a gift bestowed upon her by friends in Glasgow, and she wore it for a time in the course of the 1892 season in London, before reverting to her more accustomed buckskins. However, the costume had certainly been adopted in Glasgow as early as Christmas Eve 1891 for, as the *Glasgow Evening News*'s 'Clydeside Echoes' column announced on that date, 'Miss Annie Oakley, the shootist at the "Wild West," has donned a tartan costume, and the proud heart of the nation swells with patriotic pride and things.'

At least one of these photographs was taken at some point during the 1891–92 season at the studio of Messrs Watson & Wilson, at 83, Jamaica Street. Whether the other was taken at the same or another sitting is not clear.

An indication of the cuisine on offer at the company's Christmas dinner is given by the information that Billy Langan, the show's supply agent, had spent the then considerable sum of £12 on turkeys – another American import – and geese.

One man who got somewhat carried away with the celebrations on Christmas Day was a certain Arthur William Crawford. The *Evening Times* carried the following account of his escapade in connection with a subsequent court appearance:

> Arthur William Crawford, who is said to have been a cowboy in Buffalo Bill's Wild West troupe, was going along Duke Street on Friday, somewhat the worse for liquor. He saw his reflection in a shop window, and thinking that it was a man who contemplated an attack on him, Crawford put up his fists, charged at his phantom opponent, breaking the window of the shop, and smashing the mirror.[22]

The bench must have seen the funny side of it because: 'He was brought before Bailie Guthrie at the Eastern Police Court today, but was dismissed with an admonition. Crawford had a ticket for London in his possession, and said he was going right there today.'

The *Evening Times* retreated somewhat on the point of Crawford's Wild West provenance for, as the 'Gossip and Grumbles' columnist observed on the following day:

> I have authority for stating that Arthur William Crawford, who went on a howling burster, and painted Duke Street vermillion the other day, finishing up by 'going for' his own shadow in a shop mirror, is not, and never was a cowboy.

So was Arthur William Crawford from the Wild West or not? On balance, he had probably never ridden a horse or rounded up a Longhorn in his life but perhaps the only useful moral of the story is this: as Anno Domini 1891 drew to a close under darkening Glasgow skies and Colonel Cody's colourful entourage became an increasingly fixed and familiar part of the city scene, it was becoming ever harder to distinguish the real Wild Westerners from the local population.

Moody and Sankey

An amusing anecdote was recounted in the *Evening Times* on the 13th of January 1892 but it is likely to have originated at some point during the festive season. A certain Glasgow minister, stated to be well known but otherwise unidentified, received a sharp reminder that mature enthusiasms do not always attract the endorsement of youth.

This reverend gentleman arrived late for a Sunday School soirée, having been detained at a meeting presided over by a certain Dwight Lyman Moody, a prominent and renowned American evangelist, who, with his partner Ira David Sankey, was preaching the Gospel in Scotland at that time. The minister sought to excuse his lack of punctuality with the words, 'My young friends, I am sure you will excuse me when I tell you that I have been away hearing one of the greatest men America ever produced. Now, I wonder how many scholars can tell me whom I refer to?'

To his consternation and chagrin, there came the immediate and unanimous response – 'Buffalo Bill!' Right enough, the minister should have seen it coming.

Kilts

A few days after Christmas, a reporter from the *Scottish Leader* visited the Wild West and his impressions were published on the 30th of December. After he had been ushered into Colonel Cody's apartment by his Singhalese attendant, his host professed his satisfaction, stating, 'My trip to Glasgow has so far been a splendid success.'

Two Indians were encountered in the dressing room. These were No Neck and Short Bull and they were introduced – or rather exhibited – to the visitor by George Crager. Crager drew a parallel between the highly coloured shawls favoured by the Indian women and similar garments commonly worn in the Scottish Highlands and continued:

> As a matter of fact, many of the Indians have taken quite a fancy for the kilt, and some of them have possessed themselves of that garb, both as presents for their friends out yonder, and for their own wear.

On one of the last days of 1891, No Neck and a 'squaw' (probably his sister, Calls the Name) took a penny ride on a tramcar down to Saint Vincent Place. Another of the passengers was a young artist who sat engrossed in his pad and pencil. At the terminus, he revealed that he had been drawing the Indians and presented his sketch to them as they left the car. His gift was very graciously accepted.[23]

Notes

1 *Glasgow Evening News*, 26 November 1891
2 University students held a grand torchlight and fancy dress procession on the evening of Wednesday the 25th of November to mark the

arrival in Glasgow of their Lord Rector, future Prime Minister Arthur Balfour.
3 23 November 1891
4 29 February 1892
5 30 November 1891
6 28 November 1891
7 2 December 1891
8 *Glasgow Evening News*, 'The Voice of the People' column, letters from 'One Who Can Shoot', 28 November; 'Kicking', 1 December; Frank E. Butler, 2 December; 'Kicking', 3 December; 'W. S.', 11 December, all 1891
9 p. 22
10 Preserved in the *Annie Oakley Scrapbook*, Buffalo Bill Historical Center
11 9 December 1891
12 *Evening Times*, 'Gossip and Grumbles', 16 December 1891
13 *Scottish Leader*, 30 December 1891
14 *Scottish Leader*, 23 December 1891
15 Ibid.
16 *Evening Times*, 23 December 1891
17 Ibid.
18 *Evening Times*, 25 December 1891
19 *Glasgow Evening News*, 25 December 1891
20 *Annie Oakley of the Wild West*, p. 148
21 p. 154
22 28 December 1891
23 As reported by the *Glasgow Evening News*, 2 January 1892

8

NEW YEAR, 1892

MAJOR BURKE AT CELTIC PARK

It will be recalled that, a couple of months previously, Colonel Cody had visited Ibrox as a spectator but his general manager Major John M. Burke went one better, on New Year's Day 1892, when he turned out on the 'hallowed turf', before a sell-out crowd of fifteen thousand spectators . . . for Celtic!

In those days, Celtic Park stood in Dalmarnock Road, on the present site of the Barr's Irn-Bru factory. The club did not move to its present location until later that year.

The New Year programme of fixtures was in its formative stages. The games were friendlies then and Celtic played host to that season's eventual League champions, Dumbarton.

On such occasions, it was customary to invite a celebrity to kick off. First choice was Tim Healy MP, the champion of the East End's Irish immigrants but, as he was unavailable, the honour of commencing proceedings went to Major Burke instead.

When it comes to inspired signings, Burke was hardly in the same bracket as Henrik Larsson. The Celts didn't even win the toss that day so Dumbarton got the choice of ends. He kicked off for Celtic, only to watch as the ball was immediately picked up by the Dumbarton centre forward. By the time that Burke had lumbered breathlessly off the park, the Sons had already taken their first shot at goal. On that note, Arizona John's brief Celtic career drew to a merciful close.

The eventual scoreline came as something of a shock. Dumbarton emerged 8-0 winners and one of the shots actually burst the net. A later generation of Celts would lose by the same margin to Motherwell in 1937 but, as far as can be ascertained, the proud record set that day by the bold Sons of the Rock has never been surpassed.

In the aftermath, a joke enjoyed a brief currency. Had the Celts been overindulging the night before? Quite the opposite for the cause of Celtic's problems on this occasion was that they 'ate nothing'![1]

It could have been even worse for the Sons had two goals disallowed. The finger of blame was diverted from Arizona John as goalkeeper Duff – who, by all accounts, did his level best to live up to his appellation – emerged as the principal scapegoat.

Half a world away, in Nevada, the anthropologist James Mooney was a man on a mission. He had been sent by the US federal government to inquire into the nature and causes of the previous winter's ghost dance outbreak. It was on New Year's Day 1892 that Mooney first met with the Paiute mystic Wovoka, the same medicine man who had set an awesome chain of events in motion, the shock waves from which were now being heard loud and clear many thousands of miles away in Glasgow.

One man who certainly wasn't at Celtic Park that day was Charging Thunder, for he was in the hands of the boys in blue. No, *not* Rangers – the Polis . . .

Charging Thunder

Imagine late afternoon on the final day of 1891 in the Tobago Street police station in the Calton. Darkness has already fallen. Prisoners at the euphoric, aggressive and helpless stages of intoxication are being brought in with almost every minute that passes. The desk sergeant barks directions at the other end of the hall, contending with a discordant chorus of singing and bawling from the cells. A long and irksome night lies ahead. Then all hell breaks loose as a Lakota warrior joins the scene . . .

Of all the stories handed down from Buffalo Bill's first Glasgow sojourn, none has left a heavier imprint upon city folklore than that of Charging Thunder, the Indian who acquired a genuine measure of notoriety when sentenced to thirty days' imprisonment in Barlinnie. The tale has frequently found its way into print in a variety of garbled and wildly embellished forms but the true sequence of events, reconstructed from contemporary press coverage and the prison records, runs as follows.

An article appearing in the *Evening Times* on the 4th of January 1892, under the heading 'Remarkable Increase of Drunkenness', highlighted the fact that this particular New Year's festivities had been even more riotous than usual. On the 31st of December 1891, Charging Thunder was caught up in the Hogmanay celebrations in a city pub and got drunk. Perhaps he was a victim of the pattern of behaviour described by Colonel Cody in the course of an interview given in Bristol a few months before. When asked if the Indians drank, he replied:

> Very few of those with me do, and then it is not their fault. Unfortunately it is an article of their faith never to refuse anything that is offered to them, and consequently it sometimes happens that when they go into a town to make purchases, silly people think it is a fine thing to be seen standing them drinks, and so sometimes they become intoxicated.[2]

Returning to the Wild West in an inebriated state at about three o'clock, while the afternoon show was in progress, Charging Thunder was moved to perpetrate an unprovoked assault upon George C. Crager, as the latter stood in conversation behind the scenes with Colonel Cody, and dealt him a severe blow to the back of the head. The interpreter was knocked unconscious and fell to the ground.

While a few of the newspapers claimed that the weapon used was an Indian war club, it was actually a 2lb block of wood.

Colonel Cody quickly secured the person of Charging Thunder and the police were called. The Indian was removed to Tobago Street police station and placed in a cell.

As reported by *The Scottish Leader* of the 2nd of January 1892, 'The accused lay down on the plank bed, pulled his blanket over him, and declined to speak to anyone.'

On the following morning, Friday the 1st of January, he was roused for an appearance before the Eastern Police Court, housed on the same premises, but, since Mr Crager was unable to appear – he was reported to be stunned but recovering – the case was continued until Monday the 4th.

The building at 92, Tobago Street, where Charging Thunder once spent a thoroughly miserable weekend, has long since ceased to function as a police station and court of law. It still stands but is now derelict. A worn and faded City of Glasgow coat of arms carved upon the façade over the main entrance conspires with a vacant flagpole to hint at memories of better days.

The report in the *Evening Citizen* on the night of the 4th stated that Charging Thunder, during this court appearance, 'slouched past the bar drawing his variegated blanket closer about him, ... looking neither to the right hand nor the left'.

The Bailie, presumably on the grounds that he considered his own powers of sentencing inadequate, remitted Charging Thunder to the Sheriff Court, where the accused made a declaration later that same day. He was thence brought up to Duke Street Prison in a van, along with twenty other untried prisoners, and held there on remand.

The *Glasgow Weekly Mail* reported that: 'In the prison he was doffed of his own "toggery" and furnished with a rig out of dark moleskin. He has, however, been allowed by the authorities to wear his ornaments.'[3] The article concluded with the by now almost obligatory racial slur: 'He relished a warm bath as a luxury not often enjoyed.'

NEW YEAR, 1892

During his period of incarceration at Duke Street, Charging Thunder received a visit from two of his compatriots. The *Evening Times* identified these as 'the Sioux Chief and his sister'.[4] This is very probably a reference to No Neck and Calls the Name. They brought him a supply of cigars, which, sadly, their intended beneficiary was unable to enjoy since smoking was prohibited by the prison regulations.

The case came before Sheriff Birnie, on a summary complaint, in his chambers at the old County Buildings in Glasgow's 'Merchant City' district on Tuesday the 12th of January. Charging Thunder pleaded guilty to the charge of assault. F. R. Richardson, defending, advanced a number of pleas in mitigation. He stated that his client was just twenty-three years of age (actually twenty-four, according to the prison registers for both Duke Street and Barlinnie) and normally one of the quietest members of the show. It was also submitted that, 'like all other Indians, the slightest amount of drink was sufficient to infuriate him'.[5]

Mr Richardson explained that, on entering the public house, Charging Thunder had asked for lemonade but that, by some mischance, was given whisky instead.

Whether Charging Thunder was such an innocent abroad has to be doubted. While no mention of previous convictions is made in any of the accounts of the final disposal of the case, a remarkable statement appeared in the *Evening Times*:

> Charging Thunder, it may be mentioned, has already been through the hands of the police of the Eastern Division, he being recently found guilty of disorderly conduct in Duke Street, and admonished. Of the large number of Indians in the company, he is the only one who gives serious trouble.[6]

The Sheriff asked the name of the establishment where the whisky had been purchased. Charging Thunder, speaking through an interpreter, replied that it was on Duke Street but he could not identify the occupier.

It is unfortunate that the interpreter is not specifically named. However, it seems improbable that any Lakota interpreter other than John Shangrau or George Crager would have been available.[7]

The outcome of the hearing was reported in the *Glasgow Evening News* that night, the 12th of January, as follows:

> His Lordship said that if Charging Thunder had not been a stranger to this country he would have sent him to prison for a long time. In the circumstances, however, he would send him 30 days to prison as a warning to others. It was a shame to supply these Indians with whisky.
>
> As he went out his sister, a Wild West Squaw, gave a parcel of apples and other kinds of fruit to the incarcerated Sioux.

The *Evening Times* of the same date supplies the additional detail that Charging Thunder's sister wore a cross in her shawl and that a swarthy-looking man bearing a medal inscribed 'Lieutenant of Police' was also present. Again, this is almost certainly a reference to No Neck.

Charging Thunder was removed to Barlinnie, where he served the full term of imprisonment imposed.

A number of additional details emerge from the prison registers for Duke Street and Barlinnie, which were first made publicly available in 1988. Both records agree that Charging Thunder was five feet six and a half inches in height, which rather calls into question the description of him in the *Evening Citizen* as 'tall and muscular'.[8] The medical officers for both establishments concurred that his health was 'good'. His home address was given as 'East End Exhibition', his occupation as 'showman' and his place of birth as North America. At Duke Street, 'Religion' was left blank while at Barlinnie it was entered as 'nil'. The Duke Street registrar was clearly lost for words for, under 'Remark', he entered 'An Indian'.

On Thursday the 11th of February, Charging Thunder was released. George Crager was obviously not a man to harbour grudges, for he presented himself at Barlinnie to escort the liberated Indian back to the Wild West. The *Evening Times* for that date quoted him as confessing that he did not like prison life, and that the food had not agreed with him. However, he gave every appearance of being in excellent health, and demolished a substantial breakfast.

There was, however, a postscript. On the next day, the *Evening Times*' 'Gossip and Grumbles' column reported:

> One of the Wild West Braves had a huge drunk yesterday, and he monopolised both sides of the pavement in a highly-civilised manner. Two companion braves took the opposite side of the street from the intoxicated Redskin, but it was difficult to say whether they were most ashamed or amused at his gyrations.[9]

The possibility that the miscreant was Charging Thunder, celebrating the restoration of his liberty in his own inimitable style, is altogether too appalling to contemplate.

However, it has to be conceded that the timing was remarkable.

... Meets Doc Halliday

Charging Thunder's story is expanded upon in a scandalously unreliable – but nonetheless engaging – chapter of Halliday Sutherland's book of memoirs, *A Time to Keep*, first published in 1934. Sutherland, aged nine at the time of Buffalo Bill's first visit to Glasgow, later became a doctor of medicine and also met with success as the author of several books.

His account of the assault is of little value since there is no suggestion that he was personally present at the scene. It is obviously based on hearsay – probably not even first-hand hearsay at that – and is certainly riddled with serious inaccuracies.

Sutherland does not refer to Charging Thunder by name but rather as 'Sitting Bull' throughout. This must be qualified by pointing out that Sutherland acknowledges from the outset that there is no suggestion that this was *the* Sitting Bull. Rather, according to

Sutherland, he was the famous chief's son though even this much can be discounted.

However, he makes an interesting suggestion regarding the motivation for the assault. Colonel Cody, on noticing Charging Thunder's intoxicated state, relayed the interpreter to order him to go to his 'wigwam' and sleep it off. The Indian became so incensed by this instruction that he hit the interpreter over the head with a tomahawk. The idea that a tomahawk was used is so patently absurd that I offer no further discussion on the point. The interpreter, whom he does not identify by name, was, Sutherland tells us, a 'half-caste'. This is incorrect and it is obvious that he has Shangrau in mind.

A further error of fact is contained in the statement: 'The magistrates committed Sitting Bull to the High Court on a charge of attempted murder.'[10]

However, though there is no indication of what it is based on, Sutherland's theory concerning the motivation is as good as any other since no other explanation for what was otherwise an entirely gratuitous assault was advanced at the time.

The *Evening Times* stated: 'No reason can be assigned for the attack, Mr Crager is unaware of having acted in any way which might have roused the spite of his assailant.'[11]

Nor could the accused account for his actions. It was widely reported in connection with the hearing at which he was sentenced, for example, in the *Glasgow Evening News* that: 'Thunder entertained no malice towards the interpreter; indeed, they were friends.'[12]

Professor Louis S. Warren, in *Buffalo Bill's America*, surmises that tensions had arisen over Crager's proposed sale of Indian artefacts to Kelvingrove Museum but it is difficult to find a foundation for this conjecture beyond unaided speculation.[13]

Sutherland also states that, on his arrival in Glasgow, Colonel Cody had issued a general appeal to the city's publicans, by means of a circular letter and through the press, not to supply any of his Indians with alcohol. Whether this detail is actually correct has to be questioned as my own exhaustive search of the newspapers of the time has failed to identify any such published request. However, some support is to be found in the *Glasgow Weekly Mail*, which acknowledged that Colonel Cody had warned the publicans not to supply the Indians with alcohol.[14] By what precise means this injunction was effected is not stated.

According to Sutherland, a wave of public indignation arose against the publican who had sold the whisky (though he could not be identified in court) and sympathy was widely expressed in favour of both the Indian and his victim. This might well be an accurate summation of the prevailing attitudes. He also tells us that Crager was admitted to the Royal Infirmary.

Since it is seriously inaccurate in several fundamental respects, Sutherland's account of his experiences in connection with the Wild West show must be adjudged inherently unreliable as a historical source. The suspicion naturally arises that it was concocted not from personal experience but from press reports. This impression is enhanced by a number of interesting correspondences with details disclosed by the contemporary accounts and the same consideration also applies to his alleged encounter with Annie Oakley. It is impossible to offer an entirely positive assessment of this thoroughly garbled though fascinating primary source.

Nonetheless, it remains of great interest, in that it contains a number of tantalising details not disclosed elsewhere. In particular, Sutherland's account is to some extent redeemed by the fact that the information given concerning himself and his family, with whom he resided at 2, Cathedral Square (numbers 1 and 3 were occupied by the prison governor and the chaplaincy respectively), is confirmed by the postal, census and other official records. He was at least correct in identifying the establishment in which Charging Thunder was held on remand although he refers to it only as 'Glasgow Prison'.[15] Crucially, he tells us, correctly, that his father, John Francis Sutherland, was the prison medical officer. Dr Sutherland was well known and respected in the city and had served as convener of the Ladies' Committee in connection with the East End Industrial Exhibition.

The possibility that Sutherland's story was a total fabrication can at least be disposed of.

'YOUR FATHERS THE GHOSTS'

Sutherland provides us with some information about Charging Thunder's time in Duke Street Prison, based on recollections of his father's 'first-hand news of the Indian chief'.[16] At first, the Indian was in a state of dejection and contrition but his spirits were, to some extent, revived by positive tidings of his victim's progress: 'Not one word of English could he speak, but the prison officials by signs made him understand that the interpreter was alive, and would probably recover.'[17]

Sutherland also explains that the incarcerated Indian enjoyed certain privileges as a prisoner held on remand and awaiting trial. He was not obliged to wear prison clothes and he was permitted to receive visitors. Sutherland states that Colonel Cody and other Indians from the Wild West came to see him. The first statement is apparently contradicted by the report appearing in the *Glasgow Weekly Mail* of the 9th of January 1891 but the second is specifically confirmed by the fact that at least one party of two Indians is known (from the *Evening Times* on the same date) to have visited him during his time on remand.

One Saturday forenoon, Sutherland tells us, he went to call upon 'Sitting Bull' in his cell in the north wing of Duke Street Prison. If this is true, the visit could only have taken place on the 9th of January. The boy took him a gift of a basket of fruit,[18] which his father had bought on his behalf at Mrs Campbell's shop opposite Central Station. When the boy entered the Indian's cell, he found him sitting on his bed, under the window. Sutherland describes him as wearing his moccasins, along with, somewhat improbably, a headdress and 'pigtail of large feathers'[19] – presumably signifying a trailer. Under the watchful and smiling eye of the warder, the Indian rose to receive his visitor and gravely accepted the gift. In the course of the brief audience, Charging Thunder clasped the boy for a moment, spoke a few unintelligible words in his own language and bowed.

One week later, the account continues, 'two Red Indians came and left a headdress at our house'.[20] It would certainly be interesting to establish whether the war bonnet is otherwise known as, indeed, it would be to learn its subsequent history.

The interpreter's swift recovery had a crucial bearing on the outcome of the subsequent prosecution and Sutherland tells us that a 'light sentence'[21] was imposed. Whether thirty days in Barlinnie can be considered to be a 'light sentence' is very much a matter of personal interpretation.

Certainly, the wildest of the Wild West Indians was allowed to return to sound his famous war cry again for a couple of weeks before the season ended and his departure for America a few days later was, no doubt, a tender mercy to all concerned.

The Cowboys

For the most part, the exploits of the cowboys were overshadowed by their Indian counterparts but they did come in for an honourable mention every once in a while. On the 9th of January 1892, the ever-informative 'Clydeside Echoes' column in the *Glasgow Evening News* reported: 'Three cowboys, in all the panoply of "the wild and woolly West," rode down Renfield Street yesterday, and half-a-dozen trace-boys rode in emulation and admiration close behind.'

Meanwhile, the cowboys' bronco-busting heroics also came in for a due measure of attention for, as reported by *The Bailie for Wednesday, January 13th, 1892*, their endeavours were so highly thought of that a number of gentlemen in the vicinity engaged their services two or three times a week, in the work of taming unmanageable steeds. One cowboy, sadly not further identified, received a specific mention for the particular success he had met with in subduing a valuable horse belonging to Gavin Ralston, a landed proprietor whose mansion, Loaningdale, stood on the edge of Biggar, Lanarkshire.

On the 12th of January 1892, the *Glasgow Evening News* announced that Buffalo Bill intended to make an excursion to the Trossachs and that William Glover, the Glasgow artist who had contributed to the scenery for the show, would act as his guide.

Notes

1. *Scottish Sport*, 5 January 1892
2. *Bristol Times and Mirror*, 5 October 1891
3. 9 January 1892
4. Same date
5. *Glasgow Weekly Mail*, 16 January 1892
6. 2 January 1892
7. There is one small clue that Crager acquitted this role himself. It will be recalled that the hearing on the 1st of January was continued to the 4th because Crager was unable to attend. Witnesses would not have been heard at such an early stage in the process so it can only be taken that Crager's attendance was required in the capacity of interpreter.
8. 4 January 1892. The same adjectives had been employed in the *Scottish Leader*'s report two days previously.
9. 12 February 1892
10. *A Time To Keep*, p. 23
11. 2 January 1892
12. 12 January 1892
13. p. 410
14. 16 January 1892
15. p. 23
16. Ibid.
17. Ibid.
18. Could this detail have been prompted by the report in the *Glasgow Evening News*, 12th January 1891, about Charging Thunder's sister presenting him with a parcel of fruit as he was taken out of court?
19. p. 23
20. p. 24
21. Ibid.

9

INTERPRETERS AND MISSIONARIES

John Shangrau and the True Story of the 'Lily of the West'

The hearing in the case against Charging Thunder was not the only Wild West business conducted in Glasgow Sheriff Court on Monday the 4th of January 1892. That same forenoon, John Shangrau and Lillie Orr appeared before Sheriff Spens, to obtain a warrant for the registration of their marriage, which had taken place earlier that morning at 94, Castle Street, Glasgow, in the presence of witnesses Robert W. Cowan Service, physician surgeon, of 3, Annfield Place, and Joseph Montgomery, bookbinder, of 160, Bellfield Street. The marriage was by declaration, one of the three irregular forms then peculiarly recognised under Scots law. It may have been chosen out of a perceived affinity with informal frontier marriages.

As was the case with almost every other move made by Buffalo Bill's employees, the event attracted much public attention. Among the wedding party were two other members of the Wild West entourage, one of whom was specifically identified by the *Evening Times* as 'a gorgeously-dressed Indian lady, who had all her ornaments on for the auspicious occasion'.[1]

It may be surmised that the lady in question was none other than Calls the Name, John's aunt, returning the favour of having acted as best man at her own wedding to Black Heart in Manchester the previous August. An intelligent guess at the identity of the other guest would have to favour No Neck, his uncle.

The bride was entered on the marriage certificate as a spinster, aged eighteen, also resident at 160, Bellfield Street, a short distance from the Wild West show, on the other side of Duke Street. She was a native of Liverpool, where the couple had met during the show's visit the previous July.

In common with his colleague George Crager, Shangrau's surname lends itself to a baffling array of different spellings, in consequence of its unfamiliarity and the illiteracy of its bearers. 'Shangrau' is somewhat arbitrarily favoured here, on the simple basis that it appears thus on his Wild West calling card.

Extensive research conducted by genealogist Andrew Gingras of New Hampshire indicates that the name is ultimately of French origin and a derivative of Gingras, a surname long established in Quebec. It is also attested among the Métis population of Manitoba, which yields a clue as to the probable manner of John's forebears' westward migration and raises the likelihood that his Indian blood quantum was higher than 50%.

'John Shangraun', as he appeared on the marriage certificate, was designated as an interpreter and, at thirty-eight, he was twenty years his bride's senior. He was entered as resident at the 'East End Exhibition Glasgow' and a widower, news of his first wife's demise having been received in the early stages of the 1891 tour. The names of his parents were entered as Jule (short for Julien) Shangraun, a stock raiser, and Mary Shangraun, maiden surname Smoke (previously known as Breath Wind), both deceased. At the time of her own marriage in Manchester, Calls the Name had given her father's name as Smoke. She and No Neck were Breath Wind's younger siblings.

John was born, the second of four sons, at Fort Laramie, Wyoming, c. 1853. His brothers were Louis, William and Peter. Grandfather Smoke was the maternal uncle of the famous Chief Red Cloud, in whose band the family lived a nomadic existence during John's boyhood. Of the four brothers, William was the only one who did not pursue a career as a scout and interpreter.

Much detailed information concerning John Shangrau's career is disclosed by a series of interviews conducted by Eli S. Ricker in 1906. John and Louis were among ten mixed-blood scouts employed by the army during the Powder River campaign of 1876, operating out of Fort Robinson, Nebraska. Shangrau was also at Fort Robinson the following year, when Crazy Horse was arrested and killed there, though he was not a witness to the incident. He almost lost his life while trailing the Cheyenne under Dull Knife who broke out of Fort Robinson in January 1879, after which he gave up scouting and returned home to Pine Ridge.

That John continued to live there among the Oglalas is authenticated by the fact that as 'John Jangrau' he was a signatory to the abortive land agreement of 1882–83.

A decade of peace came to an abrupt end with the outbreak of the ghost dance disturbances in the fall of 1890. A number of frontier characters returned to the army payroll as Indian interpreters and scouts and among them were John and his brothers Louis and Pete. The manuscript *As Narrated by Short Bull* reveals that John and Louis were already known to Short Bull prior to this time.

John Shangrau's status as a bona fide historical character is assured by the circumstance that he receives a mention in the apocalyptic final chapter of Dee Brown's *Bury My Heart at Wounded Knee*, in which we encounter him as chief of scouts for the 7th Cavalry. He is quoted as counselling Major Whiteside against the immediate disarmament of Big Foot's band, fearing that it would precipitate a fight in which women and children would be killed.[2]

A short time afterwards, he was caught up in the indiscriminate firing of the soldiers and was compelled to participate in the desperate stampede which ensued.

In the wake of the Wounded Knee atrocity, a delegation of Lakota chiefs went east for discussions with the federal authorities. They were accompanied by a three-man team of interpreters, headed by the Reverend Charles Cook, himself a full-blooded Indian of the Episcopalian mission at Pine Ridge. The team also included John's brother Louis. Much light is shed upon John's own experiences by a statement made by Mr Cook on his own account, at the office of General Morgan, the Commissioner of Indian Affairs in Washington.[3]

Travelling east in the company of General Miles, Mr Cook had engaged in a chilling conversation with one of the scouts, whom he identifies only as 'John'. However, it may be inferred from external evidence that it is Shangrau to whom he is referring. Mr Cook recounted the following story. After recovering from his flight, the scout had got himself back among the soldiers. He was approached by an officer, whom he could not name, and this man gloatingly told him, 'Now we have avenged Custer's death.'[4]

Mr Cook also told how his informant had gone to the hillside and found a young woman of about twenty-three or twenty-four years old. She was so severely hurt that, at first, he thought she was dead. He wrapped her in blankets and took her to the improvised field hospital where the injured were being brought together for medical treatment. The story concludes:

> A soldier went to this poor wounded girl and offered her a shining silver dollar so that he might gratify his appetite with her, and this same scout was so maddened that he rushed upon this soldier and kicked him over and over with his boots, and he was so sympathized with by an officer near by that he said to him, 'John, if you have a gun shoot the soldier, kill him.'

GEORGE C. CRAGER AND KELVINGROVE MUSEUM

A strange and fateful sequence of events was set in motion by the Lakota interpreter George C. Crager on Thursday the 17th of December 1891, when he composed the following epistle upon 'Buffalo Bill's Wild West Co.' headed notepaper, addressed to James Paton, curator of the museum at, as Crager styled it, 'Calvin Grove'

(The Kelvingrove Art Gallery & Museum was not established at its present premises until 1901):

> Dear Sir,
> Hearing that you are empowered to purchase relics for your Museum I would respectfully inform you that I have a collection of Indian Relics (North American) which I will dispose of before we sail for America.
> Should you wish any of them after Inspection I would be pleased to have you call at my Room at the East End Exhibition Building – Please Answer when you can come.
> Yours Resp.
> Geo. C. Crager
> In charge of Indians[5]

When Mr Paton duly reported to the Galleries and Museum subcommittee of the Glasgow Town Council, the news of Crager's overture drew an interested reaction, as minuted on Friday the 15th of January 1892:

> The Curator reported that there is at present an opportunity of acquiring for the Museum a selection from a collection of genuine specimens of articles made by the Indians of the North-west provinces of America. The Chairman thereafter reported that he and Councillor Burt had, along with the Curator, inspected the collection, and the Curator submitted a list of articles it might be advisable to purchase. The sub-committee authorised the Curator to spend a sum not exceeding £40 in purchasing a selection from the collection.

The museum's Accession Register discloses that the transaction took place on Tuesday the 19th of January 1892. For reasons that are not immediately apparent, the twenty-eight artefacts were recorded in two distinct groups of fourteen items each – 1892.2.a-n and 1892.3.a-n. For the first of these, only the phrase 'purchased £40' illuminates the 'source' column while, in the case of the second, the fuller commentary 'George C. Crager, Sioux Interpreter' is appended. This second category was apparently a donation. The theoretical possibility that the first was acquired from someone other than George C. Crager remains a matter of philosophical doubt only.

In the Council minutes for the following Friday, the 22nd of January, it was further recorded that the Curator had reported the purchase and that the subcommittee 'authorised payment of the price to be made at once'.

The inventory of the artefacts acquired at this time discloses three broad categories of especial interest, in that these were represented at the time of registration as having direct associations with the site of the massacre at Wounded Knee, with the personage of the famous Hunkpapa Lakota chief Sitting Bull or else with members of the Wild West entourage.

The single item that has attracted the greatest notoriety is, without a doubt, the 'ghost shirt'. Fashioned from cotton, with feather ornamentation, it was on public display at Kelvingrove for many years. It is perforated with bullet holes and stained with what appears to be blood. The shirt's existence came to light at the time of the *Home of the Brave* exhibition at the McLellan Galleries, Glasgow, in 1992, resulting in a repatriation application by the Cheyenne River Lakota, which was attended by a blaze of media attention from beginning to end. The shirt was eventually returned to South Dakota during the summer of 1999, following a resolution by Glasgow City Council.

The precise truth of the matter will never now be established but the entry in the Accession Register alleges that what came to be known as 'the Glasgow ghost shirt' had been blessed by Short Bull, and that it was plundered from the dead body of a Lakota warrior at Wounded Knee. Sam Maddra's submission[6] that a wholesale trade in fabricated Wounded Knee 'souvenirs' existed during the period in question is accepted and it must also be concluded that the history of the artefact and of the manner in which it passed into the ownership of George C. Crager is too nebulous to admit of a definite finding regarding its provenance ever being made. The register offers the further commentary that the shirt was supposed by the Lakota to have the effect of rendering its wearer invulnerable.

The remaining articles continue to be held in the collection of Glasgow Museums. For the most part, these consist of items of clothing, baby carriers, travelling bags, purses and a tobacco pouch, many of them gorgeously ornamented with shell, beadwork and porcupine quills.

The other artefacts asserted to have been retrieved from the field of slaughter, following the fateful encounter at Wounded Knee, can be inventoried as: a war necklace fashioned from hide and fringed with sections of deer's hoof; a baby carrier, also found on the battle-field, with no mention made of what fate had overtaken its late occupant; and a pair of moccasins alleged to have been taken from the body of Across-the-Room, a son of Big Foot, the chief of the Indians slain at Wounded Knee. There is also a set of four war arrows, each with a steel head and a wooden shaft. These may or may not be the same arrows that were mentioned in the *Staffordshire Sentinel* article of the 20th of August 1891 as having been picked up at Wounded Knee. Certainly, no such representation is made for them in the Accession Register.

An article with an alleged personal connection to Sitting Bull, a 'Christening Pipe', is recorded as having been used by his daughter. It is fashioned from red catlinite with a wooden stem and ornamented with quillwork, feathers and silk ribbons.

The items connected with members of the Wild West entourage are: a pair of buckskin leggings worn by Yankton Charlie who, as it will be recalled, had returned to the United States in August; a necklace of otter skin and grizzly bear claws with a pendant of ermine skins and brass bells, worn during the 1890 disturbances by Short Bull; a marriage pipe, again of red catlinite and fitted with a carved wooden stem, as used at Short Bull's wedding; a pair of buckskin leggings, embroidered with beads, worn by Calls the Name, designated in the register as the 'Squaw Chief of the Brule Sioux in 1876'; and a canvas shield decorated with a coloured picture of two Indians hunting a bear, attributed to Lone Bull and dated 1891.

Second only to the ghost shirt in terms of historical significance is a buckskin waistcoat, handsomely ornamented in patterned beadwork and recorded as having been worn by Chief Rain in the Face.

Much effort has been wasted over the years in the futile task of seeking to establish the identity of the warrior who personally slew Custer. Sam Maddra, in her article 'Whose Ghost Dance Shirt Is This . . . Can Anyone Help?', takes the statement accompanying the waistcoat's entry in the register as inferring that this distinction belonged to Rain in the Face. However, on careful consideration of the wording, it is at best ambiguous and probably amounts to no more than a reiteration of the Wild West show's tired and standard billing of Sitting Bull as 'the killer of Custer': 'A waistcoat of buckskin covered with beadwork worn by "Rain-in-the-Face" the Minneconjous Sioux warrior, and subchief of "Sitting Bill" Murderer of General Custer in 1876.'[7]

How exactly the interpreter came to acquire the waistcoat – one of the donated items – is not touched upon by its entry in the register but it may be noted that the photograph of the Crager family taken in Manchester at the end of July 1891 showed him with it in his possession.

While almost all of the items acquired from Crager are of Lakota origin, there is also one which is in a class of its own. This is a blanket woven in coloured yarn by the Navajo Indians of the hot and arid southwest, many hundreds of miles distant from South Dakota. This blanket, probably acquired by a Lakota owner through trade, makes an appearance together with Rain in the Face's waistcoat, being modelled by one of the figures in a group photograph taken at Pine Ridge, on the 16th of January 1891, shortly after the surrender of the hostiles under Kicking Bear. This photograph is featured on the front cover of Sam Maddra's 'Glasgow's Ghost Shirt' and elsewhere in the body of the booklet but she appears not to make the connection between the items in the image and those in the Kelvingrove collection.

It might also be observed that several of the items specifically

Buffalo Bill and Sitting Bull at William Notman's studio in Montreal, 1885

Mugshot: Kicking Bear imprisoned in Fort Sheridan, Illinois, during the first quarter of 1891

Short Bull, during the same period

No Neck and Johnny Burke No Neck in Cardiff, September 1891

Courtesy of Glasgow University Library, Department of Special Collections

The Boys' House of Refuge, 1843

Courtesy of the Mitchell Library, Glasgow City Council

The official programme 1891-92, front cover

Charing Cross, Glasgow.

The Grand Hotel, Charing Cross

"All the warriors drawn together
By the signal of the peace-pipe"
Longfellow

Luncheon in honour of Colonel The Hon'ble W. F. Cody

Menu — 22nd Decem'r 1891

Argonaut Soup.

Civet de Lièvre.   Kari de Poulet.

Haggis and "Auld Scottie."
Sheep's Head and Trotters.
Black and White Puddings.

Sirloin of Beef.
Roast Turkey and Tongue.   Roll of Hunter's Beef.
Rabbit Pie.   Spatchcock Chickens and York Ham.

Devilled Kidneys.
Grilled Pigs' Feet and Salade à l'Américaine.

Pop Corn Soufflé.   Plum Pudding.
Californian Jelly.   Empress Cream.

DESSERT.

COFFEE.

Grand Hotel, Glasgow.
Guilford - Purveyor.

P.T.O.

The menu for the 1390 Club's luncheon in honour of Colonel Cody, 22nd December 1891

Annie Oakley in Glasgow

'Charging Thunder, a Sioux Indian from Buffalo Bill's Wild West Show', photographed by Gertrude Käsebier in 1899

John and Lillie Shangrau in London, 1892

The Glasgow ghost shirt

Courtesy of the Annie Oakley Center at Garst Museum, Greenville, Ohio

Courtesy of Wyoming State Archives, Department of State Parks and Cultural Resources

George C. Crager in 1902

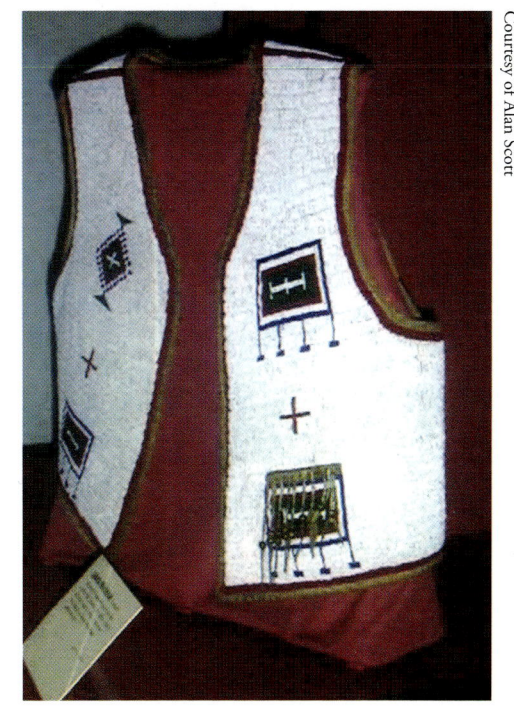

Rain in the Face's waistcoat

Mexican Joe and Company

Robert 'Montana Bill' Robeson

Kicking Bear, as photographed by the Dennistoun Photo Co., 40 Bellgrove St, Glasgow

This publicity image was used in 1894 to commemorate the Wild West's overseas tours, including the Glasgow sojourn.

Barnum & Bailey's street parade approaching Burns Statue Square, Ayr, in 1899. Jake Posey was the driver of the forty-horse team depicted here and he returned to Scotland in 1904 as the chief stud groom with Buffalo Bill.

Show posters on display in O'Connell Street, Hawick, in 1904

Roosevelt's Rough Riders with 'Princess' Nouma Hawa

Carter the Cowboy Cyclist

described and enumerated in a variety of press articles during the previous summer's tour of England and Wales fail to show up in the Kelvingrove collection.

However, the Council minutes quoted above make it clear that the collection acquired from George C. Crager in Glasgow represented merely a judicious and representative 'selection' from the total items on offer. It might therefore be that those remaining in Crager's possession after the disposal of the Glasgow artefacts were even more numerous and impressive than those left behind. Specifically, there are at least two beadwork articles on display in the Manchester photograph that make no appearance among the exhibits held by Glasgow Museums. It is therefore as tempting as it is fruitless to speculate upon whatever other items Crager might have held in his collection, how it was that he came by them or upon the manner in which he might subsequently have dealt with them.

The Missionaries

As if Glasgow were not blessed with sufficient religious enthusiasts of its own, the Indians' exile brought no respite from the attentions of American missionaries. *The Bailie for Wednesday, January 20th, 1892* reported:

> Several ladies, I understand, from the Medical Mission Training Home, visit Buffalo Bill's redskin encampment daily, and talk seriously to the Indians. These latter all believe that they have got the 'white' heart, but they find it difficult, they say, to be good when on the tramp.

Short Bull, apparently, had an enigmatic spiritual insight of his own to impart, as relayed by the *Glasgow Evening News*'s 'Clydeside Echoes' column: '"Short Bull" frankly confessed to a missionary at the "Wild West" the other day, that he would rather go to heaven four times than go to hell. This indeed was honest Indian!'[8]

One of the missionaries later recalled her experiences in Europe to the *New York Times*:

> They are very fond of singing either in English or Sioux: indeed their demand for hymns is insatiable. As two books among forty or fifty are hardly enough, they promised to copy some of their favourites before another week, and when the next Sabbath came around Revenge, who was prominent in the rebellion, had undertaken to copy a good many hymns out so all might be able to join.[9]

Since the article goes on to recall incidents of which the two local items cited above are clearly paraphrases, we may take it that this remarkable apparition of a participant in the final Indian conflict handing out the hymn books was witnessed in Glasgow. Short Bull was also reported as having responded very positively, enabling Sam Maddra to conclude that: 'Ironically, it was the Ghost Dancers, perceived by many to be backward-looking and pagan, who impressed the missionary most with their interest in and knowledge of religion.'[10]

However, I would contend that Dr Maddra has missed a crucial piece of supporting evidence for it emerges that Kicking Bear himself may have attended a Free Church service during his time in Glasgow.

Undoubtedly the most interesting item to grace the sixtieth anniversary edition of the Whitehill Secondary School magazine was a short contribution by Theodore D. Lowe. Mr Lowe was one of the school's original pupils and had retired as a solicitor in the service of London, Midland and Scottish Railway in 1943. This brief article, containing an outline of his recollections of the Wild West, concluded with the startling pronouncement that: 'I met Short Bull many times in my parents' house and walked with Kicking Bear from my father's church in Bridgeton to Dennistoun, and what more could a boy of 12 desire?'

From the postal and census records, the following picture emerges. The Reverend David Lowe resided at 1, Whitehill Gardens, an apparently self-contained ground-floor tenement apartment that is still in existence and occupied. It was to this household that Short Bull is stated to have been a frequent visitor. Mr Lowe's son Theodore D. was listed in the April 1891 census as a 'scholar', aged eleven, and this is entirely consistent with his statement that he was twelve at the time in question. There was an elder sister, Katherine, aged eighteen at the time of the census, and a letter addressed to her and bearing to be from one Charging Crow, an Indian otherwise known to have been in Glasgow, has been preserved in the collection of Whitehill Secondary School. It is dated the 1st of November 1892 and was written on 'Buffalo Bill's Wild West Co.' headed notepaper, shortly after his return to Pine Ridge. Unfortunately, the message consists mostly of general expressions of goodwill and fails to shed light upon the exact nature of the relationship between Katherine and its author, beyond a nebulously expressed concept of friendship.

The Reverend Lowe was minister of the London Road Free Church, lying just off the main thoroughfare at Boden Street, to the west of Celtic Park. The church is long gone although its battered edifice survives, reduced to a prime target for graffiti artists and other vandals. Since 1942, it has served as a 'Youth Centre' attached to Bridgeton St Francis-in-the-East Church of Scotland.

Theodore's account is uncorroborated as far as I am aware but, since he was obviously a mature and sober professional gentleman and the son of a Free Kirk minister, his story should only be discounted for good reason and with due measure of circumspection.

As Kicking Bear was a respected *wicàsa wakàn'* or medicine man and therefore, in every sense, a religious man within his own tradition, his apparent friendship with the Reverend Lowe must have been a very interesting meeting of minds and, indeed, worlds. It is unfortunate that the occasion for Kicking Bear's visit to the church is not explained and therefore the question of whether he attended a service there is unresolved. However, it is a fair walk from Boden Street to Bridgeton Cross and thence north to Duke Street so it is unlikely that this journey was undertaken without some weighty purpose in mind.

Notes

1. 4 January 1892
2. p. 440
3. Preserved in the *Crager Scrapbook*, Buffalo Bill Historical Center
4. A lieutenant, according to his interview with Ricker, p. 262
5. Glasgow Museums Resource Centre
6. 'Glasgow's Ghost Shirt', p. 14
7. *American Indian Review*, No. 15, p. 13
8. 17 February 1892
9. 15 July 1894
10. *Hostiles?*, p. 147

10

MEXICAN JOE, RUNNING WOLF AND THE NEW OLYMPIA

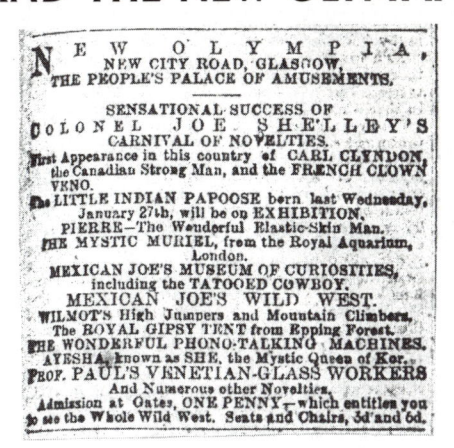

> **NEW OLYMPIA,**
> NEW CITY ROAD, GLASGOW.
> THE PEOPLE'S PALACE OF AMUSEMENTS.
>
> SENSATIONAL SUCCESS OF
> COLONEL JOE SHELLEY'S
> CARNIVAL OF NOVELTIES.
> First Appearance in this country of CARL CLYNDON, the Canadian Strong Man, and the FRENCH CLOWN VENO.
> The LITTLE INDIAN PAPOOSE born last Wednesday, January 27th, will be on EXHIBITION.
> PIERRE—The Wonderful Elastic-Skin Man.
> THE MYSTIC MURIEL, from the Royal Aquarium, London.
> MEXICAN JOE'S MUSEUM OF CURIOSITIES, including the TATOOED COWBOY.
> MEXICAN JOE'S WILD WEST.
> WILMOT'S High Jumpers and Mountain Climbers.
> The ROYAL GIPSY TENT from Epping Forest.
> THE WONDERFUL PHONO-TALKING MACHINES.
> AYESHA, known as SHE, the Mystic Queen of Kor.
> PROF. PAUL'S VENETIAN-GLASS WORKERS
> And Numerous other Novelties.
> Admission at Gates, ONE PENNY,—which entitles you to see the Whole Wild West. Seats and Chairs, 3d and 6d.

It is remarkable enough that there was even one Wild West show in Glasgow that winter but, for ten weeks, from the 19th of December 1891 until the 27th of February 1892, there were actually two. Mexican Joe operated his own attraction in the Cowcaddens, in direct competition with Buffalo Bill.

More formally known as 'Colonel' Joseph Shelley, Mexican Joe's lasting measure of notoriety is principally due to the role he had played in the strange and oft-recited episode related in the autobiography *Black Elk Speaks*. Black Elk, together with five other Lakota, had the misfortune to be left behind in Manchester at the end of the 1887–88 season and found employment with Mexican Joe in London. He was later rescued by Buffalo Bill in Paris, having fallen ill and been abandoned a second time.

If Mexican Joe's publicity materials are to be believed, his show was actually more impressive than Buffalo Bill's but whether anyone else shared this assessment is unclear. Press references to Mexican Joe's show consistently stress that it was on a considerably smaller and generally less elaborate scale than Buffalo Bill's. A further significant difference is that, while Buffalo Bill's fame was based on encounters with the tribes of the northern Great Plains, Mexican Joe's orientation was towards the Apache and the southwest.

Mexican Joe received far less attention from the press than did his more famous contemporary, so it is impossible to reproduce a comprehensive picture of his peregrinations. However, from the fragmentary record to hand, his movements can be reconstructed at least in outline. It appears that he first took his entourage to England in July 1887, only a few months behind Buffalo Bill. He continued to tour Great Britain and mainland Europe, probably on a continuous basis, until 1894.

As regards Mexican Joe's earlier career on the frontier, the *Evening Times* offered the assessment that: 'The life of the well-known scout is too well known to require repetition.'[1] It is regretted that no further elaboration was provided since, however well informed the public might have been on Mexican Joe's personal history in 1891, the subject appears to have been relegated to absolute obscurity in the intervening period.

In the spring of 1889, Mexican Joe made his first known foray into Scotland. A season at Newsome's Circus in Edinburgh commenced on Monday the 20th of May and ran for four weeks. He advertised himself in *The Scotsman* on various dates as:

America's and Mexico's Greatest INDIAN FIGHTER, BUFFALO HUNTER, TRAPPER, TRAILER, SCOUT, and GUIDE, MEXICAN JOE

With characteristic modesty, he also had himself lauded as 'THE HERO OF THE PRAIRIES', in a further advert.[2]

Included in the ambitious programme were such items as 'Love and Revenge', 'Death of the Lone Scout' and 'Capturing a Horse Thief'.

On Saturday, the 1st of June, the boys of the Leith Industrial School attended the afternoon performance at the personal invitation of Mexican Joe. The boys were accompanied by their brass band and enjoyed the occasion enormously.

The 1891–92 Cowcaddens season was clearly not Mexican Joe's first sojourn in the West of Scotland. Note for example the announcement in *Quiz* of the 8th of January 1892:

> Mexican Joe is *again* (emphasis mine) with us, and located at the New Olympia, one of the most central places of entertainment in town. The entertainment is marked by liveliness and go, and there is not a dull moment during the performance.

On the 19th of July 1889, *Quiz* had carried a lengthy review of a stage drama enacted at the 'Theatre of Varieties', in Glasgow's old barracks yard showground. For present purposes, one tantalising and unelaborated pronouncement stands out conspicuously from the rest – 'whilst at the back Mexican Joe, his own show over, has dropped in to see his fellow-performers.'

No other reference to Mexican Joe can be found in the Glasgow papers for that summer but the allusion is plain as day and the absence of accompanying commentary clearly indicates that here was an already familiar figure whose renewed presence required no further explanation.

An insight into the structure of Mexican Joe's entourage is provided by the 1891 census. At that time, the show was in Jarrow, on Tyneside. Joseph Shelley, aged forty-five, is designated as a show proprietor and entered together with his wife Ada, aged seventeen, also a rider with the show. A long-term connection with Jarrow is probably indicated by the fact that he appears there again in the 1901 census although, this time, with a new wife and employed as a phrenologist. On both occasions, his place of birth was entered as Georgia, USA, rather calling into question his alleged connection with Mexico.

In 1891, the remainder of the company were eighteen in number and encamped at 'Jarrow Circus on Pit Heap'. They included a storekeeper, a billposter, six stablemen and three 'circus riders'. Three of the stablemen hailed from the USA but the remainder of these individuals were variously natives of England and Ireland. There were five 'horse riders', all born in Nebraska and named as Frank Warner, Charles and Minnie Jefferson and John and Minnie White.

Mexican Joe's show also appeared at Paisley's Smithhills showground in August 1891, during the town's annual holidays. The coverage appearing in the *Paisley & Renfrewshire Gazette* creates the definite impression that it amounted to no more than a fairground attraction, albeit the principal one of those on offer.[3]

When 'Mexican Joe's Exhibition of the Western Wilds of America', as it was advertised, came to Glasgow during the winter of 1891–92, it was the first ever attraction at the New Olympia, on the intersection of the New City Road and the Cowcaddens Road. The New Olympia was conceived as a sort of 'people's palace of amusements'[4] and had recently been built on the site of a piece of vacant ground that, for some time past, had been the open-air location of a succession of travelling shows. *Quiz* enthusiastically offered the commentary that it was 'the finest building of the kind outside of London, being almost as large as the Waverley Market, and very much higher than that popular Edinburgh building'.[5]

Mexican Joe was beset by much the same 'vexatious delays'[6] as Buffalo Bill had recently had to contend with and the opening was postponed from the 15th of December. This was, in part, due to a fire breaking out at the New Olympia on the morning of the 16th of November 1891, causing £20 worth of damage, a respectable sum of money in those days.

Mexican Joe's entertainment had hitherto been a Wild West show pure and simple but, by the end of 1891, he felt the need to enlarge its appeal and divided it into two sections. One of these was a Wild West show, in which a troupe of cowboys and Indians continued to re-enact the familiar scenes of frontier life as before and the other consisted of a traditional funfair.

The Wild West part of the entertainment consisted of a series of tableaux, given upon a 'Colossal Stage'.[7] These successively depicted the capture of Mexican Joe in Mexico's Sierra Madre Mountains (presumably by Apaches), in 1876, as well as attacks upon a tourist party on the prairies and upon the hunter's home in the Far West.

There was also a feature, which would no doubt have been extremely familiar to anyone who had already been a spectator at Buffalo Bill's show, in which cowboys threw lassos and rode bucking broncos going by such names as Dynamite, Cyclone and Jubilee. Sioux and Apache warriors were introduced, along with their 'squaws'. An exhibition of marksmanship was given by 'Alchise, the Indian boy-shot'.[8]

Mexican Joe appears to have anticipated Buffalo Bill in conceding that a Wild West show alone was not capable of sustaining an indefinite hold upon the public's attention. For this reason, 'Colonel Joe Shelley's Carnival of Novelties' included a number of additional attractions, none of which held any obvious connection to the American West.

One penny was the modest price of admission to the fair, with admission to the Wild West charged at from 6d to 2/-. Among these curiously extraneous items were a bewildering array of enigmas, among them: 'Pierre, The Elastic-Skin Man, the Wonder of the World'; 'The Royal Gypsy Tent'; 'The Wonderful Phono-Talking Machines'; Venetian glass workers; Carl Clyndon, the Canadian strong man; 'the French Clown Veno'; 'The Mystic Muriel, from the Royal Aquarium, London'; and 'Mexican Joe's Museum of Curiosities, including, the Tatooed (*sic*) Cowboy'.[9]

Not to be outdone by Charging Thunder's brush with the law, a prosecution involving one of the Indians from Mexican Joe's show was reported, under the title of 'An Indian Raid', in the very same editions of the *Glasgow Evening News* and *Evening Times* that also reported upon the disposal of Charging Thunder's case.[10]

The substance of the case was that Charles Jefferson, an Indian from Mexican Joe's show, otherwise known as Running Wolf, had entered an oyster shop on the New City Road. Acting from motives that remain unclear, the Indian became abusive towards the young lady left in charge of the establishment, calling her by insulting names, striking her to the effusion of blood and knocking her to the floor. The case was heard that day in the Northern Police Court in Maitland Street and a fine of twenty-one shillings, with the option of fourteen days in prison, was imposed.

Further information on the desperate character of Running Wolf emerges from Alan Gallop's *Buffalo Bill's British Wild West*,[11] in connection with a somewhat sensational article appearing in the *Salford Weekly News* during December 1887, entitled 'Attempted Murder at the Wild West Show'. At a performance in Sheffield, Running Wolf, stated to be the most savage member of the troupe, had fired his gun at Mexican Joe in the course of the 'Death of the Lone Scout' sequence, having substituted a hard substance for the more conventional blank cartridge. The shot struck its target under the left eye, causing a minor wound from which blood flowed freely. Mexican Joe felt sufficiently recovered to return to the stage later in the evening, earning himself a loud cheer. It was stated somewhat implausibly that this was the fourth occasion on which Running Wolf had attempted to shoot his employer.

There are a number of clear objections to this story being accepted at face value. Firstly, it is beyond dispute that, if this was indeed intended a serious attempt on Mexican Joe's life, then it was a singularly feeble one. Similarly, while no details are available on the three previous attempts, if they ever took place at all, it is obvious that none of them had been successful. Further, there is abundant evidence that it was standard circus practice at the time to advertise a particular lion, buffalo or horse as having been responsible for the deaths of a specified number of men, thus stressing and even exaggerating the dangers assumed by the performers. This was a clear attempt on the part of Mexican Joe to extend precisely the same principle to a human performer. If an animal had indeed killed a man, even on a single occasion, it would have been put down on account of its vicious propensities, instead of being allowed to continue to pose a threat. Similarly, if Running Wolf had seriously intended his boss's death, then he would surely have been consigned to prison or some other institution. At the very least, it seems improbable that the relationship between employer and employee could have endured while, in point of fact, it continued for over six years after the fourth alleged attempt at homicide.

There is much about Mexican Joe – particularly in his vexed

relationship with Running Wolf – that stretches credulity beyond its outer limits. Suspicion naturally focuses upon the extraordinary circumstance that Charging Thunder and Running Wolf were both convicted upon the same day. Can this really be a simple coincidence? Or was the ostensibly psychotic Mr Jefferson's 'raid' upon the oyster shop – the reason for which has never been explained – nothing more than an elaborate publicity stunt, in which the shop assistant might well have been a willing and properly remunerated accomplice? It may be conjectured that Mexican Joe had been enraged to learn of the arrest and imprisonment of Charging Thunder and was determined not to let the Glasgow public draw the inference that Buffalo Bill's Indians were more savage than his. Whatever the form and level of pressure that was applied, 'Running Wolf' was the unfortunate patsy to whom it fell to take the rap.

Running Wolf hit the headlines for a second time before the month was out, when his wife presented him with a baby daughter, born at the New Olympia at 8.30 on the morning of the 27th of January 1892. The *Glasgow Evening News* reported that the New Olympians were all looking forward with keen anticipation to the christening of the little 'Scoto-Indian', whose birth certificate recorded the imposing-sounding appellation of 'Hasonega Olympia Jefferson'.[12] Mrs Jefferson's name was reported as 'Neosreleata', with variations but, on the birth certificate, it appeared simply as 'Nana'. (This is assuredly the same lady whose Christian name had been entered as 'Minnie' in the 1891 census record at Jarrow as she was entered as twenty-four at that time and twenty-seven in 1894.) Her maiden surname was given as 'Shaunga'. Mr Jefferson acted as the informant, signing the certificate with his X mark, and was designated a 'travelling showman'. The child's parents had been married in October 1885, in Dakota.

Anticipating the story of Alexandra Standing Bear, born at Buffalo Bill's camp in Birmingham eleven years later, the child was promptly placed on public display and the standard advertisement appearing in the *Glasgow Evening News* was modified on the 1st of February 1892 to include the line:

> The LITTLE INDIAN PAPOOSE born last Wednesday, January 27th, will be on EXHIBITION

A line drawing appearing in the *Quiz* 'Supplement' reveals that the tightrope walker 'Miss Nana, the Female Blondin' had been introduced into the show, along with a pillory, a merry-go-round and shooting galleries.[13] With all these guns going off all over the place, someone was bound to get hurt and, on the evening of the 22nd of January 1892, a young man named Thomas Anderson, a warehouse porter resident at 49, Holmhead Street, got himself filled full of lead.

Anderson was standing at the side of a shooting range, when a stray shot penetrated the canvas screening off the sides of the booth. The bystanders grew agitated as he fell to the ground, crying out in anguished tones that he had been shot. Dr Bruce was summoned to the scene of the accident and found that the bullet had passed clean through the victim's arm. It was a very narrow escape from more serious consequences and Anderson was permitted to go home after his wound had been dressed. The police were reported to be investigating the incident.

Shortly before Mexican Joe's show closed on Saturday the 27th of February 1892, two admirers presented a silver-mounted meerschaum pipe and cigarette holder to one of his performers, Rocky Mountain Jack.

By March, the New Olympia boasted a fresh attraction, 'The Gathering of the Clans'. This was advertised in *Quiz* as being accompanied by 'realistic scenery and effects, in which over 100 Glasgow Girls will take part. The GREATEST MILITARY FESTIVAL ever seen in Glasgow.'[14] Mexican Joe was the directing mind behind this latest spectacle.

For Sheriff Birnie, who had also heard the case against Charging Thunder, the Wild West experience was very far from over. Mexican Joe himself was summoned before Glasgow's own redoubtable lawman, at the instance of the Glasgow School Board, on the 15th of March. The case was called in the County Buildings, the charge being that Colonel Shelley had employed four children under the age of fourteen years after seven o'clock at night, in connection with this latest extravaganza. Colonel Shelley was, by now, in England and his manager appeared on his behalf. The case was adjourned for Mexican Joe's personal attendance. How it was eventually disposed of does not unfortunately appear to be recorded. But Mexican Joe was no' awa' tae bide awa' and an interview with George Smith, the 'Gypsy King' who travelled with the show, published by the *Glasgow Weekly News* on the 21st of May 1892, revealed that Mexican Joe was now encamped somewhere along the Great Western Road.

Mexican Joe is next heard of in connection with Glasgow in July 1894, when the New York press carried reports of five Winnebago Indians – two men, two women and a small boy – who, in the company of a Texan named Frank Warner, had landed at Ellis Island as exiles from his show. After a series of vicissitudes, they had successfully applied to the American Consul-General to New York at London to ship them there and were patiently waiting for the government to accept responsibility for their passage back to Wisconsin.

The *New York Recorder* narrated that:

The former went abroad for exhibition purposes with Mexican Joe, otherwise Col. Joe Shelby (*sic*), and were showing at Glasgow, when joined by Warner, who migrated thither on account of the hard times in his native land. For a time business with Mexican Joe was pretty good and salaries were paid with tolerable regularity. But after awhile the Scotchmen tired of the Wild West exhibition, and when their patronage fell off nothing was forthcoming from the management except meals.[15]

It is a singular disappointment to have to relate that there is nothing in the Glasgow papers of the time to corroborate that these financial embarrassments occurred there.

There is, however, a twist in the tale. In the unpublished autobiographical manuscript *Life Story of Montana Bill*, the subject narrated his travels with Mexican Joe from 1892 'until his failure at

Barnsley in March 1894'. Robert 'Montana Bill' Robeson is known to have operated in Scotland as a music hall turn and small-time Wild West show proprietor, at least during 1912–15. During this period, his publicity materials made much of his alleged connection with Buffalo Bill. The statement in the *Perthshire Advertiser* on the 9th of June 1915 that he had been 'the noted Buffalo Bill's right hand man in many wild adventures' is entirely typical.

Montana Bill claimed to be the son of a French-Canadian land surveyor and a Lakota woman, the daughter of Chief Rain in the Face. He further asserted that, from 1886 until 1892, he toured with Buffalo Bill in the capacity of a trick-shooting act and Indian interpreter. On Buffalo Bill's return to the United States in 1892, he was engaged by Mexican Joe. These details regarding his alleged past employment were conspicuously exhibited on his headed notepaper.

This account of his personal career, both on the frontier and as a travelling member of Buffalo Bill's show, can safely be dismissed as a tissue of transparent fabrications. However, the mention of Barnsley, upon which nothing of immediate consequence hangs, rings true even though no mention of Mexican Joe's presence there at this time can be found in any of the local papers. The correspondence with the timescale emerging from the reports of the plight of the Winnebago exiles seems too close to be coincidence. Although there is no mention of him in the record of the show's personnel in the 1891 census,[16] he appears to be included in a rare group photograph of Mexican Joe's entourage handed down by Robeson to his son, along with other mementos of his career. This one aspect of his extraordinary life story must therefore be accepted as credible.

One difficulty of course is that there is no mention in the show's publicity materials at Glasgow of a Winnebago presence but it would come as no surprise to discover that members of this long-subjugated and relatively obscure tribe were being misrepresented as belonging to the more notorious and therefore more commercially attractive Apache and Sioux nations.

The passenger list pertaining to the party has been preserved at Ellis Island and its contents are certainly illuminating. They arrived at New York from Southampton, on board the *New York*, on the 7th of July 1894.

Frank Warner, whose age was recorded somewhat precisely as being forty-seven years and four months, had his 'occupation or calling' entered as 'Indian'. The names of two of the Indians were entered as White Spot, aged thirty-five, and Minnie Ponka, thirty, his wife. These are almost certainly the same people as were entered in the 1891 census as John and Minnie White. The name of Frank Warner will also be recalled from the same source although, in that context, his native state was entered as Nebraska, not Texas.

The others were none other than our old friends Charles Jefferson, aged thirty-seven, and his wife Nana, aged twenty-seven, together with an infant son, also Charles, whose age was entered as ten months. Ominously, there is no sign of Hasonega, the little girl born at Glasgow, and concern naturally arises that she must have died in the intervening two and a half years.

The available evidence encourages the further suspicion that the individuals identified here made up the entirety of Mexican Joe's Indian contingent. Their 'intended destination' was entered as 'Black River Falls, near Chicago'.

At the time of Hasonega's birth, the *Glasgow Evening News* had referred to the proud father as 'a notorious Apache warrior from New Mexico'[17] and this billing no doubt owed much to the notoriety acquired in consequence of his then recent transgressions on the New City Road.

This new evidence places an entirely different gloss upon his character. It has to be questioned whether the reluctant savage, Charles Jefferson, could even have pointed to New Mexico on a map and, as regards his tribal affiliations, it is highly unlikely that his status as an Apache was other than fictitious.

Just as Kicking Bear was Buffalo Bill's stage villain of choice, 'Running Wolf' was Mexican Joe's. 'Running Wolf' was probably nothing more than a stage name and, as is so frequently the case with modern-day soap-opera protagonists, there was little to connect the alter ego with the real man.

Whatever bright hopes the original architects might have cherished for its long-term prospects as a Glaswegian Mecca of entertainment, the New Olympia was destined scarcely to out-distance Mexican Joe. It survived until 1902, at which time refurbishments were effected by James Miller, the architect of the previous year's International Exhibition. The building, which lay directly adjacent to the Old Normal School, next accommodated the 'Scottish Zoo', founded by E. H. Bostock, of Bostock and Wombwell's travelling menagerie fame. Even this grand attraction did not last. It closed in 1909 and was converted into a roller-skating rink. E. H. Bostock's brother Frank subsequently ran it for a time as the Bostock Arena and Jungle, in which he staged spectacles depicting such momentous events as the Relief of Mafeking and the Galveston Flood of 1900. The latter resulted from a hurricane and was a natural catastrophe on a very substantial scale, which was somehow largely forgotten until highlighted again by a very similar disaster afflicting New Orleans in 2005.

Several decades down the line, the site housed a carpet showroom, a snooker club and an Asian food hall and restaurant. A continuing measure of exoticism carries little more than a faint aroma of the site's extraordinary past.

Notes

1. 30 December 1891
2. *The Scotsman*, 29 May 1889
3. 15 August 1891
4. *Glasgow Evening News*, 30 January 1892
5. 20 November 1891
6. *Glasgow Herald*, 17 November 1891
7. *Glasgow Evening News*, 30 January 1892
8. *Evening Times*, 30 December 1891
9. *Glasgow Evening News*, 1 February 1892
10. Both 12 January 1892
11. p. 141

12 27 January 1892
13 19 February 1892
14 11 March 1892. The *Glasgow Evening News* of 1 January 1892 cited an unspecified Belfast paper as announcing that fifty Belfast girls would take part.
15 11 July 1894
16 In fairness, he did not claim to be with Mexican Joe at that time.
17 27 January 1892

11

NEW DEPARTURES

THE PERFORMING ELEPHANTS

By the end of 1891, Buffalo Bill had had his fill of Glasgow and its 'nasty winter weather'.[1] In a letter to his sister, headed 'Glasgow December 26th 1891', Cody wrote:

> Am sorry to say that I am off again. I have got the Hay fever or Grippe or something, & being so worn out and so much to do & to think of its hard. I am now trying for new attractions to put in this place to fill my vacancy when I have to leave here for my trip home. I want to leave my company playing here while I am gone. And must strengthen them with other attractions . . . I am so anxious to get in a country where I can feel & see the Sun again.[2]

Since it is unlikely that he could have contracted hay fever in Glasgow in midwinter, it is reasonably safe to conclude that Cody had succumbed to the influenza epidemic sweeping the city at that time. Certainly, Glasgow's damp and foggy climate did not agree with him and any Scot who has personally experienced the open skies and dry icy cold of winters on the Great Plains will readily appreciate this aversion.

The influenza epidemic was not confined to Glasgow alone but held Great Britain in its grip throughout January and well into February. Almost every day, the newspapers carried grim inventories of the names of prominent people carried off by the malady. The most famous was Prince Albert Victor Christian Edward, Duke of Clarence and Avondale, grandson of Queen Victoria and eldest son of the Prince of Wales, the future King Edward VII.

The young Duke, recently engaged to be married, died on the 14th of January, aged just twenty-eight. On Wednesday the 20th of January, the Wild West, in common with Hengler's Circus, permanently located in Wellington Street, and the Theatre Royal, cancelled its matinee performance as a mark of respect. No doubt Buffalo Bill was acutely sensible of the loss, being, as he was, a personal friend of the Prince of Wales. The Duke, who, had he survived, would have succeeded to the Crown instead of George V, is recalled as a somewhat dissolute character and, in recent decades, has found himself at the epicentre of highly sensational conspiracy theories implicating him in the 'Whitechapel murders' of autumn 1888, attributed to the notorious but still unidentified 'Jack the Ripper'. No doubt, had these killings taken place precisely one year earlier, during the Wild West's 1887 London season, Buffalo Bill's 'savage' Indians would have topped the lists of the many prime suspects at whom the finger of suspicion has pointed over the years.

Cody quietly left Glasgow during the final week in January and sailed from Liverpool on board the *Umbria*, arriving at New York on the 8th of February. The *Glasgow Evening News* of the 22nd of January 1892 proclaimed that he was preparing to leave Glasgow and announced, on the 28th, that he actually had. It was apparently intended that he would return before the season ended as both references mentioned a 'short trip to America' and the latter specifically stated that he would be 'back at Bellgrove in three or four weeks'.

This hope did not materialise. Given the time scales involved in transatlantic travel in 1892, it is difficult to see how Cody could have achieved such a feat, even if he had set out on the return journey immediately on his arrival home. In this light, Professor Moses' explicit statement[3] that Cody was a member of the party which sailed from

Glasgow on the 4th of March has to be discounted, particularly since there is no sign of Cody's name on the relevant passenger list.

Buffalo Bill wasn't the only one bowing out. In a letter from Glasgow dated the 11th of January 1892, addressed to the Acting Indian Agent at Pine Ridge, George C. Crager referred to Wooden Face as having recently returned to the United States.

A party of six Indians – five men and a woman – arrived at New York on the 3rd of February, having sailed from Glasgow on board the *Ancoria*. These were Close To Home, Comes Out Holy, Ice, Mrs Ice, Stands Up and White Cloud.

George C. Crager's wife, Julia, and their three children – Minna, aged seven, Cuno, aged five, and Winifred, aged three months, were not far behind, sailing from Glasgow on the *State of California* and arriving at New York on the 11th of February. Accompanying them were No Neck, a sixteen year-old boy named Two Bonnets and Johnny Burke No Neck.

Of these ten returning Indians, only Close to Home was a hostage.

'A New Era in History'

One of the guiding principles of frontier life was that nothing is certain but the inevitability of change. This truism applied to the Wild West show as much as to anything else.

The first part of the 1891–92 season represented the high-water mark of Cody's enterprise as 'Wild West' pure and simple. The acquisition as touring members of the last Indians ever to be taken by the United States army as prisoners of war was a definite shot in the arm but the entertainment, in the form in which it had originally been devised, could not be sustained indefinitely. Aside from the obvious anxiety over the precariousness of the continuing supply of Indians, the show was dependent upon enduring public favour for its long-term viability. The novelty presented by Indians, cowboys and Mexicans alone was in danger of growing stale. While the course that the process of change would eventually follow had yet to be established, the introduction of the 'new attractions' contemplated in Cody's letter to his sister would emerge as a pivotal event in the show's development.

Various contingency plans had been in place for the past year at least, ever since the alarm had been raised over questions concerning the treatment of the Indians in the show and the authorities had come within an ace of putting a stop to the whole business. The *New York Herald* had run an interview with Colonel Cody, following his return from the tour of continental Europe and reported his intention to 'explore Mexico, Peru, and other South American countries in search of cliff dwellers, Aztecs, Dodos, or any inanimate curiosity that will add strength to the big show he expects to manage in Chicago during the World's Fair'.[4]

In an influential paragraph Don Russell tells us:

> As organised in 1891, Buffalo Bill's Wild West had 640 'eating members'. There were 20 German soldiers, 20 English soldiers, 20 United States soldiers, 12 Cossacks, and 6 Argentine Gauchos, which with the old reliables, 20 Mexican *vaqueros*, 25 cowboys, 6 cowgirls, 100 Sioux Indians, and the Cowboy Band of 37 mounted musicians, made a colourful and imposing Congress of Rough Riders.[5]

Russell is a respected authority on Buffalo Bill and his writings have been accorded the status of canonical texts. An entire library of books has accrued over the years, based not so much upon original research but directly derivative of Russell. The paragraph cited above is fundamentally erroneous in respect of its timescale, since the new elements referred to would be incorporated into the show in stages, during 1892 and 1893. It is to be regretted that Russell's pronouncements have been uncritically rehashed on numerous occasions, so much so that, among American scholars, a solid consensus has formed in his favour. The clear truth of the matter, which is quickly established by the simple expedient of referring to the official programme and to the numerous accounts appearing in contemporary newspapers, is that the process of transition which he describes was not even begun until January 1892, when the need to camouflage the leading actor's

'YOUR FATHERS THE GHOSTS'

departure from Glasgow made the potential embarrassment an immediate one.

The first hint of what was to follow had come in Manchester on the 31st of July 1891, at the time of the benefit performance for the surviving local Balaclava veterans.[6] But now the movement assumed more definite form.

Lew Parker was despatched to France and in Boulogne he engaged Sam Lockhart's performing Burmese elephants. Hearing mention that a party of Africans had arrived in Hamburg with the explorer Henry Morton Stanley, he hastened there and reached an accord with Stanley's agent.[7] On the next day, the 14th of January 1892, Parker was back in Glasgow with his new recruits.

Years later, the 1910 official programme would recall: 'One hundred Zulus from South Africa were added to give a contrast to the Indian war dances by similar sports and pastimes by these African warriors. The first time that genuine Zulus were brought to England.'[8]

This statement is inaccurate. These African men, women and children were not Zulus at all but Shulis (note the spelling variation 'Schulis') from the shores of Lake Albert Nyanza, at the northernmost extremity of Uganda.[9]

And once again, with characteristic hyperbole that probably owed a great deal to Major Burke, the numbers were subjected to much retrospective exaggeration. Only 'THIRTY SHULIS AFRICAN SAVAGES, AMAZONS, and WARRIORS' had been promised as being among the 'STUPENDOUS ADDITIONAL ATTRACTIONS' widely advertised from mid January onwards.[10] There appears to have been an equal division of males and females.

The *Evening Times* stated that they had been 'among the fiercest opponents of the progress of Mr H. M. Stanley and Emin Pasha'.[11] The *Evening Citizen*, in an otherwise illuminating article of the same date, made a similar pronouncement. However, an article in *The Graphic* refers to the 'mild and docile Shulis' and identifies their homeland as falling within the settled part of the region.[12] Since savage tribesmen are more interesting than peaceful ones, a further manipulation of the facts is strongly suspected.

On the afternoon of Friday the 15th of January 1892, precisely one year to the day after Kicking Bear's final surrender to General Miles, these acquisitions were unveiled before a select gathering of invited guests. Among them were 'pressmen and professors, authors, actors and artists, clergymen and Glasgow magistrates. Surely as strange a combination as was ever dreamt of'.[13]

At some point during the proceedings, a photograph is claimed to have been taken. Lew Parker narrates:

> We placed the entire company, cowboys, Mexicans, soldiers, Indians, elephants, buffalo, elk, horses and the Africans, on an incline, the elephants at the top of the pyramid, and took a flashlight picture. After that we placed the American Indians across the arena, facing the stage, and placed the Africans in front of the stage, facing the Indians.[14]

It would of course be extremely interesting to know what became of the image to which Parker refers.

The Cowboy Band played a selection of popular tunes as the guests were arriving. Colonel Cody entered to loud applause and spoke a few words of introduction. He outlined the spectacle that the audience was about to witness – the first-ever meeting of representatives of North American and African tribes – insofar as he was able for he professed to know no better than anyone else what their reactions would be when they met. Thanking his guests for accepting his invitation, Buffalo Bill withdrew.

The Africans were the first to be introduced into the arena. They wore their native garb of short skirts for the women while the men went virtually naked and sported silver rings in their noses. The *North British Daily Mail* offered the following commentary upon their racial characteristics:

> They are dark skinned, but not full-blooded Africans with thick lips and flat noses. They have rather pleasant faces, and the women especially have a modest air. One of them is remarkably beautiful,

'YOUR FATHERS THE GHOSTS'

her cast of features being Grecian, and the wonder is how she had come to be in such company.[15]

The Lakota followed their African counterparts into the arena. Parker recalls how he called upon the Indian interpreter 'Broncho Bill' to bring out '"Rocky Bear", a celebrated Cheyenne Chief'[16] and induce him to attempt communication with the African chief by means of sign language. To the astonishment of all present, the African understood him perfectly, and within minutes the two groups were fraternising and getting along together splendidly.

The credibility of Parker's account is somewhat undermined by an apparent element of confusion over the identities of the principals in this little drama. 'Broncho Bill' Irving and Rocky Bear had both been members of the touring party on the European 1890–91 season but it can be stated with certainty that neither was present in Glasgow. Moreover, Rocky Bear was a Lakota, not a Cheyenne.

Nonetheless, the essential part of the story – that the two races succeeded in communicating by means of sign language – is substantially confirmed by the accounts given in the *North British Daily Mail* of the 16th of January 1892 and in the *Scottish Leader* of the same date.

The dances of the Indians were contrasted with those of the Africans, the latter kicking their legs high into the air. Three of the Lakota chiefs – No Neck, Short Bull and Kicking Bear – next came forward for a parley with their African counterparts, each group accompanied by their respective interpreters.

No Neck made an elaborate profession of friendship towards the Africans and offered to shake hands with them. The chief of the Africans returned this expression of goodwill and presented a dagger to No Neck, who reciprocated with a calumet of peace.

Short Bull opined that it was a great day in the history of the world and hoped that it would be celebrated by the white people. This opinion was endorsed by the assembled company with generous applause.

Kicking Bear, however, characteristically refused to confine himself to bland pleasantries. He observed that contact with white civilisation had resulted in a dramatic reduction of the Indians' land base and admonished the Africans to avoid a similar fate by making better treaties and seeing that they were kept. In his reply, the African chief diplomatically avoided this potentially contentious issue. The text of Kicking Bear's speech, transcribed in both Lakota and English, was reproduced in the *Evening Times*.[17]

All three Indians, however, stressed that Colonel Cody was their friend and that the Africans would prosper by adhering to his rules. Reciprocated assurances of friendship concluded the conference and both parties next retreated to their respective positions on opposing sides of the arena.

Mr Lockhart introduced his herd of six highly trained Burmese elephants and their clever performance greatly delighted not only the audience but the Indians and Africans as well.

Fifteen months would pass before the settled *Rough Riders of the World* format (on the lines described by Russell above) was unveiled in Chicago but already a clear comparative perspective had emerged. The elephants were contrasted to the buffalo, as were the Africans in relation to the Indians.

At the end of the reception, the audience largely took advantage of the opportunity to enter the arena and inspect the human and animal performers at closer hand.

The curtain was thus raised upon the next phase of the entertainment, which went under the title of *A New Era in History*[18] and was first placed before the general public at the evening performance on Monday the 18th of January, continuing for the remainder of the Glasgow sojourn. If an official programme was ever published, no copy is known to have survived and therefore no more detailed account can be given. It appears, however, that, during the concluding weeks, the meeting of the two Indian tribes, which had previously formed the centrepiece of Episode 1 of *The Drama of Civilization*, was supplanted by a reiteration of the dramatic encounter of the Africans and Lakota. In a further sequence, the Africans simulated the execution of a miscreant.

Cowboys now rode wild Texan steers and a detachment of English Lancers gave a display of sabre drill. The latter group had most probably been enlisted in consequence of contacts established during the previous summer's visit to Manchester.

Eastern Bells for February 1892 lamented that the involvement of the Indians was now much curtailed. Quite certainly, this was not a result of the Indians having fallen out of favour, either with the management or the public but an accommodation necessitated by practical considerations. The Indians were substantially diminished in number as the exodus back to the United States was already underway.

THE ELEPHANTS

The addition of these extraneous elements is, from several points of view, to be regretted. The purity of the original 'Wild West' concept had been adulterated and, from this watershed onwards, there is a distinct tendency for Buffalo Bill's exhibition to degenerate into just another circus.

One singular piece of inanity gracing the programme during those final weeks was a variation on the ever-popular 'bucking-bronco' theme – the show now included a bucking elephant! One of Lockhart's animals – a baby elephant, whose proud, free spirit its masters had presumably not yet succeeded in breaking – held a singular and entirely understandable aversion to being ridden. A cash prize of three guineas – then equivalent to several weeks' wages – was offered to any member of the audience who could succeed in remaining mounted on its back for three minutes. By all accounts, the money was never in any real danger for, although there was no shortage of takers, three seconds was about as much as anyone ever managed.

The newspaper ad in the *Glasgow Evening News* promised: 'Lockhart's Six Burmese Elephants will perform this week their novel, original and laughable pantomime creation entitled "Judge and Jury".'[19]

It is almost anyone's guess exactly what indignities the unfortunate beasts were subjected to during their involuntary sojourn in Glasgow. In common with the Lakota and the Africans, they were now obliged to make their way as a public spectacle in someone else's world. The *North British Daily Mail* reported that, during the concluding week of the Glasgow season, the elephants were 'hailed with delight' and that the sensation was heightened when, in an item entitled 'A Lesson in Music', each of their number was allotted a musical instrument.[20] One particularly gifted beast, named Charlie, succeeded not only in playing the cornet but also in beating a drum with his tail. An illustration in the *Quiz* 'Supplement'[21] depicts the elephants – flanked by chieftains of the African and Indian races, as well as by cowboys lassoing a horse – variously playing a pedal drum, sitting down, standing on hind legs, riding on a cylinder, wearing spectacles and balancing at either end of a seesaw.

Anyone who doubts that it was all in fun might care to note that, while Glasgow was in the grips of a bout of Arctic weather, an elephant at Bostock and Wombwell's menagerie, then appearing on waste ground on the New City Road, in the vicinity of St George's Cross, died on the night of Thursday the 18th of February. The *Evening Times* gave the cause of death as 'the effects of the intense cold on a weakened constitution'.[22] Bostock's polar bear, meanwhile, was reputedly the only animal in Glasgow still enjoying itself.

Westwards the Wagons

Meanwhile, Dennistoun, the only residential suburb in the East End, was about to face the mass departure of many of its older residents. House prices had risen sharply, particularly in Whitehill Street, in the vicinity of the new Board School. Rents were being raised accordingly and, in consequence, all but two of the residents of Oakley Terrace were preparing to join the general migration westwards. The story was featured in the *The Bailie for Wednesday, February 17th, 1892* but, if the management of the Wild West was willing to lend out their covered wagons for the purpose, nothing was said about it.

St Mark's Masonic Lodge

Records deposited with Glasgow Archives in 2001 reveal that a total of fourteen Wild West employees were admitted to the Lodge St Mark at various dates between the 14th of December 1891 and the 5th of February 1892. These were:

> William Langan, 'supply agent'; Albert E. Sheible; Fred Bowman; Bennett B. Ninian, editor of the *Wild West Blizzard*, a paper published during the Glasgow season; Barney Link, 'advertising agent'; William Sweeney 'musician'; John A. Leonard, 'musician'; John A. Flynn, 'salesman'; Henry James, 'Lockhart's elephant tamer'; Jule Keen, 'actor'; William Okey Snyder; William Ferdinand Schensley, 'musician'; Edward Yoder Snyder, 'musician'; Thomas V. Murphy, 'musician'.

In the majority of cases, the address was entered as that of the Wild West show, at 327, Duke Street, but, in the cases of Messrs Link and James, it was given as 172, Bellfield Street.

It will be recalled that William Sweeney was the leader of the Cowboy Band and the other musicians listed are also known to have been members.

The Cowboys at Celtic Park

One of the company's final acts in Glasgow came on Thursday the 25th of February, when a Wild West XI select, renewing the company's earlier acquaintance with Celtic Park, ran out for a charity match against the Brandon Club.

The match was kicked off by Albert E. Sheible, the Wild West's business representative, and Rangers' 'Tuck' McIntyre officiated as referee. McIntyre was no bit player in this particular drama – indeed, that it happened at all seems to be down to his inspiration and persistence. Two weeks after Buffalo Bill's attendance at the Glasgow Cup tie against Queen's Park, he had sent a challenge to the Wild

Westerners. Fifteen years before, Buffalo Bill had been unhesitating in his acceptance of Yellow Hand's call to single combat but, on this occasion, he proved rather more reticent. Cody's reply was quoted in the *Evening Times*, 'Gossip and Grumbles' column:

Dear Sir,
In reply to your favour of the 21st inst. [i.e. November], I will say that none of my people ever saw a game of football played, and would make a sad go of it.

Otherwise, as it is for a charitable purpose, I would be delighted to engage in it.

Very truly,
W. F. Cody[23]

Two days before the game finally did take place, certain sections of Glasgow's football-going public were no doubt reassured by the pronouncement in the *Evening Times*' 'Gossip and Grumbles' column that the Indians were to leave their tomahawks at home.

Years later, back in the States during the 1908 season, one of the items added to the programme was 'Football on Horseback', in which teams of cowboys versus Indians knocked an outsize soccer ball around the arena. There were few rules but, in concept, it was clearly a mounted version of the favourite Glaswegian sport of fitba'. It seems not unreasonable to conclude that at least part of the inspiration for this routine can be traced to the terraces of Ibrox and Parkhead.

For anyone interested in the result, it is known only that the Westerners were beaten. When asked to account for this reverse, one of the cowboys remarked that they could only play on horseback – prophetic words indeed! No Neck was reported by the *Glasgow Evening News* as so amused by this comment that he laughed uproariously and came close to swallowing his cigarette.[24] It was, however, a clear case of mistaken identity for No Neck had, by this time, already returned to America.

Notes

1. Lew Parker, *Odd People I Have Met*, p. 84
2. Reproduced by Stella Foote in *Letters from "Buffalo Bill"*, p. 71
3. In *Wild West Shows and the Images of American Indians 1883–1933*, p. 121
4. 19 November 1890
5. *The Lives and Legends of Buffalo Bill*, pp. 370–1
6. See Chapter 2, *supra*
7. This, at any rate, is Parker's story but that Stanley was involved is seriously doubted.
8. Buffalo Bill Historical Center
9. The Zulu theory is of course endorsed by Russell at p. 373 of *The Lives and Legends of Buffalo Bill* and by Professor L. G. Moses at p. 119 of *Wild West Shows and the Images of American Indians 1883–1933*.
10. e.g. in *The Bailie for Wednesday, January 27th, 1892*
11. 16 January 1892
12. 'The Emin Pasha Relief Expedition' by Robert W. Felkin, 29 January 1887
13. *The Bailie for Wednesday, January 20th, 1892*
14. *Odd People I Have Met*, p. 85
15. 16 January 1892
16. *Odd People I Have Met*, p. 85
17. 16 January 1892
18. *The Scottish Leader*, 16 January 1892
19. 15 February 1892
20. 23 February 1892
21. 29 January 1892
22. 20 February 1892
23. 7 December 1891
24. 7 March 1892

12

PARTING SHOTS

```
THEATRE ROYAL,
   MOSS STREET, PAISLEY.
   TO-NIGHT! TO-NIGHT!!
        ONE NIGHT ONLY.
   GRAND MUSICAL FESTIVAL.
BUFFALO BILL'S WILD WEST COWBOY
           BAND.
   ASSISTED BY THE FAMOUS
   ALBERGER TROUPE
             OF
   TYROLEAN VOCALISTS,
           AND
   THE SIOUX INDIANS
             OF
   BUFFALO BILL'S WILD WEST.
   MONSTRE PROGRAMME.  60 ARTISTES.
Doors open at 6.45 p.m.   Concert begins at 7.45 p.m.
Prices—Gallery, 6d; Balcony, 9d; Pit, 1s. Chairs
(Reserved), 2s. For sale at Patterson's Music Warehouse,
Terrace Buildings.
```

Kicking Bear's Last Revolt

The highly successful run of fourteen weeks finally ended with the evening performance on Saturday, 27 February 1892. Since neither Buffalo Bill nor Major Burke was present, no formal valedictory address was given but Johnnie Baker came forward to take the farewell salute.

The Cowboy Band struck up 'Auld Lang Syne', as the large and enthusiastic audience accorded the company a standing ovation. The individual performers vied among themselves for public acclaim and each was accorded a special cheer in turn.

But there was an unscripted addition to the programme for, according to L. G. Moses, Kicking Bear launched into an improvised and lengthy harangue, described in a letter from Nate Salsbury to General Miles as 'filled with menace and bravado'.[1] Moses states that: 'Kicking Bear tarried as his companions filed out of the arena. He recounted in Lakota his deeds of valor.'[2]

Kicking Bear's actions naturally raised much alarm in the minds of the Wild West management, who recognised in them a well-established ritual through which a warrior proclaimed his personal merit, in preparation for the renewal of armed hostilities.

None of the Glasgow newspapers picked up on the incident but this omission is readily explained by experience. Whenever something went disastrously – even fatally – wrong in the arena, the audience invariably applauded with polite enthusiasm and supposed that it was all part of the act.

Doubts over whether it even happened at all are partially assuaged by the circumstance that Nate Salsbury's reference to it in his letter to General Miles is substantially corroborated by George C. Crager a short time later in an interview with an unidentified Chicago newspaper.[3] Crager, however, had not actually been present on the night in question, having already set sail for New York, and so his comments are hearsay.

There are details in Moses' account that do not appear to be warranted by his sources. Sam Maddra concurs that the incident took place at the final show but errs in giving the date as the 28th, not the 27th.[4] This mistake is no doubt prompted by Nate Salsbury's statement in his letter to General Miles, dated the 29th, that it had taken place 'only last night'. This is either a clumsy mistake on Salsbury's part or else is to be taken at face value and indicating the night *following* the final show. Notice that Salsbury does not explicitly place Kicking Bear's actions in the arena.

What is clear, however, is that a great deal of paranoia surrounded Kicking Bear. In the age of the Victorian melodrama, with all of the ethical stereotyping thus entailed, he was unambiguously cast as the villain of the piece.

This status was by no means limited to his stage persona, as reflected in a number of statements appearing in the contemporary press during the tour of England and Wales, in which several journalists had been quick to discern a truly sinister dimension to Kicking Bear's character. In connection with the visit to St Paul's Cathedral, London, on the 22nd of October 1891, one journalist was moved to record:

> A wide, thin lipped mouth wore a sneer oftener than not. His black eyes gleamed as they roved ceaselessly but slyly from face to face

and one object of interest to another. When he smiled, which was seldom, the crowd stepped on itself in its eagerness to give him room. The impression seemed to be general that Kicking Bear's nature had so much malignity in it that there was room for little else. I have no desire to do the gentleman an injury, but for raw ferocity of expression I never saw his equal.[5]

A further typical example was the assessment of the *Birmingham Daily Post*: 'Kicking Bear, the fighting chief of the ghost dancers, has a face in which, even when his features are at rest, one reads plainly the bitter resentment and potential cruelty of another Sitting Bull.'[6]

The *Birmingham and Aston Chronicle* was even more graphic in its vilification, denouncing him as 'a man with a cruel-looking face, such a man as one would expect to look on unconcernedly while a prisoner was being tortured to death'.[7]

The tone of such remarks is so consistent that the suspicion naturally arises that, far from being the spontaneous reactions of independent witnesses, they were prompted and even carefully choreographed by means of Major Burke's press releases.

However, one remark, bearing the hallmarks of an honest observation, is to be found in the (Portsmouth) *Evening News*.[8] In connection with a visit to the Indians' dining tent at meal time, it was commented that, 'only "Kicking Bear", the chief upon whom the mantle of authority worn by the late "Sitting Bull" has virtually descended, sat by himself in solitary state'.

A number of remarks in confidential letters from Colonel Cody and others engaged in the management of the Wild West disclose that they strongly disliked and distrusted Kicking Bear. In his interview with the Chicago journalist, George Crager recounted that Kicking Bear and Short Bull had often been found talking in hushed tones together, only to break off their conversation at the approach of a white person.

Certainly, it is not difficult to visualise Kicking Bear sitting silently apart or else locked in conference with his friend and confidant, Short Bull, brooding endlessly on the cataclysmic events of the past twelve months and upon what destiny might yet befall.

By way of stark contrast, Short Bull was held in high esteem and the picture which emerges of the late 'high priest' of the ghost dancers is that of a misguided but thoroughly reformed character. Official correspondence and newspaper reports in equal measure emphasised his agreeable disposition and habitual benevolent smile. The *Birmingham Daily Post* even went so far as to call him 'a nice old gentleman'.[9]

But, if Kicking Bear and Short Bull were so divergent in character, why were they such close – even inseparable – friends? It is difficult to avoid the conclusion that his intimate association with the universally demonised Kicking Bear evidences a negative and largely hidden aspect of Short Bull's personality.

By the close of the winter season, Kicking Bear and Short Bull had had enough and, although over a year of their term of exile had yet to run, they were equally resolved to return home, vainly supposing that they would be permitted to return immediately to their families at Pine Ridge. This simultaneous defiance of both the Wild West management and the federal authorities provided the focus for a body of twenty-two other malcontents, including Charging Thunder and the majority of those hostages still remaining.

Exeunt

After the Wild West show finally closed its gates to Glasgow's paying public, the company broke up in stages. The arrangements for leaving Glasgow were still far from settled and, in the meantime, the greater part of the company continued to occupy the Exhibition Buildings. Lockhart's elephants departed the scene more or less immediately. On Sunday the 28th of February, the East End weans were treated to one last free entertainment, as the great animals made their way down the road, each grasping the tail of the one in front with its trunk. So unaccustomed was the sight that even the normally passive tramcar horses were panicked into a stampede.

The party of twenty-four Indians, which included Kicking Bear and Short Bull, set sail from Glasgow's Mavisbank Quay, bound for

New York on board the Allan and State Line steamer *Corean*, on the afternoon of Friday the 4th of March. Inevitably, their final departure attracted a large concourse of spectators.

Annie Oakley left town on Thursday the 10th of March. She took a brief vacation in Shrewsbury, prior to fulfilling an engagement in Paris, with the possibility of shooting at the Dublin Masonic Festival prior to rejoining the Wild West show in London in early May.

Towards the end of her time in Glasgow, Annie had succumbed to the cycling fad current at that time and learned to ride a bicycle. As the *Glasgow Evening News*'s 'Clydeside Echoes' columnist reported on the 5th of March 1892: 'Annie Oakley, of Buffalo Bill's show, is the latest cycling victim. She has been receiving lessons from a veteran wheelman.' The same source recorded that she had ordered a bicycle from the Premier Cycle Company, based in Coventry.[10]

Ghost Dance in Greenock

An improvised concert party undertook a short theatrical tour of Renfrewshire and Lanarkshire, appearing at Greenock Town Hall (Monday the 29th of February), Coatbridge (Temperance Hall, 2nd of March), Hamilton (Victoria Hall, 3rd), Govan (Govan Hall, Robert Street, 4th) and closing in Paisley's Theatre Royal, Moss Street, on Saturday the 5th.

It may be taken that Tuesday the 1st of March was purposely left free, in order to accommodate the end-of-season staff concert and ball being held that evening at the Waterloo Rooms, on the corner of Waterloo and Wellington Streets. The event was organised by the supply agent, William Langan, and it was anticipated that a number of prominent Glasgow citizens would attend.

The Cowboy Band, led by Joseph H. Hart, took top billing on the concert tour and opened with a selection of American pieces. The Arlberger Singers, the same Tyrolean vocalists who had featured in the aftermath of the attack on the emigrant train, followed with a Swiss song. The Cowboy Band returned to the stage with a fantasia named *Beauties of Scotland*, incorporating such airs as 'Bonnie

Dundee', 'Scots Wha Hae' and 'Ye Banks and Braes'. More American airs were next discoursed and then a selection from the works of Gilbert and Sullivan. The Arlberger Singers returned with 'Echoes from the Swiss Mountains'.

The performance drew to an extraordinary climax, as a party of a dozen Indians, including two women, performed native songs and dances.[11] Among these was one billed as the ghost dance, the same as had precipitated tragedy only the previous winter.

But who exactly were these Indians? Were there even as many as a dozen Indians yet remaining in Glasgow? A hypothesis can now be advanced that these were the 'lost tribe' – also twelve in number – whom the previous September had been farmed out to Viola Clemmons's *White Lily* touring production.

Alan Gallop explicitly states that the *White Lily* failed to re-open after the 31st of December 1891.[12] However, an entry in *The Bailie for Wednesday, March 2nd, 1892*, on p. 5, provides an important clue to the contrary: 'There will be no performance at the Grand Theatre during the current week, the "White Lily" Company having failed to keep their engagement. The principal, Miss Viola Clemous (*sic*) has, I believe, gone to America.'

Perhaps it may be taken that *White Lily* had been intended to close in Glasgow after the first week in March and that these Indians could rejoin the main body there prior to the departure for London. With the *White Lily*'s collapse, these dozen Indians were unexpectedly made available for an alternative production.

It is no more than a hypothesis but a measure of support is to be found in a report appearing in the *Coatbridge Express* on the 24th of February 1892, which indicates that the concert party was thrown together at the last minute. On the previous day, the 23rd, the newspaper office had received a call from Mr Hart, who was attempting to organise a grand concert somewhere in the adjoining towns of Airdrie and Coatbridge. It was further stated that, at the time of going to press, the inclusion of the Indians on the programme was merely a possibility.

The End of the Trail

The *Corean* berthed in Brooklyn Harbor on the 18th of March and, as soon as the gangplank was lowered, a sergeant and three troopers of the First Artillery detailed from Fort Columbus boarded the ship and placed the hostiles under arrest. This military presence had been arranged by George C. Crager, and the Wild West bore the costs. With a rare touch of irony, the captives were marched to an *immigrant* boarding house at 25, Greenwich Street, while the other Indians meekly tagged on behind. The entire company assembled in the barroom and sat around drinking lager and smoking cigarettes until midnight, when they were taken to the Central Railroad of New Jersey Ferry and placed on a train bound for Chicago.

On arrival at Chicago's North-western depot, the party was again divided into two. Eleven of them – Kicking Bear, Short Bull, Lone Bull, One Star, Revenge, Brings the White, High Eagle, Standing Bear, Knows His Voice, Brave and Wounded with Many Arrows were turned over to a military escort from Fort Sheridan and returned to their former place of confinement. The remaining thirteen – Both Sides White, White Horse, Bear Lies Down, Charging Thunder, Has No Horses, Holy Bird, Kills Crow, Pulls Him Out, Short Man, Shooting Star and three women – Medicine Horse, Her Blanket and Plenty Blankets – left for Pine Ridge that same evening, under the care of George C. Crager. Although Medicine Horse held hostage status, her continued confinement was apparently deemed unnecessary.

The imprisonment of these eleven at Fort Sheridan continued, lest their immediate return to Pine Ridge might precipitate a renewal of the earlier disturbances. By May, the perceived threat had subsided sufficiently to permit all but Kicking Bear, Short Bull, and Brings the White to return home. Brings the White followed in the middle of July but the final two remaining were not released until October.

For Kicking Bear and Short Bull, the apostles of the ghost dance, the Wild West trail was finally at an end.

On the Frontier Reprise

One might be forgiven for assuming that, by the spring of 1892, the Glasgow public would have had their fill of cowboys and Indians but the weight of available evidence strongly suggests otherwise.

For *On the Frontier* made a triumphant return to the Royal Princess's Theatre for a further week, from Monday the 28th of March until Saturday the 2nd of April, even while some remnants of Cody's entourage were still to be found in Glasgow. It played once more to packed houses which received the performance with obvious and noisy enthusiasm.

A front-page advert in the *Evening Times* ran throughout the week and boasted as its centrepiece a 'BAND of 20 REAL INDIANS' whereas, on the previous occasion, the number had not been specified.

Once again, a confusion of diverse incongruous themes was compressed into a single lurid frontier drama, interspersed with far more than a hint of vaudeville. A fair insight into the precise nature of the proceedings is provided by the highly favourable review appearing in the 'Entertainments' section of the *Evening Times* for the 29th of March 1892:

> *On the Frontier* – This drama, which is paying a return visit to the Royal Princess's, will prove very agreeable to playgoers with a craving for sensationalism. The plot may not be discerned without a great deal of mental effort, but the action of the play is of the liveliest kind. It is essentially a realistic drama. Horses, guns, pistols, bowie-knives, and a band of genuine Indians are among its features, and the facilities thus afforded for exciting situations are taken full advantage of.

Mr Hardie and Miss Leer appeared once more as hero and heroine respectively but, this time around, George Young took the role of the villain, Bill Morley. Of Maud Western – surely a stage name – as 'Deadwood Kate', it was said that she 'displays decided talent, and may not improbably become a shining light of burlesque. Her spirited rendering of that lyrical masterpiece "Ta-ra-ra-boom-de-ay," was one of the successes of the evening.'

The *Evening Citizen* for the same date applauded Miss Western as a 'sprightly and promising young lady'. It also transpires that the song, performed by her with such gusto, was at that time a hit 'presently on every other person's lips'. Her rendition was heartily encored' and came in the course of the somewhat surreal departure which made up the second act, when the audience was treated to a variety entertainment, consisting of 'dancing, singing, and fun'. The *Citizen* reported that 'there is no lack of enjoyment'. No doubt this gay abandon made some kind of sense to those actually present and most probably the episode performed much the same function as the inclusion of the 'horseback quadrille' and the Tyrolean vocalists in Buffalo Bill's show. To the Indian participants, it can only have seemed like the latest phases of a surreal nightmare.

There is ample reason to conclude that the ghost dance was a far more familiar concept to the people of the West of Scotland at this time than one might initially suppose. Only one month before, a similar performance had formed the exotic centrepiece of a musical company from the Wild West show. And now, once again, Sioux Indians nightly danced back their dead on a stage in the Gorbals although it might seriously be doubted that in either form an authentic reproduction of the ritual was involved.

One strange twist to the story is that the very same edition of the *Evening Times* that graphically reviewed the stage play reported a fresh outbreak of ghost dancing, this time among the Pawnees of Oklahoma.

Greater detail was provided on the same date by the *Evening Citizen*, which reported on a telegram which had been despatched from the city of Guthrie to Kansas City and thence relayed to the world. The Pawnees in the course of the past week had got up a ghost dance and, having worked themselves into a frenzy, appeared to be on the verge of going on the warpath. Three other tribes had been urged to join the militants in their proposed insurrection. The settlers who, in increasing numbers, were setting up homesteads in what was still officially designated as 'Indian Territory' were alarmed at the spectre of a frontier in flames once again. The principal action in this brief and apparently bloodless agitation came when two United States deputy marshals took into custody two Indians deemed to be the ringleaders – the Pawnee counterparts, no doubt, of Kicking Bear and Short Bull – only to be pursued all the way to Guthrie by a dozen warriors.

This threatened uprising among the Pawnees, a hitherto docile tribe who had actively assisted the army against their common enemy, the Lakota, was, on this occasion, contained through the intercession of two troops of US Cavalry which at once proceeded to the reservation and the Pawnees were spared their own Wounded Knee. This real-life drama proved to be no more that a brief curtain call, an echo of the painful and bloody process of conquest spanning four full centuries.

In that spring of 1892, the Indians were dancing still, convulsed and agonised in the death throes of their aboriginal cultures. From Glasgow's Gorbals to the Indian Territory in Oklahoma, the story was the same but for a single difference. In America, it was all in deadly earnest, as the desperation, misery and tedium inherent in the dark realities of the new life took their hold on the reservations.

Whatever agonies and aspirations were bound up in the dance of the ghosts on what little remained of the open Western Plains, in Glasgow it was no more than just another passing entertainment presented for the delectation of the patrons of the city's music halls.

Last Encounters

With the end of the season, Buffalo Bill's Indians had more time on their hands and sightings in various parts of the city inevitably increased.

On the 2nd of March 1892, the *Evening Times*' 'Gossip and Grumbles' column reported that two Indians had ventured as far afield as Argyle Street earlier that day. The two incidents may or may not be connected but that same evening an Indian, clearly the worse for drink, wandered into the Mitchell Library, which in those days was located in Miller Street. His presence was deemed a distraction and he was prevailed upon to leave. The Indian, greatly to his credit, took it all in good part and, after he had doffed his huge hat to the readers and assistants and insisted upon shaking hands with the officials, he duly obliged by stepping quietly out on to the street, where he was hailed by a spontaneous concourse of admirers.

A somewhat less positive encounter took place a week or so later – the only known instance of 'hostilities' against the local people – as related in a letter published by the *Glasgow Evening News*'s 'The Voice of the People' column on the 12th of March 1892:

Buffalo Bill's Indians
Sir – while wending my way homewards along Duke St. last night, I overtook two Indians of Buffalo Bill's troupe. They had evidently been imbibing rather freely, as one was leading the other. They came in contact with a passer-by, who returned the slight push he received. The Indian was enraged doubtless, and I unfortunately suffered for the behaviour of the white man. I was dealt a stinging blow, as revenge, I presume, for the supposed insult to the Indian. I would warn people to be careful in passing the Indians. I looked for 'Robert,' but he was, as is his wont, far, far away! I am &c., R. L. McG

Following the departure of Kicking Bear and party on the 4th of March, of course, the Indian contingent was much depleted and the *Evening Times*' redoubtable 'Gossip and Grumbles' column of the 12th of April reported the last identified sighting:

One of the few Indians who still adorn the late Wild West Show in Dennistoun has become quite a swell. He patrols Duke Street with his blanket open to show that he has one of the fashionable ladies' silk neckties, with monster bows, round his neck.

'YOUR FATHERS THE GHOSTS'

A few days later, on the 15th of April 1892, the last vestiges of Buffalo Bill's Wild West finally departed Glasgow to commence a new summer season in London.

Notes

1 Dated 29 February 1892, 27617 PRD 1892, Box 56, RG 94, NARA.
2 *Wild West Shows and the Images of American Indians 1883–1933*, p. 119
3 Colorado State Historical Society, MSS 126, p. 73, no date given
4 *Hostiles?*, p. 176
5 *The Herald*, London edition, 25 October 1891
6 8 September 1891
7 12 September 1891
8 10 October 1891
9 11 September 1891
10 28 March 1892
11 The *Greenock Telegraph* of the 1st March 1892 refers to 'ten males and two females, under their chief'. It is slightly ambiguous whether the chief is to be taken as included in the 'ten males' or as additional to them.
12 *Buffalo Bill's British Wild West*, p. 183

13

THE INTERVENING YEARS

Cossacks

A Congress of Rough Riders of the World

Returning to Earl's Court, London, Buffalo Bill's 1892 season ran from the 7th of May. The fundamental changes already indicated in Glasgow now assumed more definite form. Cody's theatrical agents were casting their nets far and wide and, just a few weeks into the run, a party of ten Russian 'Cossacks', led by 'Prince Ivan Makharadze', was added to the company. A contingent of gauchos from the Argentine arrived the next month. The British Lancers from the last weeks in Glasgow were retained.

Queen Victoria was particularly taken with the 'Cossacks' during a second royal command performance, staged at Windsor Castle on the 25th of June. But just how authentic were they? Newspaper coverage of the Wild West was often dogged by controversy and here was a clear case in point.

The *Army and Navy Gazette*[1] contained an article by Alex Kinloch, who had spent part of his life among the Cossacks. He concluded by relating that, in response to his suspicious questioning, Colonel Cody's riders had confessed that they were not Cossacks at all but members of a tribe from the Caucasus and that, contrary to their billing, they were not and never had been in any form of military service. This revelation was confirmed by the *Saturday Review*,[2] which categorically identified them as Georgians. These revelations made not the slightest dent in their popularity with the general public, for whom the precise ethnic origin of these strange riders remained a secondary consideration.

At the conclusion of two special performances given during mid September, the band of the Scots Guards was on hand to escort the audience to the gardens of the adjacent International Horticultural Exhibition.

On the evening of Saturday the 1st of October, Colonel Cody was honoured by members of the London Working Men's Association, who presented him with an illuminated address. Among the large number of delegates who attended, several had travelled from Glasgow.

The final performance took place on the 12th of October, and the company set sail on board the SS *Mohawk* on the 15th, berthing at New York on the 29th.

The 1893 season in Chicago is remembered as the high-water mark of Buffalo Bill's career as a showman. Although not officially part of the World's Fair, the show pitched on an adjacent lot for a period of almost six months. The premise was simple. Just as the Wild West had created a sensation in the Old World, Buffalo Bill now reversed the process and brought something of the Old World to the New. It was an enormous gamble as the show had not appeared in the United States since 1887. The formula, however, proved to be a staggering and hugely profitable success.

The popular Wild West elements, which had sustained the show through its first ten years, were retained but were now subsumed within a far broader concept – an equestrian spectacular of truly global dimensions. The major continents were represented – not only North America but also South and Central America, Africa, Asia and Europe.

As well as the Indians, cowboys, Mexicans, 'Cossacks' and gauchos, this new version of the spectacle included Arabian and Syrian horsemen and veteran cavalrymen from the regular armies of the

United States, Germany, France and the United Kingdom. Still others would be added as the years went on.

Buffalo Bill's Wild West became *Buffalo Bill's Wild West and Congress of Rough Riders of the World*, the name by which it would continue to be known throughout the remaining years of its existence.

In 1893, on the Gallowgate, Glasgow had a 'World's Fair' of its own – albeit on a far less celebrated scale than its Chicago counterpart. During that same summer, Paisley's Clayholes showground hosted shooting galleries operating under the superficially impressive banners of 'Can Cowboy's Far West' and 'Buffalo Hunters of the Wild West' – such was the indelible stamp that Buffalo Bill's visit to Glasgow had impressed upon the public imagination eighteen months before.

The 1894 season brought another long stand at Brooklyn, New York. The *New York Herald*[3] carried an article based on interviews with the Wild West women, among them Mrs Lillie Shangrau who, it will be recalled, had married John Shangrau, the interpreter, in Glasgow. The couple had since been blessed with the birth of a blond-haired child and Lillie was very much at home among her Lakota relations.

One singular episode prefigured the future success of the Western film genre. On the 24th of September, the inventor Thomas Alva Edison had Colonel Cody, Major Burke, Annie Oakley, John Shangrau and fifteen Indians visit him at his laboratory at Orange, New Jersey, with the object of capturing them for posterity by means of an early version of the movie camera. The second of the four film sequences shot was an Omaha dance, performed by thirteen Indians, while the other two squatted on the floor, beating their drums. Among the dancers was young Johnny Burke No Neck, still billed as the infant survivor of Wounded Knee, and Charging Crow, who had also been in Glasgow. Thus one who had befriended and corresponded with Katherine Lowe of Dennistoun came to be among the very first Indians to appear on film.

The prodigious technical advances pioneered by Edison were not without immediate practical import for the Wild West. An ambitious system of electrical illumination was installed at Ambrose Park by the Edison Illuminating Company of Brooklyn. The entire apparatus was placed under the superintendence of M. B. Bailey.

A publicity image which, by 1894, was featuring on posters and programmes, incorporated a map outlining the Wild West's overseas tours. Certain key venues were depicted in inset illustrations. Appropriately, Glasgow was represented by ships at berth on the Broomielaw.

New York, however, failed to replicate the commercial triumph of the World's Fair season. A shift in strategy was plainly required. Lengthy residencies in major urban centres were no longer viable and the key to commercial survival now lay in long and gruelling tours from one US town to the next.

It was at this time that James A. Bailey was assumed as a partner, alongside Colonel Cody and the increasingly ailing Nate Salsbury. Bailey was the sole surviving partner of Barnum & Bailey, Phineas T. Barnum having died in 1891. This crucial development heralded an effective merger with the Barnum & Bailey organisation. Relations between the two groups were thereafter conducted on a solid base of co-operation and mutually destructive competition in all its forms was systematically avoided. One show would tour in the States while the other was in Europe.

There was a substantial crossover of personnel and, particularly at the administrative and organisational levels, Buffalo Bill's operation was remodelled to absorb the touring experience amassed by *The Greatest Show on Earth*. Bailey was given the specific remit of dealing with the logistical problems involved in constantly transporting a greatly expanded company by rail.

The 1895 season set the formula that would continue to determine the basic format for the next seven seasons, as the show toured throughout the eastern United States. The vast majority of the venues were for one day only. Some of the venues, like Saratoga and Altoona, bore poetic and mysterious names derived from forgotten languages, once spoken by long-defunct Indian tribes vanquished centuries before. It was as if nothing remained of these people but a smattering of their words and, as Buffalo Bill Cody rode their way, it was almost as in celebration of their passing.

Reflecting the original path of conquest, the 1896 season ventured into the mid-western states, including into Cody's own native state of Iowa and his old stamping grounds in Leavenworth, Kansas and North Platte, Nebraska. Among the towns visited were those whose names were steeped in frontier history – Cumberland, Maryland; Forth Wayne, Indiana; Green Bay, Wisconsin; Jackson, Mississippi; and Boone and Des Moines, both Iowa.

A further ambitious itinerary in 1897 included a foray into Canada, closing in the old Confederate capital of Richmond, Virginia.

In 1898, the show penetrated to the heart of the West, performing in such recently organised states as Wyoming and Colorado.

The Wild West show had first seen the light of day at Omaha, Nebraska, in 1883, and its return in 1898 coincided with the town's Trans-Mississippi Exposition. The 31st of August 1898 was duly declared 'Cody Day' in Buffalo Bill's honour. Speeches by visiting dignitaries marked the occasion and, in his response, Cody obliquely recalled his Glasgow sojourn, in stating that his travels had taken him 'from the Platte to the Danube, from the Tiber to the Clyde'.[4]

The Greatest Show on Earth in Scotland

While Buffalo Bill was busy reconquering America, James Bailey was present in person on *The Greatest Show on Earth*'s extensive tours of Great Britain during 1898 and 1899.

The company, on arrival in England in 1898, established permanent and purpose-built winter quarters at Etruria, a district of Stoke thus named for its association with the pottery industry. It travelled in four great trains, specially designed and manufactured by Messrs W. R. Renshaw of the Phoenix Works in Stoke. Comprising seventy-four railway cars, they measured almost a full mile in length. The railway companies levied each passenger at ½d per mile and each railway vehicle at 6d per mile. £10 was charged for unloading at each station and a further £10 for loading up again. Newspaper advertisements proclaimed that, such was the show's prodigious size, it occupied twelve acres of ground, employed 1,200 people and ran on daily expenses of £1,500.

On the 1898 tour, there had been only two Scottish venues – the principal cities of Glasgow (27th June–16th July) and Edinburgh (18th–23rd July). In 1899, twenty Scottish towns and cities, commencing with Galashiels on the 29th of August and concluding in Dumfries on the 6th of October, were included on the itinerary.

Barnum & Bailey's establishment was the original three-ring circus, with two intermediate stages, a surrounding hippodrome track and a 'monster aerial enclave', the whole capable of accommodating a total of 15,000 spectators.

One hundred spectacular acts and displays were performed by human and animal performers, with a number of equestrian events. It was truly the *ne plus ultra* of travelling shows and the one criticism that was routinely expressed was that *The Greatest Show on Earth* was, if anything, rather *too* great and the bemused spectator scarcely knew which particular marvel to focus his attention on at any one point in time.

In addition to the main circus marquee, there was another tent housing the menagerie. The animal cages were arranged in the form of a horseshoe and, on a raised platform in its midst, the 'freaks' were placed on display. This subsidiary exhibition was thrown open to public inspection an hour or so before the circus performance began.

The freaks – or 'prodigies' as they preferred to be known – were, for the most part, individuals marginalised by their various physical and mental abnormalities and who, by the operation of a curious paradox, found that the very circumstances that prevented them from supporting themselves by any more conventional means also provided them with their only saleable asset. By the final years of the 'enlightened' ninteenth century – the age of John Merrick, the 'Elephant Man' – such aberrations were degraded to the level of vulgar amusements. Such entertainments took place throughout this period at Crouch's Waxworks in Glasgow's Argyle Street.

The advertisement appearing in the *Stirling Sentinel* heralded them as:

> the wonderful array of Living Human Curiosities and Queer People, Giants, Dwarfs, Midgets, Skeleton, Bearded and Long-Haired Lady, Armless and Legless Men, Tattooed People, the Dog-Faced Boy or Human Skye Terrier, Moss-Haired Girl, Lalla and Lallo, the wonderful quality of persons, together with Expansionist and Contractionist, Japanese Armless Girl, Magicienne, Sword Swallowers, Jugglers, Miramba Players and Performers upon all kinds of Musical Instruments.[5]

Lalla and Lallo were a pair of Siamese twins. Probably the strangest of all was Miss Delphi, the orange-headed girl. A native of India, her cranium lacked a proper bone structure, apart from the bones of her face. This unfortunate young woman stood scarcely any taller than the dwarf whose name was Khusania.

> She is a diminutive being, of good tempered but very monkey-like expression. Her head is round as an orange, with very little intellect. Her superstitious parents believed that a soul of the sacred monkey had taken up its habitation in her body, giving her the strange appearance she possesses. She has not the power of speech, but she regards the onlookers with evident interest and pleasure.[6]

An extraordinarily callous attitude on the part of the management towards the unfortunate individuals under its care was indicated in the *Stirling Sentinel*:

> And the proprietors are continually changing their novelties. If they get a good thing, they keep it but if indications are given that the public want a change, off goes the freak to make way for something else, and something better.[7]

A vaudeville show, admission a further sixpence, was held in the main exhibition pavilion at the conclusion of the main performance. The *Falkirk Herald* reported that: 'The programme, which was admirably sustained, was a very enjoyable one, and included character sketches, songs, dances, negro minstrelsy, musical diversions, and humorous skits.'[8]

The entertainment on the first morning at a new venue began with a huge street parade, weather permitting. It extended for fully a mile and took twenty minutes to pass any given spot. It was, of necessity, given free of charge and the route through which the procession would pass was well publicised in advance. The way was invariably lined with local people, augmented by crowds of visitors who had flocked into town from the surrounding area, and every conceivable coign of vantage was snapped up well in advance. In many places schools were given a holiday for the day of the show.

The Scotsman of the 5th of September provided a lively description of the grand parade as it made its way along Princes Street:

> This thoroughfare presented a stirring appearance, and as seen from one of the windows of the Royal Hotel the procession, stretching along the entire length of the street, the bright colours of banners and dresses set off by the green of the trees, was a very pretty and imposing sight.

For that one day, Edinburgh possessed not one 'Royal Mile' but two.

The show's immense marquee tents were unfortunately susceptible to gales. The *North-Western Daily Mail* – when the Scottish leg of the tour had only three days left to run – reported that no fewer than nine performances had had to be abandoned while north of the border.[9] These were at Montrose, Dumbarton and Paisley, as well as three in Glasgow. Both performances at Kilmarnock fell victim after the article cited had gone to print. So hopeless, indeed, did the prospects appear on that dismal morning that most of the baggage was never even unloaded at the railway station.

At Montrose, on the 18th September, the morning street pageant went ahead but, owing to the prevalence of high winds, it became necessary to announce the cancellation of the performances 'to the unspeakable chagrin of a crowd larger than has been seen in Montrose for many years'.[10] The tent containing the freaks was, at least, thrown open for a time but, at length, the gale caused the canvas to rend. This occurrence precipitated a stampede and all departments were promptly closed.

King's Park provided the venue in Stirling on the 21st but only after considerable deliberations by the Town Council. The Councillors had no wish to stand in the way of the show being held there but expressed concerns about the likely damage to the ground. A subcommittee had been dispatched to the site of the show in Dunfermline and reported that a large area of the park had been badly cut up and damaged in other ways.

Very heavy traffic was reported on the Callander and Oban railway line and three special trains were required to accommodate the crowds of people travelling into Stirling for the show:

> On the Forth and Clyde Railway no special preparations had been made, and the result was that the morning trains were packed almost to suffocation, while there were so many left behind on the platforms that the 9.30 train had to make a return journey for the remainder of its passengers.[11]

Four photographs of the street parade approaching Burns Statue Square were taken by Alfred James Thomson at Ayr, on the 4th of October.

An American Institution

The closing of the frontier ushered in a new era in American politics, in which imperial expansion beyond the seas, principally in the Pacific and the Caribbean, was briefly the order of the day. The Spanish-American War of 1898, the United States' first external war in half a century, brought armed conflict in Cuba and the Philippines for the ostensible purpose of liberating the native populations from colonial rule.

It was at this time that a curious inversion manifested itself. Buffalo Bill was no longer content merely to depict historical episodes but now took a hand in directly determining the actual course of events. At the start of the 1898 season, Buffalo Bill paraded a party of wounded Cuban insurgents in New York. This came a matter of days before hostilities were declared and was a significant factor in mobilising public sentiment in favour of war. Lieutenant-Colonel Theodore Roosevelt, who, on the back of the adventure, was elected President of the United States for two terms from 1901 until 1909, raised a fighting force predominantly composed of Western elements. It was officially designated the First Regiment of United States Volunteer Cavalry but was universally known as 'Roosevelt's Rough Riders'. The borrowing from Roosevelt's friend Buffalo Bill was both conscious and intentional. Buffalo Bill expressed a vague intention to enlist and, if his show had not been running at the time, it is probable that he would have done so. No doubt it would have been his biggest publicity coup since the ghost dance troubles. In the event, he had to content himself with sending along two of his horses, which were ridden at the front by General Miles.

The 1899 tour included a number of venues in South Dakota, the old heartland of the ghost-dance scare. During this and the 1900 season, reflecting the changing times, 'The Battle of San Juan Hill', featuring veterans of the actual engagement in Cuba, became Cody's first-ever representation of a battle outwith the Indian wars.

In 1900, the company once again travelled through myriad locations the length and breadth of the United States, many of which bore names redolent of the different phases in the nation's history. Included on the itinerary was the Lone Star State of Texas and among the towns visited was Annie Oakley's birthplace, Greenville, Ohio. Another was Mount Vernon, also Ohio, which, in common with a certain eastern district of Glasgow, had taken its name from George Washington's old Virginia plantation.

The first tour of the twentieth century introduced a brand-new battle sequence, 'The Battle of Tien-Tsin', a key engagement in the Boxer Rebellion of 1900, with the Indians pressed into service as the Chinese insurgents – a convenient metaphor, as always, for whichever side happened to be losing.

1901 also brought disaster, when, on the night of the 28th of October, towards the season's end, one of Buffalo Bill's trains was involved in a head-on collision near Lexington, Virginia. Annie Oakley was among the casualties and she sustained severe internal injuries. This accident marked the end of her long association with the show.

In 1902, Buffalo Bill utilised the ever-expanding rail network to traverse practically the entire United States, performing in Utah, Idaho, Washington, Oregon, California, Arizona and New Mexico. The 'Old West' as a living reality was by now so effectively consigned to the history books that the 'Wild West' as spectacular entertainment drew an enthusiastic welcome just about anywhere.

Buffalo Bill now boasted a sideshow. The involvement of James Bailey, taken together with the commercial pressures exerted by public demand, had led to a succession of unsatisfactory compromises. During its formative years, the Wild West had been very different from the conventional circus and it was a matter of professional pride to Cody that the essential purity of the Wild West concept was not adulterated. Posters devised by John M. Burke in 1883 had conspicuously highlighted the legend 'No Side Shows or Freaks'.[12]

Just as circuses increasingly tended to absorb Wild West elements, the reverse process also manifested itself. There was a mutual convergence between the two types of entertainment and, consequently, they had become much harder to tell apart. In particular, the partnership with Bailey resulted in the direct importation of crucial elements from *The Greatest Show on Earth*.

Buffalo Bill's 'freak show' was never on so ambitious a scale or as shocking in content as Barnum & Bailey's but that was the clear source of this influence nonetheless.

Buffalo Bill's Wild West and Congress of Rough Riders of the World had spent a decade in consolidating its position as a truly American institution. The transition to the new version of Buffalo Bill's show more or less coincided with a wider realisation that the essence of America's national genius lay not in a grand culmination of the racial destiny of a revitalised scion of the Anglo-Saxon diaspora but, on the contrary, in a wider synthesis of the uniquely diverse and cosmopolitan composition of its people. The closing decade of the nineteenth century had been a time of radical self-redefinition for the United States, no less than for the show itself. But fresh horizons beckoned as the challenge of overseas campaigns loomed once again.

Notes

1. 11 June 1892
2. 2 July 1892
3. 22 July 1894
4. Quoted by Helen Cody Wetmore, at p. 287 of *Last of the Great Scouts*
5. 12 September 1899
6. *Ayr Advertiser*, 5 October 1899
7. 19 September 1899
8. 2 September 1899
9. 3 October 1899
10. *Montrose Standard and Angus & Mearns Register*, 22 September 1899
11. *Stirling Sentinel*, 26 September 1899
12. Quoted by Victor Weybright and Henry Sell, at p. 128 of *Buffalo Bill and the Wild West*

14

GRAND ENTRY, 1902–04

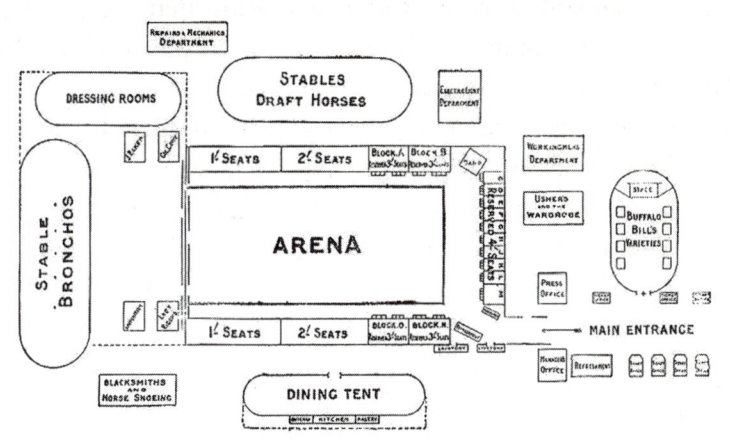

Buffalo Bill's final and most extensive British campaign came during the years 1902–04. The start of the indoor residency at London's Olympia from the 26th of December 1902 until the following 4th of April was marred by the sad news that Cody's old partner Nate Salsbury had finally lost his long battle with ill health.

Commencing at Manchester on the 13th of April, an outdoor version of the show toured England and Wales continuously for over six months, giving two representations daily, with the exception of Sundays.

Buffalo Bill's 1903 season was vastly more ambitious than either of the previous British tours, appearing at a total of ninety-two venues. Five major cities enjoyed visits of from one to three weeks apiece and eleven towns were engaged for periods ranging from two to four days. However, the overwhelming majority of the stands, seventy-six, were for one day only.

A daughter was born to Luther and Laura Standing Bear at Birmingham, on the 7th of June. Only two days later, both mother and infant were placed on public display in the sideshow tent. Crowds of visitors made gifts of money as they passed by. In 1903, ethnic diversity was in itself a qualification for exhibition status.

When the season closed at Burton-on-Trent, on the 23rd of October, the equipage was put into storage in Barnum & Bailey's wintering quarters at Etruria while Buffalo Bill and the majority of his personnel returned to the States. By an ineluctable coincidence, the ship on which they sailed from Liverpool was called the *Etruria*.

The company returned to Liverpool during April 1904 and re-opened at Stoke on the 25th. The 1904 tour covered even more ground. Of a total of 132 stands, 123 were for one day only. There was no lengthy London residency and only three cities – Newcastle-upon-Tyne, Glasgow and Edinburgh – were favoured with the maximum duration of one week. Dundee and Aberdeen received three-day visits. Cardiff, Hull, Sunderland and Inverness each hosted performances over two consecutive days.

Once again, a substantial majority of the venues – eighty-seven – on the 1904 tour were English but sixteen engagements, all fulfilled during May, were in Wales and the Scottish leg of the tour embraced twenty-nine venues.

Buffalo Bill's proud 'rain or shine' boast was soundly vindicated by the circumstance that not a single performance was lost during the course of the entire 1904 season.

Over the course of 1903 and 1904, the show visited almost every town and city of any size or significance in Great Britain, as Buffalo Bill brought his show to the people. One essential requirement, therefore, was that a prospective venue was served by an adequate railway network, both in order to convey the entourage to and from the venue and also to bring in spectators from the outlying districts.

The *Banffshire Advertiser*[1] reported a rumour that the county town of Banff had been under consideration for inclusion on the 1904 itinerary but was discounted since its rail service was insufficient to bear the weight of the anticipated traffic. The article cited the lamentations of the Macduff correspondent to the *Evening Gazette*; while local people had often been reminded that Banff was an isolated place, that sense of remoteness had never properly been impressed upon them until now. The correspondent concluded by calling upon the Great North of Scotland Railway to take immediate steps to modernise its facilities.

The Wild West travelled in three great trains, measuring an aggregate length of three quarters of a mile and weighing 1,184 tons. They comprised forty-nine of Barnum & Bailey's cars, all inscribed 'Buffalo Bill's Wild West' in large letters, with two standard brake carriages and an engine for each train. These comprised varying combinations of stock cars, flat cars and luxuriously furnished sleeping cars (eighteen, seventeen and fourteen cars respectively). The first two trains brought the workmen, the horses, the wagons, the tents and the other equipment. The third brought the performers – including Colonel Cody who slept in car number 50 – and generally arrived an hour or two after its predecessors. According to Niall Ferguson, the scale of charges concluded with the Caledonian Railway Company was the same as had been applied to Barnum & Bailey.[2]

From Stoke, the show made its way through the West Midlands into Cheshire and thence into North Wales. Moving southwards though Wales and turning once across the border into Chester, it passed through the industrial centres of the south, back into England, traversed the West Country and reached its furthest extent in Cornwall. The itinerary next continued eastward along the south coast, skirting the suburbs of London and heading northwards along the eastern side of England. Much of July was spent on Tyne and Wear, one of the very few remaining English regions not previously graced with a visit from Buffalo Bill.

An engagement on the 25th of July coincided with the Tweedmouth Feast in Berwick, a long-disputed border town over which many ancient conflicts had raged. On the following day, the eagerly anticipated Scottish leg of the tour began.

Hawick

The honour of being the first 1904 Scottish venue went to Hawick, a town boasting a proud equestrian heritage of its own. Buffalo Bill, who had once played the leading role in the stage play *The King of the Bordermen*, made his debut in the borderlands of Scotland on Tuesday the 26th of July.

The trains arrived from Berwick around five in the morning. Large crowds gathered at the station to witness the process of detraining, as well as the procession to the showgrounds. Crossing the River Teviot, the entourage rode down North Bridge Street, along the High Street, past the ancient Tower Knowe and proceeded out of town along the Slitrig Road (now called Liddesdale Road), arriving at Whitlaw Haugh, approximately midway between Hawick and Stobs. 'Haugh', it should be explained, is an archaic Scots word, denoting a tract of flat land adjacent to a river, in this instance, the River Slitrig.

This location, in a field identified by the advanceman's log as the 'near lot' and rented from James Elliot of the farm of Flex, provided one of the few pieces of flat land in an otherwise hilly terrain, set amongst the rolling and undulating Southern Uplands. The non-availability of alternative sites no doubt accounts for the unusually high price exacted for the day's rental – £50, payable two weeks in advance. It may be taken that Mr Elliot was a hard man to do business with.

A photograph of this agreeable setting, featuring the main entrance, the canvas arena, the sideshow tent and a number of wagons, was published in the *Hawick News*.[3] It was taken by John McNairn, in whose family's hands the *News* would remain for several decades longer.

In the accompanying article, the Negro troopers were referred to, unfortunately, as 'Niggers' and modern racial sensibilities jar at the headline 'Darkey Assaults A Woman', which appeared elsewhere on the same page. An element of racial confusion was also manifested in the designation of the Indian children as 'picanninies'.

While winning no awards for political correctness, it has to be acknowledged that, on the photographic level at least, Mr McNairn was most certainly a man well ahead of his time. Apart from the photograph of Iron Tail and Blue Shield, taken at John O'Groats and subsequently published in the *Ardrossan and Saltcoats Herald*,[4] the *Hawick News* photograph is the only one pertaining to the show to appear in a contemporary Scottish newspaper, as far as my extensive researches have been able to determine. To put it another way, the Hawick photograph appears to be the only one, taken locally, to grace the pages of the newspapers serving any of the Scottish venues. It is unfortunate indeed that neither prints nor negatives appear to have survived the intervening decades.

As at the other venues, virtually every available hoarding had been pressed into service and the show's posters were omnipresent. The necessary arrangements were made with George Davidson, of the Border Billposting Co., Exchange Arcade, although an accommodation appears also to have been reached with his competitor, James Grey. The *Hawick Advertiser* doubted whether any passing event had ever been so extensively and publicly advertised in the area as the Wild West had been, remarking that: 'The window display of bills was also on a very large scale.'[5] Photographs survive of posters in the window of R. Tait's confectionery shop, which was then located in O'Connell Street.

Hawick must have made a mighty impression upon Charles Eldridge Griffin, the sword swallower and manager of privileges (that is, he was in charge of the sideshow), since it is one from just four out of twenty-nine Scottish venues to be accorded a specific mention in his memoirs, *Four Years in Europe with Buffalo Bill*:

> July 20 the big Western Show made its entry into Bonnie Scotland at Hawick, pronounced by the natives, Hike, and we had a two mile 'hike' to the show grounds through a Scotch mist, which in America we would call a drizzling rain. Here I saw the first thistle I had seen for more than two years, and it seemed like seeing some one from home, as we used to have more than a plenty of them in the old Hawkeye State [Iowa] where I was raised.[6]

However, the date mentioned here is an obvious mistake and cannot be reconciled to the primary sources. The actual date was the 26th. It may be noticed that Don Russell also mentions the 20th in this connection and it is to be presumed that he is relying upon Griffin as his source.[7] This error has since found common currency among the few American academics[8] who have bothered to research the Scottish venues and it is fortunate that the O'Connell Street photographs are available to amplify the point that it was in fact the 26th. On the 20th, the show was in Durham.

Mr Griffin probably retained such a detailed and specific recollection of this particular venue because the showgrounds were normally located far closer to the station than was the case on this occasion. Such a lengthy trek was resented as an unwelcome intrusion upon the somewhat circumscribed hours of leisure normally enjoyed by the members of the company.

Visitors began to arrive in town from all parts of the surrounding countryside and, by noon, cabs were competing for their custom. Between one and two, the scene on the High Street was a particularly animated one. For almost two hours, the Slitrig Road was congested with a continuous stream of vehicles of every size and description. As had been anticipated, the thoroughfare proved hopelessly inadequate for the purpose. The traffic was handled systematically by men of the Burgh and County police forces. The Burgh Police, under the personal control of Chief Constable Morren, patrolled the road to the limits of their jurisdiction beyond Lynnwood. Over the remainder of the route, the Roxburghshire Constabulary, including two mounted men, were out in force. The County men were under the command of Superintendent Sharp, of Jedburgh.

Officers of the SSPCA were also on duty to ensure that no overzealous driver was tempted to place an excessive strain upon his horse. A few admonitions were issued but no more drastic action was found necessary.

The attendance at the afternoon performance will probably never be known as the town's three newspapers diverged extravagantly in their estimates. Two of the riders sustained minor injuries. A man fell from his horse while riding at a tremendous pace and had to be carried away. One of the female riders was later unseated and was also assisted from the arena. Neither, however, was seriously hurt.

At the conclusion of the afternoon show, a large party of Indian women and others made a visit to the local army camp at Stobs. They regarded the soldiers of the Black Watch regiment who were stationed there as objects of great curiosity and manifested much interest in 'the Kilties'. The Indians poked their noses and even themselves into the tents so that they were eventually accorded a conducted tour of the establishment. Predictably, their attentions were fully reciprocated and the crowds of onlookers who dogged their footsteps were as much amused by the strangeness of the Indians' behaviour as by the quaintness of their attire.

The performance was repeated in the evening with some slight variations. *The Hawick News* of the 29th of July 1904 estimated that 12,000 were present while the *Hawick Express* for the same date preferred the more conservative figure of around 10,000. Soldiers and volunteers from the army camp made up a considerable portion of the audience. No doubt many of them had been enticed by the visit of the Indians earlier that afternoon. One of the boxes was occupied by a party made up of Sir Richard Waldie-Griffith, Major Haddon and other officers of the Border Rifles.

Owing to the length of the journey back into town, the majority of people decided to forego the opportunity of visiting the sideshows after the main performance.

The Slitrig Road, between the showground and the town, was once again congested with vehicles and pedestrians, all making their way back into Hawick. This posed a certain element of danger, which was compounded by the road's narrowness at certain points. The occasional appearance of a vehicle attempting to make its way against the flow caused considerable difficulty.

Effective policing arrangements however ensured that only one slight accident was reported. This occurred at around ten in the evening and befell Private William Murray of the 1st Royal Highlanders. A passing motor car knocked him down near Lynnwood Lodge as he was returning to the army camp at Stobs. The soldier sustained an injury to his right knee and was conveyed to the camp hospital by the Burgh Police, utilising the hand ambulance that had recently been acquired by the Town Council.

Meals and lodgings at the Station Hotel, then in the hands of James Wilson, were procured for members of Colonel Cody's staff. Both were priced at 1/6d a time and a total bill of £10 8/6d was incurred. Additional livery was obtained from Thomas Whillens, of Slitrig Crescent. The water supply was obtained from Charles Brown, Surveyor for the Town Council, and was charged at £1 3/6d.

The Canvas City

John McNairn's photograph of the entrance to the showground at Hawick captured only a fraction of the establishment. The whole, as illustrated by a plan included in the 1903 programme, was made up of an elaborate 'canvas city', comprising the arena, together with a complex of tents of varying descriptions and sizes. Wherever the show travelled, it was always laid out according to the same plan, unless a lack of available space dictated that modifications were made, as indeed occurred at Edinburgh and Paisley.

On entering the showground, the first sight encountered was a barrow from which 'the miraculous "American silken candy"' – presumably candyfloss – was sold.[9] The next was the annexe or sideshow, lying at a short distance from the main entrance to the principal arena. This approach was lined on both sides by a number of wagons, which served as on-site ticket offices, for the full range of prices. Tickets, priced at four shillings and upwards, were additionally on sale on the day of the show from 9.00 a.m. onwards, at an outlet advertised in the local press. At Hawick, this was W. & J. Kennedy's Booksellers, 2, Sandbed.

The arena, naturally, formed the centrepiece to the entire layout. It required a clear ground space of 550 feet by 185 feet, and was enclosed by canvas walls on all sides. The accommodation for the spectators consisted of rows of seats, eighteen tiers deep, arranged along three sides, these being the two longer flanks and the near end. In contrast to the conventional circus 'big top', the arena was rectangular in shape and the ground upon which the performers appeared was left open to the elements. The patrons, however, were protected from the vagaries of the weather by means of an immense and thoroughly waterproofed canvas canopy.

Exactly how many spectators Buffalo Bill's arena could actually hold remains something of a mystery. With the usual inconsistency concerning numerical quantities, press release statements about the capacity ranged wildly from 10,000 to 20,000. There is evidence, however, that either 14,000 or 16,000 was the true figure.

At the near end of the arena lay the manager's office, the refreshment tent, the press office, the workingmen's department and accommodation for the ushers and the wardrobe. A single public entrance to the show was divided into six railed passages and programme and refreshment stands flanked the patrons as they passed. A band of courteous ushers was on hand to direct the spectators to their places and the order and comfort reigning within contrasted with the bustle and confusion that normally prevailed outside.

Along the near end of the arena were ranged the most expensive seats, reserved at four shillings each, at the far side of which lay the 'upper class' corner of the arena, containing the platform on which the Cowboy Band took up position.

Along either flank of the arena lay two blocks of three-shilling seats and in front of these and the four-shilling seats was ranged a series of private boxes. The ones on the flanks were priced at five shillings and those at the end at seven and sixpence. Further down the arena, on either side, lay the two-shilling seats and at the far end, the one-shilling seats.

Behind the top flank of the arena lay commodious tented stabling for the draught horses. This was flanked on one side by the repairs and mechanics department and by the electric light department on the other. Below the opposite flank lay the dining tent, itself fringed by three sub-departments – the butchers', the kitchen and pastry.

Beyond the far end of the arena lay one of the largest tents, which provided the stables for the performing horses. Set at right angles to it lay the dressing marquee. This tent also provided the living quarters for most of the performers and, here, men of many nationalities could be found cheerfully pursuing a variety of activities during their leisure hours. In the intermediate space between the stables and the arena were four tents set in a long rectangle and three of these respectively provided the private quarters of Johnnie Baker, Colonel Cody and the lady riders. Colonel Cody's tent, in which he frequently received visiting journalists, was both comfortable and spacious. Pine trees were stuck in the ground around its entrance, creating the illusion that a portion of the prairies had somehow been transplanted onto Scottish soil. The fourth of these tents was used as a store for the ammunition. A short distance below the stables stood the blacksmiths' tent.

Though not indicated on the plan in the 1903 programme, the tipi encampment, in which the Indians had their actual living accommodation, was pitched in the extreme top left corner, behind the dressing tent and alongside the repairs and mechanics department.

There were no seats at the far end of the arena, as it was from there that the performers made their exits and entrances.

Notes

1. 8 September 1904
2. 'The Wild West Comes to Toon', *BackTrack*, July 2005, p. 434. This article contains a far fuller account of the technical details than can be offered here.
3. 29 July 1904
4. 16 September 1904
5. 29 July1904
6. p. 45
7. *The Lives and Legends of Buffalo Bill*, p. 441
8. See, for example, Ferenc Morton Szasz, *Scots in the North American West, 1790–1917*, p. 146
9. *Elgin Courant and Courier*, 2 September 1904

15

BUFFALO BILL'S SHOW, 1904

During the tour's Scottish leg upwards of half a million people, then a very substantial proportion of the entire population, witnessed a total of eighty-eight performances over twenty-nine venues.

The entertainment began well before entering the main arena, since visitors were encouraged to perambulate the tipi encampment and other parts of the establishment.

The Sideshow Annexe

The sideshow remained open throughout the day, from eleven in the morning, three hours in advance of the afternoon performance. The price of admission was sixpence, with children under four being admitted free. While intended as a supplementary and subsidiary entertainment, part of the rationale appears to have been that those unable to afford a ticket for the main performance might at least be consoled with a visit to the sideshow.

Here, a variety of human abnormalities and small-scale circus acts were placed on display. The official programme proclaimed:

'Buffalo Bill's' Annexe,
Located near the Main Entrance of the 'Wild West' proper, contains all of the outside attractions that travel in connection with the Big Show. This exhibition includes every human extreme of living mankind, viz.:

PRINCESS NOUMA HAWA, twenty-one years of age, and twenty-one inches in height. AARON MOORE, Coloured American Giant, height, eight feet. FRED WALTERS, The Blue Man. PROFESSOR GRIFFIN, Necromancer and Sword Swallower. G.A. GIOVANNI's great Bird and Monkey Circus. MLLE. Octavia, Fearless Serpent Enchantress. PROFESSOR SACKETTO'S HARE BAND. Concerts given daily by Live Hares. PROFESSOR and MADAME DIAMOND, Thrilling Impalement Act, Hurling Bowie Knives and Battle-Axes. PROFESSOR SACKETTO'S Celebrated Military Band, etc.

The 'freaks', properly so called, were three in number. Of these, 'Princess Nouma Hawa' travelled with the show over a number of seasons. Comparing the programmes for these years, her age appears to have been permanently fixed at twenty-one. The additional privilege of shaking her tiny hand was priced at one penny.

Aaron Moore also went by the epithet of 'the Moorish Giant'. A well-proportioned man in his mid forties, his sole claim to notoriety was his outlandish size. A constant smile adorned his features and he accentuated his prodigious height with a fez and full-length coat.

Captain Fred Walters, the 'Blue Man', suffered from locomotor ataxia and a side effect of the silver nitrate which he took as medication for this condition was that his skin assumed a bluish tinge. He increased the dosage as a means of deliberately enhancing the peculiar influence upon his skin pigmentation. Captain Walters was advertised as a veteran of the 17th Duke of Cambridge's Own Lancers.

The *Fraserburgh Advertiser* reported that: 'Freaks and human wonders of all kinds were to be seen, and were duly inspected by thousands.'[1] However, the Scottish press largely ignored this immensely popular dimension of the show and the only known detailed description appeared in the *Elgin Courant and Courier*, which opined that the sideshow was a sight well worth double the price actually charged for admission. It went on to describe Professor Sacketto's Hare Band: 'For instance, it is something of a novelty to sit and listen to a band, especially when the musicians are half a dozen rabbits, who receive a supply of cabbage before performing.'[2]

The secret of how this surreal illusion was sustained is divulged in a picture postcard, based upon a photograph taken in France in 1905. The image depicts a total of eight live rabbits or hares – it is hard to determine precisely which – with their heads trapped in holes in an ornate panel, each held in place above a mechanical body, six of which play a different musical instrument, while a central figure conducts. An eighth, positioned above the rest, apparently dances.

Even greater enthusiasm was lavished upon the bird and monkey circus:

> Without doubt the most remarkable and most praiseworthy item is the exhibition by cockatoos, who, if they have not brains, have a very good substitute for them. Their performance of telling the time, days of the week, etc., by ringing on a bell was watched with pleasure and delight by a large crowd.[3]

The Main Event

The show had expanded significantly since 1892, not only in physical dimensions and size of the company but in concept too. Of the twenty-three items on the programme, the majority of the Wild West acts had endured as tried-and-tested core features in a format that was essentially unaltered, though Annie Oakley had departed and the buffalo hunt was omitted from the later overseas tours.

The various radical innovations highlighted an international equestrian dimension and, for the most part, a powerful military theme pervaded but other acts defy classification under either of these categories.

The element of continuity had been reduced to a fine art and, for about an hour and forty minutes, one engrossing sequence followed seamlessly upon another. The spectators were scarcely conceded a pause in which to catch their breath, as one group of performers made its exit and others simultaneously entered by the opposite corner. Interest was never once permitted to flag for, at any given moment, there was some absorbing spectacle to lay claim to the audience's rapt attention.

Amid a gentle hum of anticipation, the Cowboy Band struck up fifteen minutes before the show began, delivering a lively selection of classical and popular airs. That proceedings would shortly commence was communicated – as formerly – by 'The Star Spangled Banner'. Instrumentalists had come and gone but William Sweeney was a continuing presence as the band's director.

Meanwhile, in lightning obedience to a bugle call summoning them to mount up, the entire body of horsemen assembled at the stables. There they stood in readiness for the signal of Johnnie Baker, the arenic director, upon whose command, successively delivered to each detachment in its own tongue, they rode out into public view.

The orator was Edward Ackerman Totten, a tall young man of imposing aspect, who sported a broad-brimmed hat. He strode to the rostrum in the centre of the arena and, with 'a voice that could have competed with thunder',[4] he announced that what was about to be witnessed was not a 'performance' in the ordinary sense but an exhibition.

No sooner had his words died away when a blood-curdling shriek rent the air, heralding the entrance of the Indians. Instantly rumblings from the audience gave way to a low murmur of excitement as the painted mountain and woodland backdrop at the far end of the arena was raised to admit a band of galloping, howling, careering warriors in double file. Their hair streaming in the wind, they brandished their long feathered bows as they charged. The Indians lined up to face the spectators at the end of the arena and the chief who followed took up position at their head. A second cry rang out, as further bands emerged, successively introduced as representing different tribes. The chiefs, resplendent in beaded waistcoats, gaudy blankets and war bonnets, wielded feathered lances. Their followers were naked, beyond breechcloths, feathers and strange designs liberally bedaubed in body paints of chrome yellow, deep red, purple and other lurid shades. The noise of their sharp, shrill war whoops rang out continuously as the other riders fell successively into place.

The orator, in the time-honoured manner, severally introduced the performers to the audience. However, the company was far more diverse and variegated than in 1891–92 and the wonderful array of colours on display made for a tremendous kaleidoscopic effect.

After the Indians came a company of sixteen English Lancers, glorious in their dress uniform of blue and gold with red inserts and lances at rest. They were led by a sergeant, who proudly held the Union flag aloft. Next came the 'Cossacks', in loosely flowing ochre robes, girded at the waist, and cone-shaped astrakhan hats, the Russian standard at their head. Then, in turn, came: the men of the 10th US Colored Cavalry, in their regulation uniforms of blue, trimmed with yellow, blue and white, and helmets plumed with different colours; Roosevelt Rough Riders in khaki and slouch hats; Mexicans, marked by the extravagance of their headgear and sartorial brilliance of their costumes, led by Vincente Oropeza; gauchos from the Argentine; rough-looking cowboys, in sheepskin leggings, under Joe Esquivel; Cuban patriots; two 'Indian boy chiefs', resplendent in the glory of their colours and feathers; a quartet of American frontier girls, all in bonnets and some favouring the divided skirt; Bedouin Arabs, gorgeously attired, in a wild, barbaric dash; and a pair of Indian women. There was a detachment of about a dozen Imperial Japanese Cavalrymen, under ex-sergeants Tora and Sano, in European-style uniforms of dark blue and pillbox hats. Time and again, they received a special cheer, acknowledged with a salute in true military style. The breathtaking cavalcade thundered to a crescendo with the entrance of the 6th United States Cavalry.

The assembly of several hundred horsemen formed up in a square and, last of all, came Buffalo Bill himself, astride his handsome charger. Taking his place at the head of his cosmopolitan regiment and flanked by riders bearing the Union flag and Stars and Stripes, he gave a dignified bow. Raising his hat in acknowledgement of the deafening ovation ringing out all around him, from horsemen and spectators alike, he proclaimed in measured tones, 'Ladies and gentlemen, permit me to introduce to you a Congress of the Rough Riders of the World!'

In the next instant, he wheeled his horse around and led his riders through a series of intricate evolutions, a wondrous spectacle of diversity, organisation and colour, all performed with unerring accuracy. The sight, as arms clashed and hooves beat upon the hard turf, was one to be long remembered, as these horsemen of many nations swiftly departed the arena.

The 'race of races' between an Indian, a cowboy and a Mexican now additionally included Cossack and Arab participants and contrasted the characteristic attire and different riding methods of each group represented. They were normally run to a close finish. There is no evidence that the outcome was predetermined in any way.

Veterans of the 5th United States Artillery demonstrated the use of the muzzle-loading cannon, a relic of the American Civil War (1861–65), long since superseded by modern rapid-fire guns. Riding into the arena upon gun carriages – one drawn by a team of black horses, the other by a team of greys – they unharnessed, unlimbered, charged and fired their guns. After expeditiously carrying out the reverse procedure of limbering and harnessing, the men resumed their places and drove at full speed around the arena, as if in hot pursuit of a routed enemy. To illustrate their absolute control over the horses and vehicles, willow-wands were set in the ground on either side, with just a few inches of leeway given. Not one was disturbed.

A United States Life Saving Service crew, in naval uniform, graphically demonstrated the manner in which lives were saved upon the storm-tossed coasts of New Jersey, using equipment on loan from the United States government. A single mast with spars, representing a ship in distress upon the seas, was erected in the arena. A lifeline was propelled by mortar over the stricken vessel from the shore.

The line was secured to the top of the mast and a hawser followed, with a breeches buoy attached. A single imperilled mariner clambered into it and was promptly hauled to shore.

Buffalo Bill himself galloped around the arena, firing his Winchester rifle at glass balls thrown into the air by a cowboy riding ahead. The characteristic accomplishment lay in finding the mark with horse and target in simultaneous motion.

The 'Pony Express Riding' display focused upon the catlike agility with which the mail carrier leapt from one mount to the next and the rapidity with which the fresh steed bore him to the next changing place, not a moment being wasted. Lasting only about a minute, it was commonly deemed too brief to convey a proper impression of the old-time Pony Express riders.

A pair of covered wagons forming an emigrant train lumbered ponderously around and across the arena, pulled by teams of mules and attended by a body of outriders. Camp was made for the night, a fire was lit and the mules were taken to water. While others huddled around the campfire, four couples performed a horseback quadrille, providing relief from the mounting dramatic tension. This rest and revelry was interrupted as the wild whoops of a war party rang out. The marauders quickly surrounded the camp and a terrific fusillade lent a ferocious touch of realism. Just as it appeared that the settlers' valiant resistance was in vain, a ringing cheer and the deafening discharge of firearms announced the timely intervention of a party of scouts and cowboys. The tide of battle swiftly turned and the Indians fled the scene as abruptly as they had come.

Veteran English Cavalrymen, billed as having seen service in all parts of the British Empire and accompanied by a detachment of the 10th US Colored Cavalry, gave a demonstration of such military exercises as sword duels and lance drill, concluding with 'the Balaclava melee' – a grand charge in line.

A quartet of 'American girls from the frontier', as the official programme termed them, gave 'a dashing display of horsemanship which raised the enthusiasm of the spectators to a high pitch'.[5] The party was divided between those who rode side-saddle, following the convention of the time, and others who appeared no less comfortable than their male counterparts seated legs astride their mounts.

A demonstration was given of the manner in which rough summary justice was meted out in the days of the frontier, with special vindictiveness reserved for the skulking rascals who stole other men's horses. A Mexican horse thief was pursued by a band of cowboys, one of whom threw a lasso over the miscreant's head and dragged him along the ground, as the others riddled him with bullets. (At some point, a sawdust-filled dummy was apparently substituted for the actor's body.) *The Northern Scot and Moray & Nairn Express* recorded that: 'The "thief's" antics were comical in the extreme, and were received with hearty shouts of laughter and unstinted applause.'[6]

A troupe of around a dozen Mexican vaqueros, men of mixed Hispanic and Central American Indian heritage, gave a mesmerising exhibition of their dexterity with the lasso, both on foot and from horseback, dealing out amazement and amusement in equal measure.

Apart from Buffalo Bill himself, Johnnie Baker was the only survivor of the four shooting acts of 1891–92. In practically every position attainable, he brought down glass balls singly, doubly and even three at once. He performed several astonishing feats with consummate ease, rarely, if ever, missing. He fired while leaning backwards and also stooping with the gun directed between his legs. He fired back across his shoulder, sighting the target by means of a looking glass, a trick learnt from Annie Oakley. Johnnie brought his turn to a close by shattering two balls while standing on his head and firing from each barrel in turn, as his attendant held his feet upright.

'Custer's Last Fight', otherwise known as the Battle of the Little Bighorn, was restored to the 1904 programme after a lengthy absence and was, for many, the highlight of the show. Once again, however, it represented a gross travesty of the actual sequence of events and the Indians were cast as the perpetrators of a cruel, premeditated and apparently unprovoked atrocity. The sequence in which they were seen in camp prior to the battle imparted something of the former free life of the Indians upon the open plains and was enacted against an impressive background of tipis and campfires. Reinforcements arrived and the entire company of Indians, women and children included, performed a war dance, to the pounding of drums and the wild cries of the participants. The warriors' heads were plumed with eagle feathers and their faces and bodies were smeared with warpaint, giving them a terrifying appearance. The dancers worked themselves, and their audience, into a frenzied anticipation of the carnage to follow. Indian scouts stealthily trailed the advancing column. Hastening next into camp, they heralded the near approach of the solders. An ambush was swiftly prepared and the cavalrymen were hopelessly outnumbered. In Cody's version of the incident, this was ascribed to an underhand subterfuge on the part of the Indians, rather than to Custer's own gross miscalculation and ineptitude. Custer surveyed the enemy encampment and bugles sounded the order to attack. The respective white and Indian modes of fighting were contrasted as the soldiers charged but the advancing horde of Indians halted them in their tracks and forced a retreat. Forming a circle, the warriors surrounded the soldiers, gradually tightening the noose of death, and relentlessly showered deadly weapons upon them, as those within the hoop left standing sank steadily fewer in number. Their escape routes cut off on all sides and overwhelmed, the doomed soldiers died heroically, fighting to the last man. The force and bravery of the Indian assault carried a reminder of the power, now broken, which, only a few decades before, had, for a time, held back the line of settlement. A scene of slaughter, such as even the most lucid and vivid descriptions could not convey, ensued.

A display by groups of Arab and Japanese acrobats lowered the tempo and afforded the spectators a welcome interlude in which to recover their shaken composure. The Arabs formed human pyramids, a powerfully built man at the base supporting the entire weight of nine of his fellow gymnasts, and set themselves revolving in the manner of Catherine wheels. Meanwhile, at the other end of the arena, the Japanese performers walked the tightrope and balanced barrels in the air with their feet, setting them to rapid revolutions with their toes. They also executed dangerous and intricate feats at the top of a long pole, held perpendicular by one of their number. In the centre, a long-haired dervish, in a robe of yellow silk, kept on spinning rapidly like a top throughout. In a display of something akin to perpetual motion, he never once shifted position and it made his spectators dizzy just to rest their eyes upon him. This idea of placing more than one focus of attention in the arena simultaneously was apparently inspired by Barnum & Bailey. At the conclusion, the whirling dervish, whom one might reasonably have expected to collapse into a giddy heap, instead skipped casually out of the arena, turning somersaults as he went.

'Cowboy Fun', a perennial favourite, was conducted on the usual lines, as the whole troupe of cowboys and Mexicans roped and mounted nineteen bucking broncos. The *Kilmarnock Standard* noted the presence of a cowboy named Sawder, stated recently to have won the bronco-bucking championship in America, as well as two others, Minor and Brennan, who had taken the successively next best places.[7]

The squadron of riders billed in the official programme as 'Cossacks, from the Caucasus of Russia' were increased to a full score for the 1904 season. Their truly amazing exhibition of horsemanship surpassed anything else to be seen in the show for agility, originality and daring. This unique brand of equestrianism combined a wild dash and individuality of style with the seemingly irreconcilable element of discipline. The *Dumfries & Galloway Saturday Standard* detailed one typically breathtaking manoeuvre:

> With his horse at full gallop he swoops down and picks up a handkerchief from the ground, holds fast by the saddle and seems to float in the air alongside, swings himself back to his seat and throwing his feet straight up in the air rests on his shoulders, or head, on the saddle, and finally crossing his stirrups over the saddle stands upright with his toes in them, and all this without diminishing his headlong pace.[8]

Surmounting the initial indifference of the spectators, the 'Cossacks' invariably departed the arena with generous and appreciative applause resounding in their ears.

Veterans of the US 6th Cavalry, in uniforms of the style adopted on the frontier, with forage caps in contradistinction to slouch hats, exhibited characteristic military exercises mounted on bareback horses from the Western range, culminating with several riders bestriding teams of two and even three horses simultaneously, one foot firmly planted on the backs of different animals.

The Deadwood Stage was drawn into the arena by six mules and broke into a panicked flight as Indian riders approached with hostile intent. Large numbers of riders were once again brought into the arena for this engaging spectacle. The scouts and cowboys rode to the rescue, repulsing the Indians, and the coach and its passengers were saved.

Indian boys raced bareback ponies, speed unchecked by a free rein, and displayed their full array of riding skills.

The most intensely thrilling act in the show, Carter the Cowboy Cyclist's sensational leap through space, involved an aerial dimension. Starting from a platform forty-five feet above the ground, Carter, a.k.a. George C. Davis, descended a steep track, steadily building momentum until he reached the raised incline or 'take-off' at the foot. Having attained his maximum velocity of eighty-five miles per hour, he was thrust abruptly into the air, to a maximum height of twenty-two feet, and across a chasm forty-two feet wide, describing an arc measuring fifty-six feet in extent. A cannon-shot automatically fired by means of a spring gun enhanced the dramatic effect of the ascent. Hanging for an instant in midair, his front wheel pointing skywards, he suddenly pitched forward to bring both wheels onto the horizontal and landed with a heavy thud upon a receiving platform on the other side, seven feet above the ground, to the intense and sonorous relief of the spectators. From there, he shot down an incline to ground level with such force that the bicycle and rider shot clean into the wing to the right of the grandstand. So perilous was this item that the management reserved the right to cancel in heavy rain or high wind. However, to the immense credit of all concerned, this proviso was seldom, if ever, invoked. Minor mishaps, however, were a regular occurrence.

The spectacle reached its thrilling climax as the Indians attacked a settlers' cabin, setting it ablaze. As the flames leapt in the air and all seemed lost, the homesteaders were relieved by the last-gasp arrival of reinforcements. Reversing the convention subsequently established by Hollywood, according to which Indians never attack at night, this sequence was seen to best advantage during the hours of darkness.

The show ended with a parting salute by the entire congress of rough riders and the cries of the Indians were once again the predominating sound as the horsemen passed out of the arena. Buffalo Bill himself was last to depart. The Cowboy Band played 'God Save the King' and the spectators made for the exits, barely able to credit the wonderful exhibition that had just passed before their eyes.

The entire performance was repeated in the evening, illuminated by seventy-six electric arc lamps suspended at regular intervals around the arena and augmented by a pair of powerful limelights operated from a high platform in front of the pavilion end, which highlighted all the striking features of the show.

Minstrel and Variety Concert

For a further sixpence, a 'Great Minstrel and Variety Concert', lasting half an hour, was held on a specially constructed stage, with appropriate scenery, in a corner of the main arena in front of the four-shilling seats, immediately after the end of the principal entertainment. Five hundred was a normal attendance.

This additional amusement, advertised in the official programme as 'presented by a company of America's foremost Singers, Dancers, Comedians, and Instrumentalists', was a further direct importation from *The Greatest Show on Earth*. Part of the rationale may have been to ensure that the audience broke up in stages.

The concert was scarcely noticed by the press but the *Falkirk Mail* was unusually forthcoming and offered the following commentary upon the specific attractions:

> The caste (*sic*) included Major Sitherland (Sutherland?), champion baton and gun spinner; Clark and Gold, banjoists, dancers and singers; Charles Whalen, comedian; Charles Diamond, original harp, song and dance artist; Mdlle. Beatrice, saxaphone (*sic*) soloist; and Boyd and Lovely, American negro (*sic*) comedians.[9]

After several hours of saturation entertainment of almost every character imaginable, formidably assaulting each one of their senses, the spectators made their way homeward, their minds no doubt swimming with a lifetime's supply of tangled memories.

Notes

1. 2 September 1904
2. Same date
3. Ibid.
4. *Arbroath Herald*, 25 August 1904
5. *Aberdeen Daily Journal*, 26 August 1904
6. 3 September 1904
7. Same date
8. Same date
9. 20 August 1904

16

GALASHIELS AND THE INDIANS

The first intimation of Buffalo Bill's coming took the form of a letter from his agent to Galashiels Burgh Council, dated the 11th of March 1904. A request for use of the town's Victoria Park for one day the following July, the precise date to be established later, was read out at a Council meeting on the 14th, at which it was unanimously resolved to grant the application. After various proposals and counter-proposals, the rental was fixed at £15.

In the early hours of Wednesday the 27th of July, the special trains moved northwards from Hawick, on the North British Railway Company line. The company took up occupation of almost the whole of Victoria Park, which survives today, its boundaries substantially as they were in 1904.

The entire camp was in place by seven in the morning. The dining tent was erected in seventeen minutes flat and breakfast was served just half an hour later.

Once again, the streets were thronged with thousands of excursionists. The more expensive tickets were available on the day of the show from A. Strachan's Piano Warehouse, located at 42, Bank Street.

The weather left little to complain of. A mist fell in the afternoon but soon lifted. The afternoon show was well attended and the more expensive seats were well filled. The attendance in the evening, however, was very much larger.

Robert Kerr, of the Abbotsford Hotel, provided accommodation and additional livery, the billposting arrangements were concluded with William R. Laing and a water supply was provided by J. B. Lumsden, the Town Clerk, at a cost of £1.

The *Scottish Border Record* carried a lyrical description of the Indian encampment:

> Something amazing was seen at every turn. Perhaps it was a highly coloured Sioux, with his feathered scalp waving above a painted face and a braided attire of as many colours as the rainbow can boast.
>
> 'How coola?' muttered the Sioux with an alarming expansive grin. And the joyous greeting of 'How are you, Big Little Sitting Standing Bull?' elicited the response 'Was-ahte', or may be 'Lil-a-was-ahte,' meaning 'good' or 'very good' as the case might be. It depended on whether he had had breakfast or not.
>
> Perhaps it was a comfortable squaw, with a little jingling papoose trotting by her side. The papooses wear many bells on their deerskin trousers, and when they run they sound like a rippling stream. They seemed to derive infinite enjoyment from the fact.[1]

THE INDIANS

The *Stirling Journal & Advertiser* carried an interesting proposition concerning the Indians:

> Several times while his 'Wild West' has been exhibiting in America, Colonel Cody has been called to Washington by the Government authorities and requested to proceed to the Indian reservation for the purpose of suppressing any uprisings which appear imminent. In consideration of the valuable services which he has rendered to the Government for many years, a special permit was granted to

Buffalo Bill to take representatives of the various tribes from their reservations to travel with his exhibition during its stay upon this side, the only stipulation exacted being that he would personally be responsible for their care and good treatment, and when the company completed their tour, see that they were safely returned to their reservations. In order to obtain this permission it was necessary to have a special law passed by the United States Congress, in as much as the Indians are not now allowed to leave their reservations, and it is very much doubted if such a concession could have been obtained by any other person than Buffalo Bill.[2]

This text clearly originated in one of John M. Burke's press releases as it is also attested in a number of other newspapers. It has to be doubted, however, if any such legislation ever existed since, following a landmark court case of United States *ex rel.* Standing Bear v Crook[3] in 1879, the legal basis for the government's continuing attempts to control the movements of its 'wards', the Indians, during peacetime was very far from clear.

However, a great deal of pressure was indeed brought to bear by federal officials, who strove to resign the Indians to a settled life within the confines of their reservations. The tipi had effectively vanished as a permanent dwelling two decades before. The more 'progressive' now made a living out of cultivating the ground, rearing cattle or breaking wild horses. Many, however, their glory days behind them, were content to subsist on government rations.

As the Dundee public was conveniently reminded by an article appearing in *The Courier*,[4] Kicking Bear had died in May and no doubt much of what spirit of resistance there remained perished with him. Performing in the Wild West was considered, in influential circles, a dangerous distraction from the programme of accelerated cultural assimilation to which the Indians were relentlessly subjected. A roving life, in which they were encouraged to breathe fresh life into the old ways, ran directly contrary to this objective.

The force of the official discouragement, together with its ultimate futility, is apparent from the notice served upon those who were gathering to enlist with the Wild West for the return to England:

Pine Ridge Agency, S.D.,
April 4, 1904.
TO INDIANS WHO ARE NOW CONGREGATED AT RUSHVILLE, NEBRASKA, FOR THE SUPPOSED PURPOSE OF JOINING BUFFALO BILL'S WILD WEST SHOW WITHIN THE NEXT FEW DAYS:-

You are hereby notified and warned that it is strictly against the rules and regulations of the Indian Office for Indians of Pine Ridge or any other agency to hire out or to join shows of any sort for exhibition purposes.

You are familiar with the rule which requires that when you are away from the agency you must first obtain a permit from the Agent. Non-compliance with this rule subjects you to punishment and the dropping of your names from the ration rolls.

You are hereby requested and ordered to return to the reservation, go to your homes, take care of your families, stock and other belongings, plant your gardens, fix up your fences and try to do something towards earning a living for yourselves and families. This will be much better for you than running around trying to join wild west shows.

(Signed) J. R. Brennan.
U.S. Indian Agent[5]

For the Indians, the 1904 season could scarcely have begun less auspiciously and there must have been several among their number who would shortly come to regret their disregard of Agent Brennan's admonitions.

In *Land of the Spotted Eagle*, Luther Standing Bear, who had been Lakota interpreter during the previous year's tour of England and Wales, recalls that, while he was preparing for the trip to Rushville, he was approached by a friend, *Wakan' Han'ska*, signifying 'Tall Holy'. Standing Bear attributes to this man the power of the *wakin'yan*', or Thunderbird, which conferred upon him 'great intuition and the ability to foretell events'.[6]

Tall Holy solemnly warned him not to go to Rushville but, although he respected his friend's abilities, Standing Bear continued with his journey just the same. At Rushville, amidst the bustle of excitement, two young men, who had been in England the previous year, approached Standing Bear and sought leave to withdraw from the party. They told him that on their journey, having stopped to camp for the night, their slumbers had been broken by a terrifying, and apparently simultaneous, vision. Around midnight, they were roused by the noise of a deafening crash and the screams of frightened people. Rushing outside into the stillness of the night, they realised that the nightmare was a premonition.

Luther Standing Bear concludes his account:

> Just before we reached Chicago the disaster occurred. Our train, while stopped for a few moments, was crashed into by a swift-traveling one, and a passenger car filled with Lakota braves was torn to splinters, and human bodies crushed in among the wrecked steel and timbers. When I returned home, recovering from what seemed fatal injuries, Wakan Hunska came to see me. 'Nephew,' he said, 'what I saw came to pass!'

A missive addressed to the Department of the Interior, United States Indian Service, by Agent J. R. Brennan, writing from Pine Ridge Agency on the 9th of April 1904, takes up the grim story. The accident described by Luther Standing Bear had taken place on the 7th. Three Indians – Comes Last, Philip Iron Tail and Kills Ahead – were killed and twenty injured. The injuries were naturally of varying degrees of seriousness. Luther Standing Bear himself sustained dislocations of the hip and collarbone and took no further involvement in the 1904 season. Iron Tail ('contusion of chest and abrasion of heel, not bad') and Philip Blue Shield ('two ribs broken'), along with four other Indians – Ellis Cut or Cuts, Abraham Good Crow, Good Crow and James Stand or Stands –

who suffered cuts and contusions, were able to continue on the tour.[7]

Considerable difficulties arise regarding the precise number and identities of the Indians participating in 1904. As with 1891–92, there is no surviving official roster or route book that would provide a definitive listing. Neither the official programme nor *The Rough Rider* for 1904 gives the least assistance in this respect. The publicity materials are inherently unreliable since they were always prone to exaggeration and other forms of misrepresentation.

One of the standard newspaper advertisements held out the prospect of '100 Redskin Braves'.[8] Another widely published version of the advert, however, conceded that this figure was inclusive of women and children as well:

100 AMERICAN INDIANS.
Genuine 'Blanket' Red Men, Chiefs, Warriors, Squaws, and Papooses from the Uncapappa, Brule, Ogallalla, Arapahoe, Cheyenne, Yankton, and Sioux Tribes.[9]

It will be recalled that this (dishonest) attempt to create the impression of a veritable convocation of several distinct Native American nations was an enduring feature of the Wild West show. With only marginal exceptions at most, all members of the entourage were Lakota from Pine Ridge Reservation, SD.

The *Aberdeen Daily Journal* narrated that there were 'nearly' one hundred North American Indians so that, even in its modified form, this conveniently rounded figure requires to be treated with considerable suspicion.[10]

The *Edinburgh Evening Dispatch* unusually advances the substantially lower figure of sixty-five.[11] This is supported by the *Aberdeen Free Press*, which refers to '60 or 70 Indians'[12] and, since the show's publicity machine is unlikely ever to have adjusted the true figure sharply downwards, it is contended that sixty-five was at least close to the true figure.

Sixty-five is precisely the aggregate figure entered on the passenger lists for the crossings from New York to Liverpool. Twenty-seven Indians arrived on the *Lucania*, on the evening of Saturday the 16th of April and a further thirty-eight followed on the *Umbria* a few days later.

There were fifty-six adult males, five women accompanying their husbands, two small boys and two infant girls. The *Huntly Express* subsequently carried a report of 'squaws with sleepy papooses on their backs',[13] presumably referring to the little girls.

The *Liverpool Daily News* had described the arrival of the *Lucania* and foreshadowed the subsequent newspaper adverts by maintaining that fifty Indians were on each ship – although this is inconsistent with the passenger lists – and by maintaining that the Indian contingent was composed of representatives of a variety of different tribes.[14]

All of those identified as having continued after sustaining injuries in the train crash and, presumably, the replacements for those who did not, sailed on the *Umbria*. The *Liverpool Daily News* blamed blizzards and other supervening causes for the delay that had prevented them from joining the *Lucania* but made no reference to the crash.

By way of comparison, just forty-six Indians appeared on the roster for 1902. Sixty-two names were listed for 1896. This further establishes that the figure of one hundred Indians travelling with the show in 1904 was pure hyperbole.

In the best traditions of double entry accounting, the books do not balance for the figure of sixty-five Indians does not match the passenger list for the return voyage. When the *Campania* sailed from Liverpool on the 22nd of October, only fifty-one Indians were on board. All were entered as being ordinarily resident at Pine Ridge Agency in South Dakota. On board were two women, two boys and one little girl. The remaining forty-six were adult males.

A detailed comparison of the inward and outward passenger lists reveals some alarming discrepancies, which are not easily explained away. As well as seventeen arriving but for whose return to the United States no record can be found, at least three individuals returned whose arrival is not documented. Perhaps some remained in England for the 1905 season and it may be presumed that some, as on past tours, were taken ill and returned home in mid season. It is also possible that others came to replace them.

The 'chiefs', at least at the outset of the tour, can be identified as Charging Hawk, Thomas American Horse, Whirlwind Horse, Two Elk, Samuel Lone Bear (also chief of the Indian police) and Young Sitting Bull, otherwise William Sitting Bull, a son of the famous chief. Neither Two Elk nor Sitting Bull appears on the *Campania* list. Both, however, had been entered as passengers on the *Lucania*, on the inward voyage. The apparent absence of any record relating to Young Sitting Bull's return to the United States has to be considered an irritating loose end since his (alleged) presence was a consistently reported attraction, standard references to him appearing in several Scottish newspapers.

However, as demonstrated in connection with the 1891–92 season, Buffalo Bill's publicity machine was not above advertising the presence of prominent Indians who had already returned home. The ostensible involvement of a son of the famous chief is clearly a continuing point of interest but, without an entry on a return passenger list or other supporting evidence, the presence of William Sitting Bull in Scotland cannot be authenticated as hard fact.

Alan Gallop, who, unfortunately, does not disclose his source, states that:

> The new recruits from Pine Ridge would also take part in the re-creation of the Battle of the Little Big Horn – Young Sitting Bull playing the part of his famous father and Johnnie Baker (wearing a long blond wig and built-up boots) in the role of General Custer.[15]

William Sitting Bull had appeared as one of the five 'chiefs' on the show's roster for 1902 but, beyond the associations of his illustrious surname, he appears to have left no great impression upon the historical record.

Iron Tail was the principal chief on the 1904 tour but his name is strangely absent from newspaper accounts of the first days of the tour. Although he arrived in England on board the *Umbria*, it is suspected that he took no active part in the show until he was sufficiently recovered from the injuries sustained in the train crash. In a photograph taken in Cornwall at the end of May, he appears using a crutch.

The Courier contains an informative account of a visit to the Wild West camp by a journalist, at some town or city preceding Dundee in the itinerary, most probably Edinburgh. Samuel Lone Bear acted as cicerone and it emerges that this urbane gentleman was a wholly different proposition from his predecessors on the 1891–92 tour. Of boyish appearance and in his late twenties, he could have had little or no first-hand recollection of the Indian wars:

> Chief 'Lone Bear' politely conducts us round the camp, introducing us to various men and whispering their Indian names to us so that they will be pleased at our attempts to talk Dakota. Like the rest of the younger men, he has been to school, and can talk English well, despite his modest disclaimer, and can write in a manner which would put to shame many a one who has had greater advantages. In the show, he, with another chief, leads the attack on General Custer, and conducts the Ghost Dance on horseback.

This is one of the few occasions on which any indication was ever given of who did exactly what in the show.

An encounter with the ubiquitous Iron Tail followed:

> The head chief, 'Iron Tail,' comes up with his red blanket, his fine Indian face wreathed in smiles, shaking hands cordially as he recognises a friend. 'Iron Tail' is a dignified warrior and not one to extend friendship too easily. On our first meeting with him some time previously, he was distinctly dubious, and it was only after a lengthy explanation and the exchange of some magic Indian word that he deemed us worthy of his friendship, and though he cannot speak a word of English, he extended his hand and said, 'Kola' (friend), and was all right. 'Iron Tail' has been in the wars, and took part in

the great battle of Little Bighorn, which now he helps to depict in mimic warfare.

There is also a rare reference to the Lakota interpreter. In contrast to Messrs Crager and Shangrau, he appears only in occasional glimpses in the press coverage this time around:

> The Indian interpreter, himself an Indian, named David Bull Bear, in virtue of his office does not wear the garb of his blanketed brethren, and gathers his long hair carefully under his sombrero. In his younger days he was in the battle of Pine Ridge, though he was then 'only a kid,' on the side of the whites. True to his early training, he now acts as guide to the emigrant train across the prairies, and is foremost in repelling the attacking Indians. He says there will not be any fighting among the Indians now, because they are civilised, and the old braves are learning the arts of peace.[16]

One significant difficulty arising is that he appears also to have gone by the name of David Arapaho. However, the reference in the *Courier* article is immediately familiar and an Indian matching the description can be identified in a few photos taken on the 1904 tour, notably the group photograph taken at Land's End on the 31st of May.

The otherwise unnamed wife of Spotted Weasel and Mrs Short Bear, also known as Kills Deer, appear on the *Campania* list but none of the other three women can positively be established as having continued with the entourage until the end of the tour. This accords with the *Falkirk Herald and Midland Counties Journal*, which recorded the presence in the opening review of 'two squaws riding in alone'.[17] The *Dumfries and Galloway Saturday Standard* commented upon the presence of 'a couple of corpulent squaws'[18] in the same context.

Notice, however, the statement in the *Courier* article: 'The squaws, of whom there are several here, are square, solid ladies, with their hair neatly braided at each side.'

The Courier also mentions the children with the party:

> One tiny boy is dressed up like his father, and as he capers about he rattles the bunch of feathers on his back like a little porcupine. In the ghost dance no one joins with greater zest than does the little brave Spotted Weasel. Small Laura Short Bear, a little maid, with her funny little face painted yellow and red, and her quaint little dress, stares unblinkingly at her visitors.

It is unclear whether the 'tiny boy' refers to 'the little brave Spotted Weasel' (first name Washington) or to Willie Ghost Dog, the other little boy in the party, both known from the *Lucania* list. *The Scotsman* recorded that 'two chubby papooses'[19] participated in the war dance. It will be noticed that 'ghost dance' and 'war dance' were now presented as direct synonyms.

Only about half of the adult Indians, judging by the ages entered on the passenger lists, could have been alive at the time of the Custer battle of just over twenty-eight years previously. Only about one quarter of the men could possibly have been combatants, even if one fixes the minimum age at the almost impossibly low figure of twelve. These were a new generation of Indians, for whom the old free life was at best a fading memory.

Buffalo Bill's publicity materials did much to disseminate and reinforce the negative stereotypes to which the British public had already been exposed on previous tours. The Indian's role within the entertainment – which in due course of time would be inherited by his Hollywood successor – was purely that of wild aggressor and implacable opponent to the predestined spread of civilisation. Once again, (gravely misplaced) imagery from the literature of the colonial period of a century and a half before was promiscuously employed. The offensive words 'squaw' and 'papoose', designating 'woman' and 'child' respectively and both originating in the eastern woodlands, were further established in English usage as if they were authentic Lakota terminology.

As the *Border Advertiser* obligingly proclaimed:

> The American Indian, who is now fast assimilating with the White Man, is disappearing from the stage of life as far as regards his

picturesque personality. In a few years, there will no longer be any Blanket Indian, so fast has civilisation spread her luminous wings over the American Continent.

Colonel Cody brings with him some splendid specimens of these, the really last of the Mohicans.[20]

Almost every statement concerning the Indians in the press releases emphasised the cruellest and most warlike aspects of their racial characteristics, with ubiquitous references to torture and scalping. For the *Hawick Express*, they were 'the decadent race of Indians'.[21] The judgement of history was upon them.

The image of the American Indian consistently presented was an amalgam of every negative preconception that had been accumulated over four hundred years of more or less incessant warfare. The stage was set for yet another curtain call for the vanishing race.

Meanwhile, back in Galashiels ...

Even after Buffalo Bill had come and gone, the dust generally took time to settle and there were often sundry miscreants and wrong-doers to be rounded up and censured. Galashiels was no exception.

The case against Patrick O'Donnel, on a charge of obstructing the roadway, was heard in the Police Court on Monday the 1st of August. A chipped potato vendor, he had, on the evening of the show, taken up a strategic position at the gateway to Victoria Park just as thousands of people were departing. He disregarded a police request to move his cart and it had to be removed by force.

A fine of five shillings was imposed.

Notes

1 29 July 1904
2 26 August 1904
3 Case No. 14,891 Circuit Court, D. Nebraska 25 F. Cas. 695; 1879 US

App. LEXIS 1667; 5 Dill. 453. See Dee Brown, *Bury My Heart at Wounded Knee*, Chapter 15, 'Standing Bear Becomes a Person'. Note that this Standing Bear belonged to the Ponca tribe and was not related to any of the other people of that name who are referred to in this book.

4   13 August 1904
5   Document J. R. B. (L), copy held at the Buffalo Bill Historical Center
6   p. 72
7   Copy of Brennan's missive held at the Buffalo Bill Historical Center
8   For example, the *Stirling Journal and Advertiser*, 2 September 1904
9   For example, the *Perthshire Advertiser and Strathmore Journal*, 26 August 1904
10 17 August 1904
11 6 and 9 August 1904
12 30 August 1904
13 2 September 1904
14 18 April 1904
15 *Buffalo Bill's British Wild West*, p. 237
16 13 August 1904
17 17 August 1904
18 17 September 1904
19 9 August 1904
20 26 July 1904
21 29 July 1904

17

INTO THE WEST OF SCOTLAND

Colonel W. F. Cody

Motherwell

The arrival of Buffalo Bill on the 28th of July, just at the close of the local Fair holidays, brought a welcome distraction from the impending parliamentary by-election, then being keenly contested in Lanarkshire's Middle Ward. The camp was pitched in the field adjoining the Tramway Power House, on the main road to Hamilton. This location was ideally placed for access by streetcars from the surrounding districts as it contained the depot and headquarters of the Lanarkshire Tramway & Omnibus Company Ltd. Trams were a relative innovation in the district, having been introduced to Motherwell only the previous year.

It was probably through design that the showground, then lying at a distance west of the burgh boundaries, was almost equally convenient for the inhabitants of the adjacent town of Hamilton and it is not difficult to visualise animated crowds of people streaming briskly eastwards across the Clyde Bridge.

The Advancemen

Ground rental of £20 was payable on the day of the show to one 'Robert Hamilton, Low Motherwell'. This was in all probability the same Mr R. Hamilton who had rented out a field on Airbles Road to Barnum & Bailey five years previously. The contract further provided that the manure and refuse were to be left on the ground. The water supply was obtained from Motherwell Town Council, for which one pound and five shillings was payable to James McCallum, the Burgh Surveyor.

A clear indication of the dramatic manner in which most people – in 'Steelopolis' and elsewhere – received their first intimation of the Wild West's advent appears in the *Motherwell Standard*'s 'Local Notes' column:

> The townspeople were this week treated to an object lesson in the pushful Yankee methods of advertising. On Tuesday a small army of billposters and advance agents swooped down upon Motherwell and literally took possession of the streets. The hoardings were rapidly covered with illustrated posters, special boards containing stirring pictures were planked down at intervals all along the principal thoroughfares, illustrated periodicals were scattered broadcast in the town, and within a couple of hours after the arrival of the 'army' it was pretty generally known in the district that 'Buffalo Bill' would visit Motherwell on the 28th.[1]

The Tuesday referred to was the 12th of July, two weeks and two days prior to the show's arrival. Essentially the same paragraph appeared in the *Hamilton Herald* on the 15th, with only a couple of minor modifications. The first newspaper adverts appeared on the 14th and 15th respectively. The advertising campaign did not, however, extend to either of Hamilton's newspapers.

The billposters engaged were Matthew McMillan, of 2, Muir Street; Alexander Morrison, of Condie's Buildings, East Cross; and A. F. Aitkenhead, of Dechmont View, Uddingston. Mr Aitkenhead's remit was to take care of business in Bothwell and Uddingston. A. E. Peachey, McMillan's local manager, got into hot water with his employers for contracting at a rate of 1½d per sheet, although this had been the sum paid on the occasion of Barnum & Bailey's visit. A note on the advanceman's log referred to Peachey's desire to work on Buffalo Bill's advance staff and directed that, if he were to be discharged by his present employer on this account, he was to be taken on.

The advanceman's log preserves an interesting source for the various transactions entered into for the coming spectacle, as his department travelled ahead of the show by rail in the advertising car, otherwise car number 1.

On the evidence of a standard contract surviving from 1893, the billposting firms did not necessarily put the posters up. That was done by the advancemen themselves. What was contracted for was the 'exclusive privilege' of posting bills and the billposters' cooperation in ensuring that they were not defaced, covered or destroyed until after the expiry of the agreement.

The showground would generally have been secured months ahead but there were details to be settled and a water supply to be obtained. On the show's arrival, large water wagons were filled at the town's supply and drawn into camp by draught horses.

Hotel accommodation had to be arranged for Buffalo Bill's staff of agents and representatives as it was in the nature of their duties that their movements did not precisely coincide with that of the show itself. In Motherwell, this was provided by William Duffy of the Royal Hotel, at rates of 1/6d for meals and 2/- for lodgings. He also supplied the additional livery, three country teams and two town wagons, apparently used by the advancemen themselves.

The sheer scale of the operation presented something of a challenge and the Caledonian Railway Company was obliged to make special arrangements at their Merry Street depot for the accommodation of the show vehicles, with special rails being laid and the entrance widened.

Indians, Cossacks, Japanese and other performers made an appearance on the streets of Motherwell and the attention which they attracted was a powerful factor in publicising the show.

The Tramway Power House lay on the south side of the Hamilton Road, on a site now bounded by Malcolm Street and Nigel Street on the west and east respectively. It is unclear whether the showground lay to its immediate left or right but, either way, the open spaces then extending to Motherwell's south-west have long since been built over and transformed quite beyond recognition.

COATBRIDGE

Weather conditions in the 'Iron Burgh' on Friday the 29th of July were all that could be desired. The venue was the West End Public Park, for which a rental of £10 plus £25 deposit was payable to John M. Alston, the Town Clerk.

Lodgings were obtained at the Royal Hotel, then under the management of Robert C. Crozier, with meals charged at 1/6d and lodgings at the same figure, yielding a total bill of £5 3/6d.

The local billposters were engaged – John Mills of 10, Ross Street, Coatbridge, and John Gibson of 3, Broomknall Street, Airdrie.

Livery was provided by James Munro, of 5, Main Street, Coatbridge, consisting of two country teams at 15/-, with an option on one or more town wagons.

Structural alterations were needed once again. Part of the wall at the West End Park was demolished in order to facilitate access for the show's wagons.

An outbreak of smallpox, the dread disease which had claimed so many Native American lives over the centuries since first contact, was causing much concern in Coatbridge and Airdrie and regrettably coincided with Buffalo Bill's visit. In 1904, outbreaks were still a regular occurrence and there was a smallpox hospital somewhere on the periphery of most Scottish towns.

West End Park still exists today, within the triangle of land formed by Blair Road, King Street and Bank Street. It was originally Greenmuirs, the pleasure park of the nearby Drumpellier estate. It came to be known as the Yeomanry Park but, by 1904, had acquired its present title.

Dumbarton

The entourage moved on to Dumbarton overnight, arriving around three in the morning of Saturday the 30th, at the town's Lanarkshire & Dunbartonshire goods station, and took up occupation of virtually the entire surface area of Meadow Park or 'Broad Meadow', as it was alternatively known.

The advanceman's log refers to 'Meadow Park, belonging to the City' and a rental of twelve pounds and ten shillings was paid to John Henderson, the Chief Constable.

Griffin would later recall his impressions of this particular site: '[O]ur tents were pitched in another beautiful park, with all the trimmings – lakes, swans, etc., while Giant Ben Lomond, famous as the rendezvous of Rob Roy, loomed up in the distance.'[2]

Elizabeth Grame Hartley, a celebrated poetess from Alexandria, graced the front page of the *Lennox Herald*, with her epic ten-stanza 'A Welcome to "Buffalo Bill"'.[3] This was essentially an extended and updated version of an earlier eight-line opus that she had originally penned to greet the show's arrival in Glasgow back in 1891 and which appears in Alan Gallop's *Buffalo Bill's British Wild West*.[4]

Dumbarton's strategic position on the north bank of the Clyde estuary provided the inspiration for the second stanza:

> Thou, in war's wild commot'on nursed,
> Who danger wont to mock,
> We're proud that thou should visit first
> Our old town of the rock.

This is certainly a piece of artistic licence – Dumbarton was only 'first' if you find some grounds for disregarding Hawick, Galashiels, Motherwell and Coatbridge. But it has to be conceded that 'We're proud that thou should visit fifth' doesn't have quite the same emphatic ring.

A kindly and heart-warming act on the part of an unspecified group of show employees was recounted in the *Lennox Herald*.[5] Early in the morning, a small and down-at-heel laddie, who had already attained the status of a local character, presented himself on Dumbarton Common and befriended the labourers who were engaged in erecting the tents. He made it his business to entertain the showmen, singing them several songs and performing a 'break-down' dance. The men reciprocated by feeding him, washing him and replacing his ragged clothing with a completely new outfit. They treated him to a visit to the sideshows and a box at the main performance. As he took his leave of his friends that night, they presented him with a parting gift of about five shillings in cash. No doubt that wee boy had occasion to remember for the rest of his life, with gratitude and affection, that day of days, on which real Sioux Indians had pitched their tipis on Dumbarton Common.

At least one other local youngster could be counted on to keep the memory alive. Fully two weeks later, an intrepid one-legged laddie from nearby Vale of Leven's Cannon Row was still providing a remarkable – and free – nightly entertainment by the banks of the River Leven. He had taken to riding a rickety old bicycle down Dummie's Brae at breakneck speed, all to the manifest amusement of the local residents and in homage, it seems, to 'Carter, the Cowboy Cyclist'. How it was that the young daredevil had come to part with his missing leg is unfortunately not recorded and I have to confess myself curious to know just how much longer he succeeded in keeping the remaining one!

The lakes and swans referred to by Griffin are sadly no more but the flat expanse of Dumbarton Common survives as a public amenity. In 1998 it was the subject of litigation in the Court of Session, after an (unsuccessful) application was made by the local authority to dispose of it as the site of a proposed Sheriff Court building.

Glasgow

The advancemen experienced some surmountable difficulties with the local billposters, who insisted on having their bills delivered at least three days before the Glasgow Fair holidays started on Saturday the 16th of July.

On Sunday the 31st, the show made a triumphant return to Glasgow for a week's engagement from Monday the 1st until Saturday the 6th of August. The first train rolled into the Caledonian Railway's Gushetfaulds goods station on the south side at half past three in the morning, the others following shortly thereafter. The process of unloading began at five.

The Stars and Stripes and the Union flag fluttered gaily over the Third Lanarkshire Rifle Volunteers Drill Ground, Dixon Road, a location admirably served by Crosshill Railway Station, on the Cathcart line. It was wedged between Aikenhead Road and the recently vacated (and original) Cathkin Park, the home of the Third Lanarkshire Rifle Volunteers Football Club (Third Lanark) – an offshoot of the regiment – from 1875 until 1903. The northern extremity lay just above the eastern extension of Allison Street. It was known locally as the 'Baun Park'. 'Baun' is apparently 'Parliamo Glasgow' for 'band', doubtless an allusion to its military associations. Rental of £120 was paid two weeks in advance to Captain John Davidson of Oldfield, Pollokshaws. The site has long since been built over and is occupied today by an undistinguished housing estate.

In the course of the day, local people turned out in their thousands but had to be content with glimpses of the various comings and goings through the uprights of the enclosure. (The barricade around the ground blew down in a storm c. 1910 and was never replaced.) The Indians, attired in their native paints and costumes as if they were about to commence a performance, proved the foremost objects of fascination.

More privileged were the several Glasgow pressmen. They attended by invitation and, on entering the enclosure by the east end of Dixon

'YOUR FATHERS THE GHOSTS'

Avenue, were accorded a guided tour of the establishment by Messrs Burke, Wells and Small, Buffalo Bill's press agents.

Colonel Cody cordially received this deputation in his personal tent, which 'looks out on the Cathkin Hills, which if lacking the magnificence of the Rockies, is (*sic*) not without pictorial charm under the August sun'.[6]

The newsmen found the Colonel enjoying the society of his frequent companion, Chief Iron Tail, whose bright yellow shirt, with points of red, and brilliant blanket contrasted sharply with the dark and sober suits of the Glaswegians. They were slightly at a disadvantage when Iron Tail greeted them with 'Hau kola', approximately translating from Lakota as 'Hello, friend', and conducted a pipe-smoking ceremony in their honour. An interpreter was also on hand. The gentlemen of the press were afterwards entertained to dinner, which was served in the dining tent at four.

A priceless and unique photographic record of the Glasgow sojourn survives in the form of five images captured by local amateur photographer Thomas Lindsay, then aged twenty-two. Two of these depict the emigrant train sequence in progress, while a third splendidly portrays an Imperial Japanese Cavalryman. The two remaining depict groups of Indians and local people on Dixon Road; these have an admirable 'fly on the wall' quality to them, which is entirely absent from the heavily contrived posed photographs professionally taken elsewhere.

According to information passed down by Thomas McAllister, the Indians frequented the pubs in nearby Polmadie, where they soon placed themselves on friendly terms with the locals.[7]

'Carter the Cowboy Cyclist' created a minor sensation in Glasgow. On the opening day, strong winds forced him to think twice about his leap. After a few minutes' delay had kept the spectators in a state of nervous tension, they watched, in what the *Glasgow Herald* termed 'breathless excitement',[8] as the cowboy successfully completed his stunt, much to the 'comfort and relief'[9] of all present. But, on Friday afternoon, Carter swerved to the right and fell from the wooden staging to the ground, as a shiver ran through the crowd. Showing no sign of serious injury, he jumped instantly to his feet, mounted a horse in the usual fashion and rode away to wild applause.

The crowds which turned out in Glasgow were particularly enormous and, over a comparable period of time, greatly exceeded those of any other city on this side of the Atlantic, with 11,000 people watching the opening performance. As the week went on, the attendances steadily increased, as interest in the show built up an unstoppable momentum. After the massive demand for seats that was encountered on the first two nights, it was decided, for the first time in the history of the show, to provide seating for an additional 4,000 spectators on the Wednesday evening. Even this was found to be insufficient and thousands were again turned away. A total of 30,000 people attended the performances that day and the *Daily Record and Mail* estimated that, if all the spectators who had been present in the evening had been placed shoulder to shoulder in military fashion, the line would have extended to beyond the town of Johnstone or to a distance of ten and a half miles.[10] It was the biggest-ever attendance for any one single day in all the twenty-one years' existence of the show but even this was exceeded on the Thursday, with 16,000 at the afternoon performance and 18,000 in the evening. Once again, thousands more were turned back.

On the Friday evening, it was deemed prudent to relieve congestion by admitting the audience to the arena at six thirty. By seven the arena was full of people and, as the long and tedious wait began, someone struck up a traditional Scottish song. Everyone present joined in and kept up singing until the show commenced. Buffalo Bill recalled, 'Everybody sang with great heartiness, and the effect as heard in my tent was remarkably good.'[11]

On the morning of Saturday the 6th, Chief Lone Bear made a visit to the Glasgow Health Exhibition, held under the auspices of the Sanitary Institute, in the Exhibition Buildings on Duke Street, the Wild West's home back in 1891–92. He was highly impressed with the various exhibits and was presented with a sample of baby food and a box of chocolates for the 'papooses' at home. He professed regret that his obligation to return for the show's afternoon performance denied him the opportunity of seeing the exhibition in full swing.

In a week that had been remarkably free of mishaps, 175,000 people saw the show. Not one single accident befell the spectators for, as Buffalo Bill himself acknowledged in his final interview, the people had been most orderly in their conduct and amenable to the directions of the staff. Buffalo Bill must have deeply regretted his absence of foresight in booking for one week only. Much longer stands in major English cities had been included on the 1902–1903 tour and it is difficult to conceive of a single valid reason why the same consideration could not have been accorded to the second city of the British Empire.

Taking his leave of the reporters before entraining for Edinburgh, Buffalo Bill fired a parting shot:

> Please express through your journal to the citizens of Glasgow my heartiest thanks for and profound appreciation of the magnificent support they gave us during the week. Glasgow has beaten all records for attendances on this side of the Atlantic, and comes second to the Chicago World's Fair record in 1893. You may take it from this that I am more than satisfied. I expected much from Glasgow, but not so much.[12]

The Lawmen

Charles O'Neill, a 'well-known thief',[13] then residing at 144, Trongate, was apprehended in the act of attempting to pick pockets within the Wild West grounds, after he was observed acting in a suspicious manner. He was brought before Bailie Taggart at the Queen's Park Police Court and sentenced to forty days imprisonment.

The Wild West brought problems in crowd control without obvious precedent and an associated wave of petty crime. In rising to the challenge, local constabularies were placed under the able direction of Assistant Superintendent Christopher C. Murphy, formerly of the Pinkerton National Detective Agency. He had numbered among the most successful and famous of the New York detectives, before devoting his career to travelling with the show, and discharged a similar capacity for Barnum & Bailey in 1898 and 1899. It was a matter of considerable professional pride to Mr Murphy that such was the extent to which he and his associates had brought the criminal element to bewilderment and ruination in one place after another, there had not been one successful theft within the showgrounds for fully four years.

It is a striking instance of the complex cultural interplay between Scotland and the United States that the Pinkerton National Detective Agency's founder, Allan Pinkerton (1819–84), was a native of the Gorbals. The precise birthplace of the original 'Gorbals diehard' was a squalid third-floor tenement flat at the junction of Muirhead Street and Rutherglen Loan, within ready walking distance to the north of the Gushetfaulds goods yard, Buffalo Bill's point of arrival and departure. By a singular set of coincidences, James Mackay[14] locates the influential lawman's birthplace upon the site of the present Glasgow Procurator Fiscal's Office, while that of his baptism now accommodates the Sheriff Court of Glasgow and Strathkelvin.

Notes

1 14 July 1904
2 *Four Years in Europe with Buffalo Bill*, p. 45
3 30 July 1904
4 p. 162
5 6 August 1904
6 *Evening Times*, 1 August 1904
7 Letter from Thomas McAllister to Barry Dubber, 4 April 1990
8 2 August 1904
9 *Daily Record and Mail*, 2 August 1904
10 4th August 1904
11 *Daily Record and Mail*, 8 August 1904
12 Ibid.
13 *Daily Record and Mail*, 6 August 1904
14 *Allan Pinkerton – The Eye Who Never Slept*, pp. 21 and 22

18

EDINBURGH, FALKIRK AND FIFE

Edinburgh

The work of transporting the show to Edinburgh began immediately after the final Glasgow performance. The trains arrived at Princes Street Station at around five the following morning, Sunday the 7th of August.

Princes Street Station then stood at the western extremity of Princes Street and was the Edinburgh terminal of the Caledonian Railway Company. In 1904, it presented credible competition to the North British Railway Company's more famous and enduring Waverley Station but, in later decades, fell into decline and was closed during the Beeching era.

The horsemen and wagons rode out into Shandwick Place and thence turned toward the West End, heading for the showgrounds in Gorgie, by way of West Maitland Street, Dalry Road and Gorgie Road, proceeding past Heart of Midlothian's Tynecastle Park and turning finally into Westfield Road. Here, a highly successful week's residency, from Monday the 8th until Saturday the 13th, lay in prospect.

Westfield Road was the location of Damhead Farm. Ground was rented from W. S. Robertson, dairyman, at £75 for the week's tenure.

Presumably Mr Robertson was the nearest equivalent to a 'cattle baron' that Gorgie could muster. The location was widely advertised as Gorgie Road so it may be taken that public access was by way of Westfield Street.

A retrospective article, 'Wagons Roll . . . it's off to Gorgie with Buffalo Bill' claimed to identify the site: 'Today, strangely enough, 80 years on, although Gorgie Station is no more, the waste ground has survived – a desolate spot, lying between Gorgie and Slateford Roads, the property of the Post Office.'[1] However, this information is highly suspect since the location recorded in the advanceman's log lay on the opposite side of Gorgie Road.

The contract specified that Mr Robertson was to make an entrance fifty feet wide and also provide ground nearby for the horse and cook tents, if so required.

As the *Edinburgh Evening News* observed: 'Quietly, almost surreptitiously, as if the sanctity of the Scottish Sabbath was the first consideration, the great exposition of Western life took up its quarters at Gorgie yesterday morning, hours before the city was awake.'[2]

But the old bastion of Edinburgh was not taken entirely by surprise. Once again, a crowd of people had turned out at the station to witness the arrival and unloading.

At the showground, the canvas city, covering an area of roughly five acres, was once more in place by eight in the morning.

The venue was well located for the nearby Gorgie Road tramway terminus and the Edinburgh and District Tramway Company Ltd laid on a special service. It was equally well favoured by the North British Railway's suburban service, which conveyed its passengers to the adjacent Gorgie Station, virtually at the doors of the show. The North British Railway ran special trains before each performance, from Musselburgh, Joppa, Portobello, Leith, Abbeyhill, Waverley and Haymarket, with a return service departing at 4.15 p.m. and 10.15 p.m.

Malcolm Cant, in his book *Gorgie and Dalry*, states that an amphitheatre, providing cover for 18,000 spectators, was already in place.[3] However, this information has to be seriously doubted as

Mr Cant's source appears to be the *Edinburgh Evening News* of the 8th of August 1904, in which the 'amphitheatre' turns out actually to be a clear reference to the show's own canvas arena which, it is respectfully suggested, he has misconstrued.

The ground surface was somewhat rough. The same journal commented on the following day that 'as a show ground, the rough and ready nature of the place leaves almost of necessity a little to be desired . . .'

The overall impression created by the contemporary press coverage, as well as by the advanceman's log, is that the site was quite simply a 'field'.[4] *The Scotsman*[5] and the *Edinburgh Evening Dispatch*[6] specifically refer to the presence of the canvas marquee.

A party of journalists was accorded a conducted tour of the showgrounds during the relative quiet of the Sunday afternoon. They were entertained by Colonel Cody in his private tent and were introduced to Iron Tail, Lone Bear and a few other Indian chiefs. A peace pipe was quickly produced and a ceremony was conducted, similar to the one which had taken place in Glasgow the week before.

The description of the establishment witnessed by the newsmen provides an insightful picture of a Sunday in the life of the performers:

> A glance at the encampment of the Redskins revealed an interesting side of savage life under civilised conditions, and a visit to the large tent which provides a home for the widely-assorted members of the world's congress of rough-riders found quite a little army of these enjoying their leisure in various ways. Some were sleeping, others, careless of Sabbatarian ideas, were playing at cards; here and there were small groups smoking and chatting.[7]

During the afternoon and the early part of the evening, the police had a busy time, in consequence of the 'extraordinary numbers' of sightseers who gathered outside the enclosure and watched the proceedings with keen interest.[8] In the meantime, the *Edinburgh Evening Dispatch* went as far as to say that *most* of the company had absented themselves from the showground and were sightseeing in Edinburgh.[9]

During his original research on Buffalo Bill's Scottish venues undertaken during the early 1990s, Barry Dubber interviewed Mrs Christine Carse, who was born in the Damside Cottages, Gorgie, at some time in the final years of the nineteenth century. Her father, Dick Heseltine, was a well-known local character, who worked as a boiler man in the employment of Thomas Topping, builder, whose yard on Wheatfield Road lay adjacent to the showground. In an undated letter to Barry, Mrs Carse related her first-hand recollections:

> I am 93 years of age, but have lots of memories of B. B. My father's yard was next to the show & I spent all my time running in and out of the show. I remember him well with his leather coat & fringes & he always carried a rifle. I remember touching it once & got a sharp clout & told never ever to touch guns (I never did). I also remember his Indians & Cowboys . . . I used to run around after B. B. & he used to pull my long black hair . . .

Large crowds turned out for all twelve of the week's shows and the evening performance on the first day was attended by Lord Provost Sir Robert Cranston, who was accompanied by Lady Cranston.

That opening day was favoured with brilliant summer weather, enabling it to be viewed to full advantage.

On Wednesday the 10th, the 'San Toy' company, who were appearing at the city's Lyceum Theatre, attended as invited guests of Colonel Cody. A number of the young actresses were accorded the privilege of riding as passengers in the Deadwood Stage, during the sequence in which it was attacked by the Indians.

Miserable weather conditions set in on the Thursday but this did not prevent a total of almost 140,000 people seeing the show in the course of that week in Edinburgh. As in Glasgow, the attendances tended to rise as the week went on.

The ancient Scottish capital was singled out for specific mention by Charles Eldridge Griffin, who deemed it to be one of the grandest cities he had ever visited. Acutely conscious of the traditional Glasgow–Edinburgh rivalry, he concluded: 'While Edinburgh is "in it" for beauty, it does not compare so favorably with Glasgow for business, notwithstanding our success was very pronounced.'[10]

Two stories concerning Winchester rifles are associated with Buffalo Bill's Edinburgh sojourn. The first of these found coverage in a number of contemporary newspaper reports. On Saturday the 13th, Buffalo Bill acquired a Winchester rifle alleged to have been used by Sitting Bull at the Battle of the Little Bighorn in 1876, together with proper identification papers. It is possible that the rifle was purchased at an auction although the idea that it chanced to come up for sale precisely when Buffalo Bill was in town presents an unlikely coincidence. While Sitting Bull was exiled in Canada with a band of followers, during 1877–81, the weapon passed into the hands of a Scottish nobleman, Sir Thomas Dawson Brodie, Bart of Idvies, either though gift or sale. On his subsequent return to Scotland, Sir Thomas brought his acquisition with him.

Colonel Cody, apparently feeling the need for a break from the normal routine, passed the weekend in Edinburgh, instead of travelling to Falkirk with the remainder of the entourage. He no doubt recalled his day trip to Scotland's capital more than a dozen years previously with some affection and desired to repeat the experience.

He wrote a letter home to his niece Josie, headed 'The Royal Hotel, Edinburgh' and dated the 13th of August 1904, the day of the concluding performances in the Scottish capital and on which he purchased Sitting Bull's rifle. It is brief and mostly unremarkable in its contents. One sentence however does stand out and attests to Cody's positive frame of mind at this time: 'I am feeling first rate and business is big.'[11]

The second story concerns a rifle that Buffalo Bill allegedly left behind. In 1946, the police offered an amnesty for the handing in of illegally held guns and ammunition. One of the many weapons surrendered was a Winchester rifle which, it was alleged, had belonged to Buffalo Bill. Commentary on the affair appears in George Baird's *Edinburgh Theatres, Cinemas and Circuses 1820–1963*. Baird avers:

'Chief Superintendent Robert Cribbes, C.I.D, told me, "Buffalo Bill left a Winchester rifle in St Cuthbert Stables, Grove Street, where his circus 'stood in equipage.'"[12]

A link to the stables cannot be corroborated, nor can the Winchester rifle's provenance be established beyond reasonable doubt. However, putting the various elements together, a very definite hypothesis emerges. It should be recalled that the contract with Mr Robertson called for him to provide additional space for the horses if necessary. This is significant and it cannot have been a standard term as Edinburgh is the only Scottish venue in connection with which such a note appears. It must have been realised that the space available, around five acres, would be insufficient and that additional accommodation would be required – the show would normally occupy an area of ten acres. This is confirmed by the *Edinburgh Evening Dispatch*, which stated that the smaller of the two stabling tents was placed in an adjoining lot.[13] It was also commented that the site was somewhat smaller than the show was normally accustomed to and that it had been necessary to make an effort to utilise the available space economically.

It might well therefore be that some portion of the equipment was put into storage at the stables in Grove Street. Most logically, this would have consisted of the wagons and other equipment utilised in the work of transportation, none of which would have been needed from the show's arrival until its departure, an interval of almost a week. Having replaced his old Winchester (the one handled by Christine Carse?) with the rifle formerly belonging to Sitting Bull, the old one might well have been deemed surplus to requirement. It is entirely reasonable to suppose that this was one of Buffalo Bill's frequent acts of spectacular open-handedness and that he left the gun at the St Cuthbert stables as a characteristically idiosyncratic token of his gratitude for kind assistance received in the course of the week.

The precise facts of the matter will probably never be known but the foregoing is at least a reasonable hypothesis.

Only one photograph is known from Edinburgh, a studio portrait of three 'Cossacks' – Aleksandre Murvanidze, Simon Oragvelidze and Pavle Makharadze – taken at the studio of Ovinius Davis, at 16, Princes Street.

FALKIRK

It had clearly been a week of portents and prodigies in the town of Falkirk, as was duly observed by 'Argus' in the 'Casual Comments' column of the *Falkirk Herald & Midland Counties Journal* on the 17th of August 1904. A perfectly ordinary domestic hen resident in the burgh and of previously unblemished character succeeded in 'setting all natural laws and precedents at defiance' by bringing forth two chickens from the one egg. No less remarkable was the circumstance that 'the strange, eventful history of the gas works question' was finally resolved and, at long last, excavations for this important municipal undertaking were underway – as 'Argus' observed, the millennium felt appreciably closer. Somewhere towards the end of the column, mention was eventually made of the visit of Buffalo Bill.

The entourage arrived in town on Sunday the 14th of August, by means of the North British Railway at the Springfield Goods and Mineral Depot, on the present site of the Central Retail Park, a short distance to the north-east of Grahamston Station. The company thence proceeded to Randyford Farm, on the south side of the Grangemouth Road.

The former site of Randyford Farm has long since been built over and is now occupied by the housing estate directly opposite Falkirk College and is commemorated in the names of Randyford Street and Randyford Road. The neighbourhood is certainly more noteworthy than first appearances might suggest for a little further along towards Grangemouth lay Westfield Farm, which had itself hosted *The Greatest Show on Earth*, for one day in 1899, and is now occupied by the Falkirk Stadium.

The site rental was £6. The water supply was contracted from Charles Massey of the Falkirk and Larbert Water Trust, at £1 for the two days.

The tents were pitched long before the first of the town's steeple bells began to ring out but the erection of the canvas walls of the arena was postponed until the Monday morning. As little work as possible was done on the Sabbath to permit the company their customary day of rest. Sergeant Smith and three constables, all placed under the direction of Mr Murphy, were on hand at different parts of the field to deter and restrain the excessively curious among the crowds of local people who were continuously present from morning to night.

One man who made the journey along the Grangemouth Road that Sunday, and probably wished he hadn't, was John Sullivan, the warder of the corporation model lodging house. While strolling along Kerse Lane, at some time between eleven and twelve in the forenoon, he received an unwelcome and probably unnecessary reminder that gratuitous violence was a concept entirely familiar to the lieges of Falkirk and by no means a preserve of the North American Plains. He was ambushed and set upon by one Alfred Monson, a labourer of Garrison Place, who laid about him with as much vim and enthusiasm as Buffalo Bill's Indians ever set about the Deadwood Stage. Monson punched his unfortunate victim in the face, to the effusion of blood. The case was one of several which came before Bailie Russell at the Falkirk Burgh Police Court on the Monday morning, when the Procurator Fiscal led evidence that the attack had been carried out without any provocation whatsoever. A somewhat different version of events was offered by Monson but was not accepted. Monson was fined thirty shillings, with the option of twenty days imprisonment.

The modern visitor to the neighbourhood would require a considerable leap of imagination if ever he were to suspect that it had welcomed a tipi encampment. But, in truth, it resounded to strange cries and pounding drums and witnessed an uncommon incident, narrated in full by the *Falkirk Herald & Midland Counties Journal*:

THE INDIANS AND THE RAIN

The Red Indian still holds firmly to his superstitious notions, as was exemplified in the showground on Sunday night. Heavy showers had descended during the evening, and the prospects of favourable weather for the performances on the following day were not bright. The Indians held a council to discuss the weather, and the outcome was that they decided to make 'medicine' and give offerings to the sun god to induce him to come out and scare away the rain. In the Indian encampment tom-toms were beat all night for the purpose of scaring away the unfavourable weather; but notwithstanding their superstitious efforts, when morning broke the meteorological conditions were still adverse. As the forenoon advanced, however, the sun came out, the rain-clouds disappeared, and splendid weather followed. The Indians it may be mentioned, took to themselves the credit for this welcome change in the weather.[14]

A discrepancy over the extent of the transformation arises between this account and that given in the *Falkirk Mail*, according to which leaden black clouds still hung obdurately and threateningly overhead[15] but, at any event, the consensus was that the rain stayed off for the duration. Either way, the ritual was essentially a rerun of the Brighton 1891 scenario and a cynic might be tempted to interpret it as a publicity stunt.

On Monday morning, Colonel Cody himself rolled into town following his weekend break in Edinburgh.

In order to cope with the greatly increased traffic, six extra carriages were attached to the Polmont and Grangemouth train in the afternoon and four more were added at night. The Caledonian Railway Company ran a special service from Larbert at 7.05, as did the North British Company on the Polmont and Philpstoun line. At night, the North British ran a special train for the return trip back to Philpstoun, with a connection to Bo'ness.

The large crowds, for a provincial town like Falkirk, came as a pleasant surprise. About 10,000 attended the afternoon performance and 11,000 in the evening, when large numbers of people regretfully turned back, all the shilling seats having been taken.

One of the girl riders, who favoured the side-saddle, was thrown as her horse stumbled in the course of its mad career. Fortunately, she escaped with just a slight injury to her leg.

Inspector Sempill took charge of the police arrangements on the Monday. Under his control was a force of fourteen men – sergeants, acting sergeants and constables.

It must all have made for a doubly memorable evening for Detective-Inspector Alexander Davidson, who was also present, in company with a detective from Edinburgh. This was the final occasion on which he reported for duty, prior to his well-earned retirement from the force. Mr Davidson, originally from Aberdeenshire, had been employed by Stirlingshire Constabulary since 1871. His exploits as a young constable in the mining village of Slamannan, where his talents were principally deployed in stamping out shebeening and bringing proper regulation to the licensing trade, and his subsequent work in Falkirk were outlined in an article on his career in the *Falkirk Herald & Midland Counties Journal* and sound as if they could have inspired a dime novel or two in their own right.[16]

At the conclusion of the evening performance, the scene on the narrow road back into town was one of severe congestion and the police struggled to control the one-way flow of pedestrian and vehicular traffic. The situation at times was critical and was aggravated by the brakes and carriages plying for hire, as well as by the show's wagons, already headed back to Springfield siding. However, not a single accident was reported.

An interesting footnote to Buffalo Bill's brief sojourn among the bairns of Falkirk is provided by an observation in the *Falkirk Mail*, on one final prodigious happening in a most extraordinary week in the long history of the burgh: 'Not the least remarkable feature of "Buffalo Bill's" visit to Falkirk was made prominent on Tuesday morning when there was not a single case to be tried at the Burgh or the Sheriff Courts.'[17]

Dunfermline

On the 16th of August, the show appeared at the Race Field near to McKane Park and just a short walk from where Scottish-American industrialist and philanthropist Andrew Carnegie was born into humble circumstances. This venue is now an ordinary field, lying to the south and west of the corner of Lovers' Loan and Coal Road.

Respected local historian Ronald Watt recounts a story about Buffalo Bill acquiring a particularly Caledonian souvenir from the Shetland pony farm on the Transy Estate, the property of a Mr Mungall. There, animals were sold, some as pets, the less fortunate ones going to the mines as pit ponies. The pony bought by Cody, although perfectly formed, was particularly small, even by the diminutive standards of the breed. It was subsequently exhibited as the smallest horse or pony in the world. Mr Watt states that his grandfather, Alexander Watt, was the stud manager of the farm. It seems that Ronald's father, Robert Watt, was at that time a boy of five or six years of age. He had developed a particular fondness for the pony and was broken-hearted when he returned from school one day to witness Mr Mungall in the act of selling it to Colonel Cody. The pony ended its days in New York Zoo.[18] Sadly, although this was possibly the same pony as is referred to in connection with the 1908 season in Don Russell's *The Lives and Legends of Buffalo Bill*,[19] I have searched in vain to corroborate this story.

Two songs, written by local folk icon John Watt and appearing on his *Heroes* CD, present an enduring echo of the occasion. These are 'The Day that Billy Cody Played the Auld Grey Toon' and 'The Wild West Show'. John's late father, Gordon Watt, as a boy of thirteen, witnessed the performers making their way down Dunfermline's Douglas Street and saw the show later that day. His later recollections provided the inspiration for these songs. He is quoted in the sleeve notes as having offered the assessment: 'A tremendous show, the largest I have ever seen.' In the first of the songs, John has allowed himself an even wider artistic licence than Colonel Cody himself –

his highly colourful and fanciful lyrics make mention not only of Sioux, as well as the Cheyenne and Arapaho who were alleged to be present, but also of Shawnees, Pawnees and Paiutes! But, for all of its studied (and confessed) inaccuracies, the song remains an important record of the excitement of the occasion and underscores the fact that people's perceptions of the unaccustomed figures they beheld in their old familiar streets and wynds were much wilder than even the admittedly sensational reality. 'The Wild West Show', in contrast, is essentially factual and its air of stark realism lucidly reflects the writer's obvious grasp of his subject.

One myth must end here, though. In the sleeve notes, there appears the following commentary to 'The Day That Billy Cody Played the Auld Grey Toon': 'Billy Cody aka Buffalo Bill played Dunfermline, Fife on August 16th 1904 and paraded in Kelty, Fife on the 19th and Cowdenbeath, Fife on 23rd.' This theme is expanded upon in the lyric:

Billy packit up and jackit up, and moved doon tae the coast,
He'd paraded up in Kelty where they thocht he was the most.

Following consultations with the man himself, I can reveal that the sole basis for this story lies in John's misinterpretation of the words appearing in a newspaper advert in his possession:

WILL VISIT KELTY, FRIDAY, August 19th. COWDENBEATH, TUESDAY, August 23rd.

Closer examination, however, reveals that this line does not pertain to the Wild West advert at all but to the one for Harry Lauder immediately above it. John also concedes that his reference to the appearance of an Indian fancifully identified as 'Spotted Sloth' in the 'Goth', otherwise the 'Gothenburg' public house in Kelty, holds no foundation whatsoever beyond his (discredited) yarn about the show parading in Kelty.

It is a shame that such enthusiasm was not expressed at the time:

On Tuesday afternoon, its neglect of a courteous expression of appreciation of an entertainment it evidently highly enjoyed, was specially, almost painfully, noticeable when at the close Colonel Cody having advanced to the front and respectfully tendered his acknowledgements – and then in the most knightly fashion retired, displaying the backward paces of his beautiful and perfectly trained horse.[20]

The departure of the 'overflowingly large' evening audience produced serious congestion in the narrow Lovers' Loan exit, spilling into West Nethertown Street over a period of almost half an hour.[21] The bairns only made matters worse by running around in a state of high excitement, imitating the strange prairie cries still ringing in their ears. As pressure built up, a fence was levelled and many people walked home to the northern parts of the town across the fields. Half a dozen potato chippers, exercising scant regard to public safety, took up position at the foot of Coal Road. Dozens of wagonettes and other vehicles, several of them driven in a distinctly careless fashion, posed a constant danger to the personal safety of the departing throngs and, in the darkness of the night, it was thanks to luck more than judgement that no serious accident occurred.

Accommodation for Buffalo Bill's representatives was obtained at the City Arms in Bridge Street, which, I am delighted to report, as the City Hotel, is still doing a roaring trade in 2007.

Kirkcaldy

At Kirkcaldy, on the 17th of August, a special tramcar service ran from Oswald's Wynd and the park gates along the upper route to the Gallatoun terminus. The canny folk of the 'Lang Toon' were obviously hard to impress since, beyond the sudden upsurge in the transport authority's fortunes, just about the only mention to appear in the town's four local papers in the wake of the show was an oblique reference under the 'Fifeshire Table Talk' column of the *Fifeshire Advertiser*: 'They have been trying to train an American mustang at Auchterderran, and Buffalo Bill being absent they used a whip handle. Fine, £1.'[22]

Just the same, the locals had more important things on their minds. The papers were full of flower shows, seemingly a national obsession at that time, not to mention a recurrence of that perennial Scottish entertainment – a church secession crisis. Also, the fitba' season was about to kick off and, the night after Buffalo Bill hit town, local favourites Raith Rovers beat Lochgelly United at Stark's Park by one goal to nil.

With all of this going on, it is scarcely to be wondered at that local worthies barely deigned to notice the fleeting presence of the Wild West encampment – practically under their noses – on 'Ritchie's Field'. This location, as the newspaper advert and the advanceman's log alike attest, lay 'near Fife Pottery' and a day's tenure was acquired for £8 from John Ritchie, of 15, Roslyn Street.[23] This probably refers to the open space that lay to the immediate south of Fife Pottery, now dissected by Roberts Street.

Notes

1. *Evening News*, 4 August 1984
2. 8 August 1904
3. p. 203
4. *Edinburgh Evening Dispatch*, 8 August 1904
5. 8 and 9 August 1904
6. 8 August 1904
7. *Edinburgh Evening News*, 8 August 1904
8. *Edinburgh Evening Dispatch*, 8 August 1904
9. Ibid.
10. *Four Years in Europe With Buffalo Bill*, p. 45
11. Stella Foote, *Letters from Buffalo Bill*, p. 58
12. p. 474
13. 8 August 1904
14. 17 August 1904
15. 20 August 1904

16 23 July 1904
17 20 August 1904
18 See letter, 'Buffalo Bill and the Shetland Pony', in the *Dunfermline Press*, 3 March 2000
19 p. 449
20 *Dunfermline Journal*, 20 August 1904
21 Ibid.
22 20 August 1904
23 *Fife Free Press*, 13 August 1904

19

FORFARSHIRE AND ANGUS

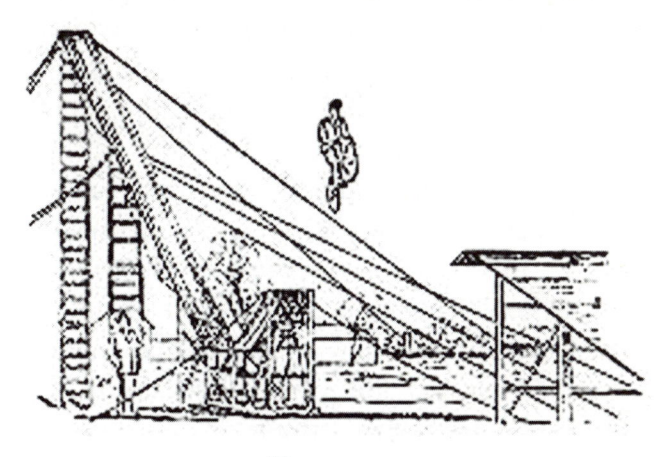

Dundee

The creation of the Esplanade Extension had been a major civic preoccupation for the fifteen years preceding 1904. It sits on a spur of reclaimed land on the north bank of the Firth of Tay, in the prosperous West End, and has been further augmented since. It provided Buffalo Bill's venue for three days from Thursday the 18th until Saturday the 20th of August.

Dundee Town Council, at a meeting held on the 17th of August 1904, considered reports which Mr Harvey of the Caledonian Railway Company had obtained from the Burgh Engineer and the Deputy Chief Constable, regarding the stability of the public footbridge at the adjacent Magdalen Green railway station. For reasons of public safety, the Council issued a proclamation regulating traffic over the footbridge. On the days of the show, it would only be open to people crossing southwards to the Esplanade – i.e. going *to* the shows – between the hours of twelve noon and three and again from six until nine in the evening. Between three and six in the afternoon and again between nine and eleven in the evening, it was to be opened only to people proceeding in the opposite direction

– i.e. coming *from* the shows. Railway company employees and passengers arriving at or departing from Magdalen Green were specifically exempted from this provision.

It was further ordained that the footbridge would be kept free of all obstructions, caused by persons loitering or otherwise.[1]

The Caledonian Railway Company ran special trains between Dundee West and Magdalen Green, supplementing an augmented service of tramcars and omnibuses.

Disaster attended Thursday's afternoon performance as the painful news raced through the crowd that a boy had drowned in the Tay, having fallen into the water below while amusing himself on the Esplanade Extension wall with a number of companions from the Benvie Road district. The alarm was raised and an unspecified Wild West show employee raced along the wall and hurled a lifebelt in the direction of the stricken lad, who was by now too far out and soon sank from view. The tragedy presumably cast an ironic shadow over the demonstration of the life-saving equipment, which regrettably had not been to hand. There was to be no heroic last-gasp rescue this time. At half past two that afternoon, as cheers and gunshots doubtless resounded from the arena, mingling surreally with the horrified gasps of onlookers, a body was retrieved from the Tay, near to the point of the Esplanade Extension wall. It was identified as that of John Fraser, aged ten, who had resided with his father, Walter Fraser, at 14, Cleghorn Place. Dr Templeman, who attended, not unreasonably entered the cause of death as 'probably drowning'. A poignant discovery was made when the dead boy's shoes and stockings were found upon the esplanade wall.

The opening day was also marred by the unpredictable Scottish weather. At the evening performance, the large crowd watched from under the canvas canopy, while the performers went through their routines under what *The Courier* termed 'a terrific downpour of rain'.[2]

A wet track caused by the torrential rain and high winds spelt danger for Carter the Cowboy Cyclist. However, he gallantly resolved not to disappoint his public. He went ahead with his act and, in the event, gave rise to a 'sensation'[3] as the adverse conditions caused him to skid from the landing stage. Losing control of his bicycle, man and machine together rolled over and over on to the track. Attendants promptly rushed to the scene. He had to be helped on to a horse and was conducted from the arena, nursing minor injuries. Nonetheless, he was back in the saddle for his performances on the following day.

The Lord Provost attended the afternoon show on Friday the 19th, together with many of the leading citizens of the city and district. In the evening, a substantial party of boys and girls, newsvendors for the *Evening Post*, attended at the charge of their generous employers:

> The lads and lasses, who numbered over two hundred, gathered at the office of the 'Evening Post' about seven o'clock, when they were treated to refreshment before they left for the great show. It was indeed a delighted band who wended their way out the Nethergate to the Magdalen Green in happy anticipation of spending a pleasant evening.[4]

The youngsters followed the entire programme with wide-eyed, rapt attention and gave shrill vent to their appreciation. The cries of the Indians, which they did their best to emulate, were a particular source of fascination.

Between shows that same day, Buffalo Bill accorded an interview to a journalist, who found Colonel Cody in the company of Chief Iron Tail, in the process of planning their annual autumn hunting trip in Wyoming. Buffalo Bill outlined the genesis of his career as a showman and, when asked for his opinion on the character of the American Indian, stated him to be 'a noble and grand man'.[5] He also spoke of the country that he was developing in Wyoming's Bighorn Basin and stated his intention eventually to settle in the town there that bore his name. At the conclusion of the interview, his intention was expressed that:

[O]n the highest peak in the district there will be erected a mammoth figure of a buffalo, beneath which, when his day comes, Col. Cody will be laid to rest, so that even in death his spirit may hover over the land he loves so well.[6]

Sadly, this desire would never be realised as Buffalo Bill's mortal remains were eventually received not by Cedar Mountain, Wyoming, but by Lookout Mountain, Colorado, for reasons unconnected with his wishes.

On the final day, Saturday the 20th, proceedings were blighted by heavy rain once more. The Cowboy Cyclist's daring leap through space was again placed in jeopardy and efforts were made to dissuade him from executing his feat but, with his usual indomitable pluck, he went through with it just the same, apparently without any greater incident than usual.

The Dundee performances were witnessed by a total of 72,400 spectators, averaging out at a little over 12,000 at each of the six performances. This was, in relative terms, better than any of the cities visited recently, with the sole exception of Glasgow.

Buffalo Bill departed Dundee in a blaze of glory – well, in a blaze anyway. After the entourage had returned to the Caledonian goods yard – to the immediate west of the gasworks, roughly in the area bounded by East Whale Lane, Foundry Lane, Peep O'Day Lane, and Dock Street – and, as the wagons were being loaded on to the trains, one large truck – containing 'water oil', used in illuminating some of the smaller tents – ignited and spat out a huge tongue of fire, as a leak came into contact with a lighted torch. Within seconds, flames were leaping almost forty feet into the air. The burning wagon was immediately detached and shunted apart from the remainder of the train. But the danger was by no means diminished as the fire threatened to spread to adjacent buildings.

Buffalo Bill's staff, co-ordinated by Fred B. Hutchinson, the manager of the exhibition, and Mike Coyle, the superintendent, combined with the city's fire brigade, under the direction of Captain Weir, to combat the conflagration. The railwaymen hastily produced a water hose but Weir ordered that it be redirected on to the buildings, which, by now, were crackling under the heat.

Workmen, mostly show employees, set to work with picks and shovels, digging earth from a nearby embankment, which they threw onto the blaze together with a quantity of sand commandeered from another wagon in the yard.

A highly hazardous operation was mounted to stop the blaze spreading. The oil tanks were detached and drawn from the stricken vehicle, using chains fitted with hooks. A tank containing about thirty-five gallons of oil was thus removed intact. Another tank, however, had no sooner touched the ground when its base gave way. The wave of spilt oil immediately burst into flames and Captain Weir, a fireman named McLean and one of Buffalo Bill's staff were enveloped in the resulting inferno. All three managed to scramble out with their clothing on fire. Almost incredibly, no serious injuries resulted.

The fire was eventually brought under control but not before the wagon's superstructure was entirely destroyed and damage to the value of about £50 was incurred.

Events in Dundee had proven even more dramatic outside of the arena than within and presumably the unscheduled spectacle was witnessed in full by the crowd that had assembled to watch the loading arrangements. At least some of the bemused locals must have wondered if it was all part of the entertainment and whether a similar display was routinely given at every town on the itinerary.

Local youngsters reaped a harvest of empty cartridges, coppers and even coins of greater value from the vacated showground. A similar bonanza befell the city's tea rooms and other eating establishments, which did a roaring trade during the days in which the show was in town. Not everyone was happy, though. One man complained to 'The Bellman's Budget' columnist that his slumbers were disturbed nightly by imitation Indian war whoops echoing from the street outside.[7]

Local postcard publishers J. Valentine & Son, whose speciality was local events, issued a set of at least three black-and-white cards, based on photographs taken in Dundee. One image records a crowd of visitors set against the background of the main entrance and sideshows. The second depicts the Imperial Japanese Cavalry riding around the arena, while a third shows a party of Indians on horseback, preparing to make their entrance. These were subsequently offered for sale at retail outlets in towns and cities visited later on the tour.

Magdalen Green is still an attractive public park and, although the railway station of the same name has long since been closed, the Esplanade Extension remains a flat, open expanse of grassland, now dissected by Riverside Drive.

Japanese and 'Cossacks'

During a guided tour of the Wild West camp at Dundee, a reporter noted the presence of a 'number of intelligent young Japs' eagerly following his paper's latest accounts of the war in the Far East.[8] The Russo-Japanese War of 1904–1905 – from which Japan would rise to global prominence after successfully resisting Russian expansionism – was then raging but, despite the hostilities between their respective countries, the Japanese and 'Cossacks' in the company were consistently observed to be on good terms with one another and confined themselves to vying in friendly rivalry for public acclaim.

British public opinion firmly favoured the cause of the Japanese or the 'little allies', as they were affectionately known.[9] For this reason, they were, in the words of the *Aberdeen Free Press*, 'hailed with acclamation wherever they went'.[10] From a modern perspective, it is a shock to the system to learn that in 1904 'Jap' was a friendly rather than a pejorative term. Clearly, the cataclysmic events of just four decades later were wholly unanticipated.

Conversely, the 'Cossacks' were received on the streets and in the arena with reserve, verging on outright hostility, and it was only by virtue of their extraordinary horsemanship that the spectators were finally won over.

However, *Wild West Georgians*, by Irakli Makharadze and Akaki

Chkhaidze, published in 2002, vindicates the doubts concerning the authenticity of the 'Cossacks' first expressed in 1892.[11] That they were billed as 'Russian Cossacks from the Caucasus' is in itself sufficient to set the alarm bells ringing in the mind of the informed reader.[12] The real Cossacks were natives of the Steppes, a large expanse of grassland akin to North America's Great Plains, while the Caucasus is a mountainous region, in the north of Georgia, then a part of the Russian Empire.

In almost every case, the surnames of the 'Cossacks' ended with the suffixes '-idze', '-adze' or '-vili'. This will strike an immediate chord with Rangers supporters since two Georgian players, Shota Arveladze and Zurab Khizanishvili, have graced the team in recent years.

The 'Cossacks' were headed by a 'Prince' and it is understood that, in 1904, David Kadjaia acquitted this particular role. This rank was as fictitious as that of 'Chief', which was arbitrarily conferred upon certain Indians. The impressive medals they wore were equally bogus. The Georgian riders paid to masquerade as 'Cossacks' were clever horsemen and actors and nothing more.

Arbroath

For Monday the 22nd, a field on the Auchmithie Road was rented from Arthur Allison, the farmer of the Culloden Farm. The site, now a built-up area, is commemorated by Culloden Terrace, which runs into the Montrose Road.

A front-page entry in the *Arbroath Guide* announced that Arbroath Station's goods department, in order to devote itself to the requirements of the show, would be closed to the delivery and reception of all traffic, other than livestock and perishables, between certain hours from Saturday the 20th until Tuesday the 23rd. An advert directly below this one offered a storage facility to bicycle-riding patrons of the show at the Red Lion Hall, Barngreen, at 2d per cycle.[13]

Colonel Cody was briefly reunited with an old Civil War comrade. David Anderson, born in the town's Anderson Street more than seventy years previously, had migrated to the United States, where he served with the young Cody in the Grand Army of the Republic, under Generals Grant and MacPherson. He remained there for long enough to vote for President William McKinley in 1897 but returned home to Arbroath at some time thereafter.

Cody entertained Anderson in his tent, where they talked about old times over a cigar, and he presented his visitor with a copy of his biography, which he inscribed:

With the compliments of the subject, W.F. Cody, 'Buffalo Bill', to Comrade David Anderson, Arbroath – August 22, 1904.[14]

A reporter attempted to interview Mr Anderson but that laconic gentleman could only be induced to offer two observations. The first was that there was no 'caste system' in America, of the kind that dominated British society. Secondly, he corroborated the story about Cody being a strict teetotaller. How he came to know of just what his old pal had been getting up to in the intervening four decades and what degree of prompting was required are matters which were not enlarged upon.

It is doubly regrettable, therefore, that the Wild West caused one local publican – James Bell Mustard, of the George Hotel, Commerce Street – to fall foul of the licensing laws. He appeared at Arbroath Police Court on Thursday the 8th of September, charged with having, on Sunday the 21st of August – the night before the shows – committed a breach of his certificate by serving a glass of whisky to each of two men, who were neither lodgers in the hotel nor bona fide travellers. They were James Simmons, an English lancer, and Roman Lozano, a Mexican. Buffalo Bill's entourage had inadvertently succeeded in making its own colourful and distinctive mark on Scottish legal history.

The case hinged upon the phrase 'bona fide traveller'. The intention behind the legislation was to prevent local people and semi-permanent residents from seeking alcoholic refreshment on the Sabbath, while creating specific exemptions in favour of hotel guests and true itinerants who, of necessity, were dependent on hostelries for their sustenance. Were Simmons and Lozano 'bona fide travellers'? Much discussion revolved around the arrangement whereby their food, drink and sleeping arrangements were provided for them in the Wild West establishment. Their names had been entered in the hotel book but the place from whence they had come had negligently been omitted. Whether they had arrived in Arbroath with the show trains or come in the forenoon from Dundee by a regular train was not established. Evidence was, however, led by the police witnesses that, when they left the George Hotel, a dozen more of Buffalo Bill's men were waiting to get in and that the accused closed the door against them and would not admit them. Both hotels on the west side of town were closed. None of Buffalo Bill's men were to be found at the White Hart Hotel for there was a man on the door keeping them out.

Police Sergeant John Brand gave evidence that, at two of the hotels he visited, Buffalo Bill's men were being turned away and 'about the other he would say nothing at present' perhaps because a further case was pending.

In the end, Bailie Alexander wisely took the pragmatic view. Nowhere did the legislation provide a satisfactory definition of what a 'bona fide traveller' actually was. Cases were cited in which the Judges of the High Court of Judiciary had failed to agree among themselves upon the point. Bailie Alexander did not therefore feel qualified to resolve the issue and, under the whole circumstances, found the case against Mr Mustard not proven and dismissed him.

The *Arbroath Guide* attributed the following remark to Bailie Alexander: 'The accused told the constables that there were Buffalo Bill's men sleeping in the hotel, but they had only his word for it.'[15]

In his evidence, Mr Mustard reiterated that some of Buffalo Bill's men had stayed with him, two of them since the previous Friday.

Somewhat belatedly, admittedly, I can come to the assistance of the court. A reference to Mr Mustard appears in the advanceman's log, identifying 'The George, James B. Mustard' as the hotel at which lodgings were found. Meals were priced at 1/6d, with overnight accommodation at the same sum, and a total bill of £10 16/- was incurred. There is therefore no reason to doubt the veracity of Mr Mustard's testimony.

Mr Mustard was not the only one to get into hot water. The Wild West show also occasioned some adverse comment at the monthly meeting of the Arbroath School Board, on Monday the 5th of September. Mr Murray demanded to know on whose authority the children of the town's schools were given a holiday on the day of the show. The Board's chairman, who had been out of town, said that it was the first he knew of it. It emerged that certain members of the Property Committee had taken it upon themselves to assume the full powers of the Board, on the grounds that, firstly, a day off had been declared on the occasion of Barnum & Bailey's visit on the 19th of September 1899 and, secondly, it was feared that mass absenteeism would result had the authorities not gone with the flow and accorded the de facto holiday official sanction. Under the circumstances, the officials in question 'had presumed on the indulgence of the Board in the emergency'.[16] The offending members were soundly taken to task and the hope was expressed that they 'would not again go so far astray as to take upon them the powers of the Board even in the matter of a show'.[17] However, given the number of times that the word 'Laughter' appears in brackets (five in this immediate connection and one in another matter), it may be taken that the matter was resolved and a proper balance of influence restored, without any real recriminations or ill-feeling resulting.

It is not therefore surprising that the dust had still scarcely settled almost half a century later when, in April 1951, the film adaptation of the Irving Berlin musical *Annie Get Your Gun* played at the Palace Cinema for six days. Other films billed as playing in Arbroath at the same time confirmed the enduring popularity of the Western genre; these were *I Killed Geronimo*, *The Gunfighter* and *Hills of the Brave*.

The *Arbroath Herald* deemed this a suitable opportunity for a retrospective feature, under the erroneous title of 'When Annie

Brought Her Gun to Arbroath'.[18] This story must have been a matter of some importance to the editorial staff for, in that week of all weeks, they were hardly short of news. In the course of the past few days, the Stone of Destiny, 'liberated' from Westminster Abbey on Christmas Day last, had turned up at Arbroath Abbey and naturally provided a glut of headlines for the local press.

There was obviously a certain measure of confusion over when exactly Buffalo Bill's visit had taken place for it was stated that: 'And celluloid Annie, now visiting Arbroath, recalls the great day *at the close of last century* (emphasis mine) when the real Annie frightened the birds on Hayshead hill with her marksmanship.'

Of course, Annie Oakley had departed prior to the 1904 tour. Insofar as can be established, Annie Oakley *never* visited Arbroath in her life, apart, of course, from when she came in the guise of Betty Hutton. This is quite a standard error and Annie was very much the ghost haunting the 1904 version of the show.

If the article can still be taken as a credible source at all, it observed that the canvas entrance to the show was pitched on the site occupied in 1951 by Horologe House.

Forfar

On Tuesday the 23rd of August, an aggregate of 16,000 spectators watched the show on Forfar's Market Muir, braving the dismal weather, which was showery and dull. *The Forfar Herald & Kirriemuir Advertiser* commented that the ten – about seven, according to the advanceman's log – acres available at that site was a bit cramped for the show's requirements.[19] A rental of £5 was payable on the day of the show to D. M. Morrison, the Market Master, at the Weigh House. Lodgings were obtained at Jarman's Hotel, then opposite the Caledonian Railway station, at 97–99, North Street, on the corner with Market Street.

William Petrie's livery stable, at 15, North Street, provided four country teams at 14/- each and one or more town wagons at 10/-. A hundred-by-twelve-feet billboard was ordered from local contractor

A. Esplin and sited at Alexander D. Strachan's sawmill yard, which was also in the vicinity of the hotel.

The water supply was obtained for £1 from the Town Council's appropriately named Burgh Surveyor, Alex Watterson.

The Forfar press were hard men to impress because, for at least one of their number, the event was an anticlimax: 'The much boomed and greatly belauded "Buffalo Bill" has come and gone. He promised much in his big show, gave much, and, perhaps, left much to the imagination.'[20]

The Market Muir still hosts travelling shows today. It is situated in the north part of town, a short distance to the west of Station Park, the home of Forfar Athletic FC.

The railway station, which gave its name to the football ground and at which the show was unloaded, is no more. The line has similarly vanished almost without trace though, a short distance to the north-west, a railway bridge remains in place. The line ran between the Market Muir and Station Park, touching the Muir at its north-eastern corner.

Montrose

On Wednesday the 24th of August, the entourage made its way from the Caledonian Railway goods yard to Burgess Park. Crowds of people from the Angus countryside followed with every train and the town soon assumed a holiday appearance.

The precise location of Burgess Park is problematic since the name is not recognised today. The suspicion necessarily arises that this was an ad hoc designation, after the manner of King's Field in Stirling. Certainly, it appears not to have been what would normally be thought of as a public park as the advanceman's log reveals that it was rented from David Ritchie, a dairyman, at the cost of £6. The strongest clue comes from the *Montrose, Arbroath and Brechin Review*, which located it opposite the House of Refuge.[21] The fact that this clarification was needed at the time strengthens the 'ad hoc designation' theory.

Local youths follow the Indians along Dixon Road, Glasgow, August 1904

Indians entering the showground, Glasgow

Photograph by Thomas Lindsay, courtesy of Maeve Dixon

Westward the wagons . . .

A member of the Imperial Japanese Cavalry in Glasgow

Photograph by Thomas Lindsay, courtesy of Maeve Dixon

Photograph by Thomas Lindsay, courtesy of Maeve Dixon

and the ensuing battle scene

'Cossacks' on Princes Street

The sideshow tent, the main entrance and the ticket wagons at Dundee

Courtesy of the Postcard Club of Tayside

Opening Review – the Imperial Japanese Cavalry enter the arena

Courtesy of the Postcard Club of Tayside

Mounted Indians stand in readiness to attack

Buffalo Bill and his Indians on the South Pier, Fraserburgh

Indians on the rocks below the Wine Tower, Fraserburgh

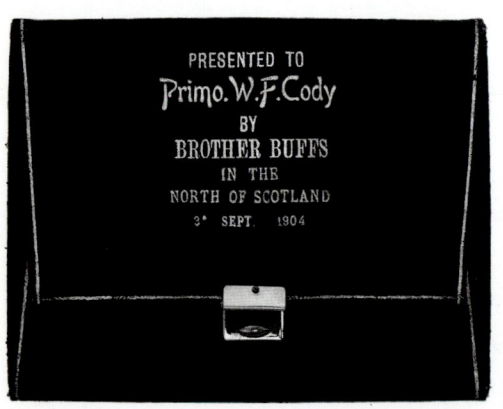

Courtesy of Buffalo Bill Historical Center, Cody, Wyoming: 1.69.1554

The morocco-encased affiliation card presented to Colonel Cody by 'Brother Buffs' at Inverness

Iron Tail and Philip Blue Shield at John O'Groats, 3rd September 1904

A party of Indians at Land's End, Cornwall, 29th May 1904

An unidentified Indian lays a wreath upon the tomb of Robert Burns, Dumfries. Michael B. Bailey and Johnnie Baker look on.

Wild West personnel and local people at the Burns Mausoleum, Dumfries

Courtesy of The Buffalo Bill Museum and Grave, Lookout Mountain, Golden, Colorado

The medal presented to Colonel Cody by Provost Glover at Dumfries, 14th September 1904

'Colonel' Samuel Franklin Cody

Courtesy of Buffalo Bill Historical Center, Cody, Wyoming; Gift of The Coe Foundation; 1.69.469

Painting by James Watterston Herald, photo courtesy of Paul Reid

Buffalo Bill at Arbroath?

Photograph by Alfred James Thomson, courtesy of Valerie Dean

Buff Bill, the true subject of the James Watterston Herald paintings

Additional livery was supplied by the Star Stables, telephone number Montrose 25. The wall opposite the North British Station was acquired as a billboard lot, 10/- being payable to R. L. Sinclair. The advanceman also noted that a good lot for a 100-foot billboard had been identified near the park. The owner, unfortunately, was out of town but Mr Sinclair was trying to obtain it on the show's behalf.

A strong flavour of the time is provided by the report in the *Montrose Standard and Angus and Mearns Register*, that several attractions had taken place in Montrose in quick succession.[22] The first of these was Harry Lauder, the next was the Montrose Flower Show, followed by the prize gathering of the Angus and Mearns Rifle Association, then a visit from Walker's Cinematographic Company and, as the culmination of all this series of interesting and colourful events, Buffalo Bill's Wild West. It was all the more enthusiastically received since the locals still felt aggrieved at having missed out on *The Greatest Show on Earth* five years previously.

The great disappointment of 1899 had been keenly shared by the pupils of St Cyrus Public School, Lunan Public School, the inmates of Dorward's House of Refuge and also the boys of Rossie Reformatory, all of whom had attracted the generous attentions of wealthy patrons. However, in 1904, the Reformatory boys were not to be disappointed. A certain local philanthropist, Edward Miller of Rossie Castle, was kind enough to foot the bill for the admission of the boys and officers to Buffalo Bill's show. This generous gesture was greatly appreciated and the boys thoroughly enjoyed the performance.

Between 8,000 and 9,000 spectators were present at the afternoon performance and from 10,000 to 12,000 in the evening. All the local schools were closed for the day.

One man who found the show a highly arresting and captivating experience was an unnamed pedlar apprehended at one of the performances. He was subsequently convicted at Montrose Police Court, on Saturday the 27th of August, for attempted theft by pickpocketing and was sentenced to twenty-one days imprisonment.

Notes

1. Minutes of Dundee Town Council and of Dundee Water and Gas Commissioners 1903–1904 11311B, p. 995
2. 19 August 1904
3. *Dundee Advertiser*, 19 August 1904
4. *The Courier*, 20 August 1904
5. Ibid.
6. Ibid.
7. *The People's Journal*, 27 August 1904
8. *Dundee Advertiser*, 19 August 1904
9. *Aberdeen Daily Journal*, 30 August 1904
10. 27 August 1904
11. See Chapter 13, *supra*
12. *Aberdeen Daily Journal*, 13 August 1904
13. 20 August 1904
14. *Arbroath Herald*, 25 August 1904
15. 10 September 1904
16. *Arbroath Herald*, 8 September 1904
17. Ibid.
18. 13 April 1951
19. 26 August 1904
20. Ibid.
21. 19 August 1904
22. 12 August 1904

20

THE NORTH-EAST

> Buffalo Bill and his Indian Braves
> ON THE PIER AT FRASERBURGH.
>
> Photographs of this Unique Event—
> Whole Plate, mounted or unmounted, 2s each;
> By Post, 2s 3d.
> Cabinet, mounted or unmounted, 1s each; By Post, 1/1
>
> Also a fine group of Indians on the Rocks at Kinnaird. Same prices.
>
> These Photographs are Copyright and will be supplied by W. NORRIE only.
>
> 28 CROSS STREET, FRASERBURGH.

ABERDEEN

The Kittybrewster goods yard was swiftly transformed as the three trains with their light yellow coaches and bogies were shunted into the sidelines. Unloading began shortly after five o'clock, almost completely occupying the extensive yard in the process. A large crowd of spectators gathered in Bedford Road.

Over three days, from Thursday the 25th to Saturday the 27th, six performances were given at the Central Park Auction Mart, on the opposite side of Clifton Road. Rental was £60, payable to J. K. Moir, the manager, on the day of the first show.

By seven-thirty, the canvas city was in place and the workmen were enjoying a well-earned breakfast. Over by the Clifton Road wall, the Indians raised their tipi encampment.

Directly beneath the Wild West advert appearing in the *Aberdeen Daily Journal*, 'The Bon Accord', of 17–19, Market Street, took out an entry of its own, advising that visitors for the performances should avail themselves of 'the largest and best appointed dining rooms in Scotland'.[1] Another local business detecting the scent of opportunity was Sangster and Henderson. An advert in the *Aberdeen Free*

Press incited the firm's out-of-town clientele to take advantage of the cheap day returns, ungrammatically proclaiming:

> The Great Events in the City for To-day is SANGSTER & HENDERSON'S SALVAGE SALE and BUFFALO BILL'S WILD WEST SHOW[2]

John Ledingham and Sons, of Rosemount Bakery, were awarded the contract to supply bread, biscuits and aerated waters to the touring company.

In anticipation of heavy traffic, Mr Moonie, the superintendent of the Corporation Tramways, put every available car on to the Kittybrewster route, while maintaining normal service on the other lines. For fully two hours prior to the afternoon and evening performances from Thursday the 25th until Saturday the 27th, a continuous procession of 'heavily-loaded clanging tram cars'[3] ferried human cargoes northwards along George Street, arriving at the showground every couple of minutes, then returning to St Nicholas Street to load up again.

Two relatively minor accidents took place at the opening performance. A 'Cossack' was thrown to the ground when his charger suddenly turned while galloping along at speed. The rider limped painfully to the edge of the arena, where he collapsed. Professor Stephenson, who was fortunately in the audience, attended. During the Custer's Last Stand sequence, a horse rolled over on its rider, who received a nasty gash on the scalp from a hoof.

The opening day's total of 23,000 spectators was far exceeded on Friday, when 13,000 people came in the afternoon and 14,000 in the evening. Carriages, cabs and even a few motor cars kept up a steady stream. In particular, the tramway officials struggled to cope with the extraordinary flow of traffic from Union Street to Kittybrewster.

The *Aberdeen Free Press* recorded:

> The town was full of strangers, and peculiar scenes were witnessed. At any corner one might have run up against an eager motley

crowd surrounding a swarthy group of North American Indians, in feathers and ornaments whose copper-coloured complexions and – considering the ferocious lines of former savagery – good-humoured visages looked as well pleased as the delighted and curious onlookers.

The same article went on to elaborate:

Opportunities were eagerly awaited by snap-shottists to obtain photographs of one of the most photographed men in the world – Buffalo Bill himself. It was the ambition of every amateur with a camera and a day off to capture a portrait of the veteran Colonel. Speaking of photography, Ameen Abou Hamad, the fine-looking Arab who at the performance 'understands' eleven Bedouin athletes in a pyramid, was seen going around with a hand camera getting snap-shots of the city as souvenirs of his visit. The chief performers have their 'off time' in the forenoon only and early yesterday morning in cars and carriages they could be seen disporting themselves sight-seeing in and around the city. At Bieldside and Bankhead, on the early Deeside trains, and at the Beach, the 'lions' of the place were being viewed by the men of the Wild West, accompanied by their lady friends.[4]

The opening review was marred by a cloudburst of torrential rain, letting up exactly as Colonel Cody took his place at the head of his horsemen. This incident provided an additional spectacle:

Immediately the rain had ceased quite an army of men appeared on the scene, and, acting the part of a great cleansing department, had within comparatively few minutes removed every pool and trace of mud, and had strewed the wet ground with pine wood shavings, so that the place was perfectly dry within a few minutes – a remarkable manifestation of the complete organisation and preparation for every imaginable contingency.[5]

This unscheduled addition to the programme neatly underscored an assertion in *Bon-Accord* that the phrase 'rain or shine' had been introduced into the English vernacular by advertisements for Buffalo Bill's appearances in London, seventeen years previously.[6]

Crowds of people of every age and description turned out in force in the Granite City, pouring along George Street and Causewayend, all of them headed in the selfsame direction. *Bon-Accord* estimated: 'I suppose it was seen by nearly half the population of Aberdeen over the age of childhood.'[7]

On Friday, the Wild West's officials declared that never before had they seen so large a crowd assembled in advance of a show, as on that evening. The *Aberdeen Daily Journal* described the scene: 'Looking along George Street from "Split the Winds," the sidepaths, as far as the eye could see, were thronged with people, all moving in the direction of the Wild West show.'[8]

In order to ease the unrelenting congestion at the entrance, it was deemed prudent to admit the public to the arena half an hour earlier than normal. The ticket sellers were hard pressed to keep up with the unremitting clamour and the ticket boxes were in danger of being swept away. As an additional measure, fifty ushers and attendants, whose normal duties lay in other directions, were deployed to the front, where they assisted the police in regulating the crowds by guarding the ticket wagons. These were closed every so often and then opened again after one batch of spectators had been shown to their seats. The 1/- and 2/- seats were soon occupied to capacity and a notice was posted to this effect. Over and above that night's capacity crowd, the *Aberdeen Free Press* estimated that 5,000 had to be turned away, unable or unwilling to pay for the more expensive seats.[9] Consequently, even the tramcars returning to the city were packed.

There was another accident in the arena, one of the riders being thrown heavily from his horse during the cavalry exercises.

Drawing upon the experiences of Friday evening, the gates were opened at twelve-thirty and six-thirty, instead of one and seven o'clock respectively, for the third and final day. It was just as well for Saturday afternoon brought no remission and, from eleven o'clock onwards, a steady torrent of humanity made its way to Kittybrewster.

The Great North of Scotland Railway Company ran a record number of special excursions on the Deeside, North and Buchan lines, all stopping at Kittybrewster, and people travelling on the Deeside trains were thus spared the inconvenience of having to travel to and from the Joint Station.

Upwards of thirty tramcars ran on the Woodside section alone and, as each empty car arrived at Queen Victoria's statue, it was instantly besieged. People waiting to board at intermediate stops along the way were disappointed as each began its journey filled to capacity. Even the best efforts of the public transport system's management proved inadequate and people in their thousands gave up and walked.

Over the three days, Frank Small, of Colonel Cody's press bureau, a former journalist himself, took great care of the Aberdeen newsmen, plying them with copy and hosting guided tours of the Wild West establishment. At the Saturday afternoon show, he invited an *Aberdeen Daily Journal* reporter to ride as a passenger in the Deadwood Stage. Apart from being well and truly shaken up as the coach jolted along, the newsman was quite unnerved by the continuous fusillade from a large party of mounted Indians on the warpath, some of whom even ventured to peer menacingly in through the windows at their prospective victims.

At the conclusion of the final show that evening, Buffalo Bill took his customary farewell bow, amidst what the *Aberdeen Daily Journal* termed 'a perfect storm of cheering'.[10]

An interview with Buffalo Bill appeared in the *Aberdeen Daily Journal* on the 30th. Cody commented upon the world-famed thriftiness of the canny Aberdonians: 'What I have found is that the Scotchman is evidently a man who does not squander his money foolishly; and thus, when he sees anything he wants, he has the more with which to get it.'

The Colonel had formed a high estimation of the Aberdeen audiences. He opined that they were intelligent rather than demonstrative and knew the exact and proper time to applaud. He also referred to a scouting, camping and hunting acquaintance of his, a Scotsman named Keith,[11] who had assured him that the show would receive a hearty welcome in Scotland and specifically that it would do great business in Aberdeen. So pleased was the Colonel with the way things were going, he sent Keith a cablegram, to which the answer came: 'Didn't I tell you what Aberdeen would do?'

Colonel Cody also expressed his gratification in a letter to the *Aberdeen Free Press*, in which he deemed the Granite City 'one of the most beautiful as well as substantial in appearance I have ever visited'.[12]

In aggregate, 74,000 spectators saw the show at Aberdeen, almost 2,000 more than at Dundee, and the tramway's takings over the three days stood at £367 – about £240 in excess of the returns over an average three-day period.

The process of removal and entrainment went off without a hitch, under the able direction of Mr Murphy of the show staff, assisted by William Deuchar, passenger superintendent for the GNSR, Mr Kidd, the Stationmaster at Kittybrewster, and Inspector Norrie.

Quite remarkably, there had not been a single casualty outwith the arena.

Well, unless of course you count the fishing industry, that is. It seems that, during his time in the north-east, Buffalo Bill even managed to throw the fish markets into turmoil. The *Aberdeen Daily Journal* reported on the 31st of August 1904:

> The glutted markets and poor prices last week, it is said, was the result of the fishermen planning to get into port during the visit of Buffalo Bill's show, and the scarcity of Monday and yesterday, and consequent advance in prices, were attributable to the same cause.

One final piece of disruption came on the final day, which had been set aside for the annual 'Pearson's day in the country' when 2,000 children were to have departed Aberdeen for an excursion to Milltimber, on Deeside. However, the Great North of Scotland Railway

Company was desperately short of railway carriages since all those available had been pressed into service as 'specials' for Buffalo Bill's show. In consequence, the outing had to be postponed until the following Saturday.

Professor Ferenc Morton Szasz identifies a 'persistent legend'[13] that several of the Indians were so taken with Aberdeenshire that they settled there permanently and married local women but, once again, hard evidence is lacking.

Kittybrewster Goods Yard is now a retail park. Central Park, which in its time accommodated not only Buffalo Bill, but also Barnum & Bailey's *Greatest Show on Earth*, remained a cattle market well into the 1990s but has since been redeveloped as a housing scheme.

Peterhead

Early on Sunday the 28th, Buffalo Bill's trains pulled into the 'Blue Toon's' now defunct station on the Great North of Scotland Railway Company's Buchan line and the company made the short journey to the nearby showgrounds.

The venue was advertised as the Roanheads (or Ronheads, the spellings were apparently interchangeable) Park, which was built over c. 1930. However, the *Peterhead Sentinel & Buchan Journal* discloses that the shows actually took place on the adjacent field known as the Feuars' South Enclosure.[14] Writing many decades later, Alex Sutherland,[15] who had witnessed the visit as a small boy, identified this location as the site later occupied by the municipal bowling greens and tennis courts. The *Aberdeen Free Press* supplies the detail that the site was opposite the Gadle (or Geddle) Braes and that an undulating piece of ground was selected for the arena.[16]

Buffalo Bill got a special deal on the rent – James Sutherland settled for just £10, provided that the horse manure was thrown in as well!

The water supply was contracted from T. H. Scott, the Burgh Surveyor, at £2 for the two days. Accommodation was obtained from Agnes J.

Smith of the Royal Hotel and James Reid and Son supplied both the livery and the billboard lot. The livery consisted of three country teams and one town wagon, all at 10/- each. The rental of the billboard lot, in Queen Street Park, was charged at 5/- and four 4/- tickets.

Immediately after breakfast that Sunday morning, a substantial body of Indians ventured out to explore the rocky and sandy shore. In search of shells and other curios, they wandered a mile northwards along the coast to the village of Buchanhaven where, being dressed in traditional costumes, their appearance raised considerable alarm. The local people were, however, soon reassured by the party's far from warlike disposition.

Three of the Indians, in paint and feathers, attended that afternoon's Salvation Army meeting. What exactly they made of this particular variety of 'bluecoats' is unfortunately not recorded, beyond the fact that they took up position in the front seats and manifested intense interest in the proceedings. Colonel Cody later wrote a letter to the adjutant, expressing gratitude for the interest taken in the spiritual well-being of his company.

The day of the shows, Monday the 29th, was one of the warmest and brightest that had been experienced that year and, by noon, the thoroughfares were thronged with holidaymakers, all headed for the Wild West. Throughout the day, the Gadle Braes and all the streets in the vicinity of the Roanheads Park were overrun. The ticket vans opened for business at one but, long before the appointed hour, substantial and expectant crowds laid siege to the entrance.

In 1904, motor transport was still in its infancy and, for all but the most well to do, the bicycle represented the slickest mode of private transport to be had. As at the other venues, the roads into town were filled with a far greater number of cyclists than are ever likely to be witnessed today. Many, no doubt, took advantage of the service advertised by John Johnston, junior, of 28, North Street. Mr Johnston undertook to take care of cycles at a small charge, for the duration of the show, and Charles Ingram, of 15, Queen Street, advertised a similar service.

On the day of the shows, cheap return tickets were issued at

Maud and intermediate stations, for the special trains departing at 10.33 a.m. and 5.42 p.m., and returning from Peterhead at five past seven and eleven in the evening. Similar facilities were run to and from Fraserburgh on the following day.

Once again, several performers ventured out on to the streets of the town, individually or in parties, and, of these, the *Peterhead Sentinel & Buchan Journal* recorded:

> Cossacks in turbans and gabardines, vaqueros with broad and curly-brimmed hats, cowboys with shirts and ties that did not seem to call for much washing walked jauntily along the pavement, not neglecting the lasses. Stalwart Indians stalked through the streets, their coal black hair and coloured plumes showing high above the heads of the crowds that followed wherever they appeared.[17]

Around 9,000 people attended the afternoon performance, with a further 12,000 in the evening. Both of these appearances 'were pronounced to be unqualified successes'.[18]

A generous measure of the obvious enthusiasm was reserved for Colonel Cody. The bicycle leap through space was witnessed with 'awe and wonder' but '[w]hen 'Buffalo Bill' himself appeared in the arena, he was greeted with cheers, and his rare marksmanship on horseback called forth hearty encomiums from the onlookers.'[19]

A signed photograph of Buffalo Bill survives, inscribed 'Peterhead' and dated 29th August 1904, in the collection of Joseph G. Rosa.

A letter to an associate at home, headed 'Peterhead', bears the same date as the autographed photograph. Its main preoccupations lay in Cody's vexed and complex business interests elsewhere but he did take the time to express his obvious satisfaction at the show's warm reception in Scotland: 'The first part of this season was not the best but of late business has been immense.'[20]

Until half past one on the following morning, no one seemed to want to go to bed. Then it was all over. An expanse of waste paper on the showground, a partly collapsed wall and posters which would continue to cling to the walls for some days yet to come – these things remained, in the words of the *Peterhead Sentinel & Buchan Journal*, 'to attest the visit to Peterhead of the greatest show that ever came to the district'.[21]

Major Burke's press releases frequently lauded the show's educational qualities but, sadly, it sometimes left a less elevating impression upon the minds of the young. In the days following Buffalo Bill's departure from Peterhead, an element among the local juveniles took to lassoing ladies' hats, one young miscreant proving so persistent that the police were obliged to intervene!

Fraserburgh

Every place that Buffalo Bill's show ever visited has its own treasured memories and anecdotes but the Broch holds a virtually unanswerable claim to having been *the* most eventful and incident-packed of all the Scottish venues in 1904.

The entourage commenced to unload its three special trains at five o'clock on the morning of Tuesday the 30th and cavalcades of the finest horses ever seen locally cantered out to the exhibition grounds, by way of Saltoun Place and Maconochie Road. The fishing was light and so the day was practically recognised as a holiday. The weather conditions were appropriately perfect.

The show's great canvas city occupied the whole of the Links, extending from the South Church down to where the tool works was later sited. The *Fraserburgh Advertiser*'s 'They Say' column lamented that 'Buffalo Bill got the use of the links at a mere song' and 'the clearing of the rubbish and the putting to right the ground will absorb B.B.'s payment'.[22]

The advanceman's log reveals that the actual sum paid to M. Tarras of the 'Town House' was the admittedly lenient figure of £5 5/-.

As at the other venues, unprecedented crowds flocked into town from the surrounding districts so that accommodation for both man and beast was at a premium. Between 20,000 and 25,000 people visited the show, over 3,000 of whom arrived by special trains, and the day's aggregate takings came close to £2,000.

The de facto holiday extended to the nearby town of Rosehearty, where the streets were almost deserted and, all day long, the horse-drawn omnibuses were kept busy ferrying people back and forward on the Fraserburgh road.

The eighteen police officers under Inspector Middleton obviously performed their duties admirably since no disturbances were reported in connection with the show, notwithstanding that the numbers of people seen in Fraserburgh that day constituted a record figure.

Quite apart from the brisk commerce generated by the crowds of visitors, a number of people from the town's business community did rather well for themselves. A. G. Gavin, of 80, Mid Street, was engaged to put up gaily-coloured posters, whose appearance throughout the town did much to add to the sense of anticipation, as well as to the holiday atmosphere on the day itself. A 'small daub' was posted inside the fish market, for which A. Tarris was remunerated with two 4/- tickets. A billboard was erected at the entrance to the Links by David K. Cumming, a contractor of 51, Charlotte Street, for a fee of £5. In payment for the billboard lot, William Alexander, the Burgh Surveyor, who had also arranged for the water supply, received 10/- and two 4/- tickets. Accommodation was obtained at the Grand Hotel, then under the proprietorship of Mrs W. Morrison. A. McKay, of the Saltoun Hotel, supplied additional livery, in the form of three country teams at 10/- apiece. The more expensive tickets were placed on sale by John Trail, stationer, at 9, Mid Street.

William Norrie, a professional photographer whose studio was at 28, Cross Street, created an excellent souvenir of this unique occasion. The surviving photographic record of Buffalo Bill's visits to Scotland is sparser than might be imagined but Fraserburgh is very much the honourable exception. Prints of several superb shots taken by Norrie were advertised for sale in the wake of the visit.

The first of these depicted Cody and a large band of Indian men on horseback on the South Pier. Colonel Cody was next introduced to John Cranna, the harbour treasurer, and the pair stood in animated conversation for several minutes.

A group of nine Indians were photographed standing on the

rocks below Kinnaird Head and the Wine (otherwise Aric) Tower, looking out to sea. The progress of a small sailing boat in the background enables us to determine that the shot in which the Indians are seen gazing intently out to sea was taken first, while a second, more relaxed, grouping was taken a minute or so after.

The Indians were accorded a guided tour of the Kinnaird Head Preserve Works and were delighted when their guide, Councillor Mackie, presented them with a tin of McConochie's Canned Herrings apiece.

The Wild West show certainly had its share of thrills and spills. Riding at breakneck speed is an inherently risky business and accidents of various kinds, even resulting in occasional fatalities, inevitably occurred.

During the afternoon performance, an Indian named Little Bear injured himself in a riding accident painfully reminiscent of the mishap at Sheffield, in 1891, which had cost Paul Eagle Star his life. His horse slipped and fell upon its rider while crossing the Links Road, which, somewhat unusually, traversed the arena. He was at once carried to his tipi, where he was attended by Dr Slessor.

Little Bear got off comparatively lightly but remained behind at the Thomas Walker Hospital for almost a full week, suffering from a festered foot. It was not until the following Monday, the 5th of September, that he was able to rejoin the entourage at Perth.

Little Bear must have been greatly impressed by the Roman Catholic missionaries, who, by 1904, along with other denominations, had made considerable inroads on the reservations. He presented himself at the morning service at the local chapel on Sunday the 4th, in full warpaint, and attracted much attention from the other communicants. On the following morning, the day of his departure, the fast-recuperating Little Bear was virtually mobbed by the scholars, who were assembling for their lessons, while he paced up and down outside the Senior School to exercise his injured foot. To his great credit, he just smiled back and took it all in his stride. I have no doubt that this Lakota warrior in particular was fondly remembered for decades thereafter.

The Links, an expanse of grassy land lying between Maconochie

Road and the shore, still exists in essentially the same form today, though a certain amount of peripheral development has taken place during the intervening period.

Notes

1. 26 August 1904
2. 27 August 1904
3. *Aberdeen Daily Journal*, 27 August 1904
4. 27 August 1904
5. *Aberdeen Daily Journal*, 27 August 1904
6. 1 September 1904
7. Ibid.
8. 27 August 1904
9. Same date
10. 29 August 1904
11. Possibly John Keith, mentioned by Sam Maddra at p. 89 of *Hostiles?*, as one of Cody's companions in his ill-fated mission to bring in Sitting Bull. Merrill Keith, a neighbouring stock raiser in Nebraska, is also known, from p. 13 of *Buffalo Bill's Great Wild West Show* by Walter Havighurst.
12. Dated the 27th and published on the 30th August 1904
13. *Scots in the North American West, 1790–1917*, p. 146
14. 3 September 1904
15. Letter to Barry Dubber, 2 May, year not given but probably 1990
16. 30 August 1904
17. 3 September 1904
18. *Aberdeen Daily Journal*, 30 August 1904
19. Ibid.
20. Sarah J. Blackstone, *The Business of Being Buffalo Bill – Selected Letters of William F. Cody, 1879–1917*, p. 28
21. 3 September 1904
22. 2 September 1904

21

THE HIGHLANDS

HUNTLY

Wednesday the 31st of August was the turn of Huntly, 'the capital of Strathbogie'.[1] The Market Muir, an expanse of ground belonging to the Town Council, was obtained in a lot contract for £10, payable to Mr Shearer, the Burgh Surveyor. This included the water supply and the use of a billboard at the venue.

A further billboard lot, adjoining the railway, was rented for £2 from the Great North of Scotland Railway but the stationmaster was tenant of the ground and used it to grow potatoes. Erecting the billboard necessitated the destruction of part of the crop, and proper restitution had to be made. A handwritten note appended to the advanceman's log indicates the nature of the ad hoc compromise adopted: 'Squared station master with 5 tickets for potatoes.'

Before the hour of four in the morning, 'hurrying feet and excited voices'[2] were already tripping towards the station through the grey and chilly dawn – all were anxious to be present at the detraining. Hundreds of people, in their reckless haste to secure a good view of proceedings, took their position so close to the line that, in the interests of safety, they had to be moved back by the station authorities with the assistance of the police. At ten minutes past four, the whistle of the first train sounded and, in the next instant, the engine emerged from the gloaming as it rounded the Greenhaugh corner.

The account given in the *Huntly Express* was firmly focused upon the proceedings at the railway station and the description of the unloading process is without peer.[3] The order in which the trains arrived reflected a carefully devised plan as they carried personnel and equipment in precisely the order in which they were required.

The first train, drawn by a pair of powerful locomotives, appeared to be endless as it completed a forward and backwards shunting manoeuvre. It was then divided into two and unloaded from separate bays. The first portion contained the wagons and the tents. Behind those were the sleeping cars in which the small army of workers had rested during the journey from Fraserburgh. In the second came the stabling cars for the dray horses.

First upon the scene were the station officials, with three of Buffalo Bill's agents who had arrived in town on the previous evening. Within minutes, the labourers had sprung into position on every side. Most appeared remarkably fresh for such an early rise, although there were of course exceptions.

The first task was to unload the horses and, while this was in progress, the second train, bringing more equipment, came in at quarter to five. The wagons were always run on to the flat cars already loaded so that they could be run off again, without delay, on arrival at the next venue. A 'skid' was attached to the end car and a powerful pair of draught horses pulled the wagons down the incline. Their places were then taken by teams of four, six or eight as required. A total of 144 dray horses were employed by the show and their intelligence and smart appearance were frequently remarked upon. It was clear that they knew precisely what was required of them and little, if any, cajoling was needed to bring each to its appointed task.

At twelve minutes past five, the first of the wagons set off for the showground. The departure of the second coincided with the passing of the early morning train for the north and the attention of its passengers was instantly drawn to the operations in progress.

The third train, which brought the performers, pulled in on the north line, between the Bleachfield gates and the station. The onlookers watched incredulous as a cornucopian supply of Indians and other showmen spilled out on to the platform. The *Huntly Express* observed: 'Many of the Indians had a pleasant smile for the white-faced stranger, whose scalp, under other conditions, might have been a trophy for the dusky warriors whose rude customs are now but matter for our amusement.'[4]

The blinds on Colonel Cody's car remained drawn and it was not until nine o'clock that he emerged and drove to the Market Muir in a buggy drawn by a pair of beautiful horses.

At the same hour as many of the country people would have been setting off for town, rain began to fall. Cheap day returns were issued from Keith, Insch and intermediate stations – 2,020 passengers came from the direction of Keith and 1,500 from Insch. 'Busses were run from such places as Aberchirder, Turriff, Alford, Strathdon, Cabrach, and Glass. Never had such crowds been seen in Huntly – the only parallel which suggested itself to the *Aberdeen Free Press* being a great revival meeting that had taken place there in the 1860s.[5]

The bedraggled condition of those arriving by horse-drawn carriages left no scope for enquiry about the weather experienced on the way. By twelve, rain fell in torrents and the *Huntly Express* was generous in its praise for whoever had had the presence of mind to throw open Stewart's Hall for the shelter of the women and children.[6] The rain continued unabated until one o'clock, after which conditions brightened, broken only by the occasional spell of drizzle. The main casualties were the soft drinks vendors. After two days of glorious weather beforehand, certain expectations had arisen in that direction, only to be disappointed as the anticipated bonanza failed to materialise. The demand was mostly for tea, pies and sandwiches instead.

John Wilson, of the Square, was awarded the contract for the show's supply of groceries and vegetables, while Councillor Kennedy of Bogie Street received the order for bread.

Between showers of rain, parties of Indians emerged from their tipis and went shopping in town, where they were hailed with interest wherever they appeared. Groups of Japanese were warmly cheered by schoolboys, and at times even the adults joined in the tribute as well.

Carter the Cowboy Cyclist sustained an awkward fall in the afternoon, in consequence of the wet conditions, but there was no such mishap in the evening, by which the time the weather was much improved. The aggregate attendance over both performances was estimated as approaching 20,000.

In the evening, large crowds of people awaiting the returning specials gathered on both station platforms, their numbers augmented by many townspeople. By the golden light of the waning moon, they watched entranced as the entraining operations were carried out in the same smooth and meticulous fashion as the unloading.

To the *Huntly Express*, we are once again indebted for the following account:

> The final picture left on our memory is not without interest. At night, as at morning, the Red Indians claimed our special interest. The horses had just been locked up for the journey, and the squaws with sleepy papooses on their backs were waiting for their stalwart consorts. One by one they entered the car. A stout squaw was amongst the last. Removing her child from its resting-place on her back, she held it up to the burly Indian by her side, who tenderly kissed the little one, whose hands crept among the jet black hair and lingered in what was, doubtless, a loving and good old-fashioned 'cuddle.' Thus in all ages, and amongst all peoples, 'one touch of nature makes the whole world kin.'[7]

It had been a busy time at Huntly railway station and, for Mr Mitchell, the stationmaster, presumably the recipient of the tickets in compensation for the ruined potato crop, it was probably the biggest challenge of his career. Through the pages of the *Huntly Express*,[8] he expressed his appreciation to the local traders for having been so prompt in removing coal, timber and other commodities from the goods yard on Monday and Tuesday, thus clearing the way for Buffalo Bill.

The Market Muir survives as an open space, although it is now largely given over to sports fields. In recent years, Aberdeenshire Council proposed to sell it off for a supermarket development but the local Community Council mounted a successful campaign in opposition.

Elgin

Of all the Scottish venues on the 1904 tour, Elgin is among the best documented, thanks to the writings of the late Walter Jack. After reading a feature about the Old Stag pub in the *Northern Scot*, stating, inter alia, that the establishment had enjoyed a record day's takings on the occasion of the visit of 'Buffalo Bill's Circus',[9] Mr Jack was inspired to compose an article, 'Buffalo Bill Brings the Wild West to Elgin' which appeared in the *Scottish Field* for September 1987. A chapter entitled 'There's A Cowboy In The Gerden' was also included in his book, *In Days Gone By*.

The Cathedral City's first intimation of the visit was received when huge billboards were erected at Fife Arms Close, Lossie Wynd and Glover Street. So many posters were put up in every available space that the town soon resembled 'one huge picture gallery'.[10] This result was all the more remarkable for the fact that the local bill-poster, James D. Yeadon, of 62, High Street, had initially proved uncooperative. The advanceman's log records: 'No contract; he would guarantee nothing.'

As before, a large crowd converged upon the station to witness the unloading and a substantial number of cyclists rode in especially from Knockando, Aberlour and other parts of Speyside. Some had walked the three and a half miles from Llanbryd and even further afield. All the local schools had a half holiday.

A. Watt, superintendent, and John Ross, assistant superintendent, were both in attendance, while the shunting operations were carried out under the direction of John Anderson, the stationmaster.

A mad rush resulted when the performers began to emerge on to Station Road by way of the railway crossing. The *Northern Scot* reported: 'The "Redskins" in particular excited the greatest wonderment. There they sat on their steeds closely wrapped in their cloaks. It was a scene which will never be forgotten by those who were privileged to witness it.'[11]

The Japanese cavalrymen received an enthusiastic ovation when they cantered into view, duly acknowledged with a military salute.

The entourage rode out to the Public Park, by way of Duff Avenue or, as it was more specifically identified in the advanceman's log, 'Rear of Public Park, belonging to City'. The sum of £5 was paid to Acton A. Turriff, the Burgh Surveyor, with an additional charge of £1 for cleaning. A further charge of 15/- secured the water supply.

Two heavy wagons sank into the soft ground and one was extricated by a team of sixteen horses. The other had to be unloaded where it stood.

James Falconer, the baker, supplied several hundredweights of bread to the show and it may be surmised that the ovens were kept blazing for several hours in order to meet this massive order.

The site selected for the Indian camp stood on the riverbank. There the Indians cast multicoloured reflections upon the dark and placid waters of the Lossie, their variegated garb setting an effective contrast with the foliage. Meanwhile, the cowboys passed this leisure time fishing in the river but without any obvious measure of success.

A number of Indians later went shopping in town and a crowd gathered and followed them from one shop to the next. One old warrior desired to buy a particular type of bootlace but, being unable to communicate his requirements in English, he was quite at a loss as to how to carry out this transaction until some of his comrades interpreted for him. Much attention was paid to the elderly Indian by the crowds, a fact which seemed to please him greatly.

'Cossacks' also appeared on the streets of Elgin. The *Elgin Courant & Courier* recorded that:

The Cossacks have a high opinion of Elgin and its people. One young Russian gentleman was quite enthusiastic about it, and said Elgin was very beautiful, there were good men and women and nice girls, the latter remark being accompanied with a broad grin.[12]

Both local papers estimated the aggregate crowd at 30,000 so that, in both the afternoon and evening, the arena must have been full to capacity or else very close to it. Packed special trains arrived on both the Highland and GNSR lines, with between 5,000 and 6,000 travelling from Keith and Forres alone. The presence of a number of distinguished visitors was noted, among them Lady Caroline Gordon Lennox and party from Gordon Castle.

Between shows, groups of Indians strolled about on Ladyhill, where they perched upon the ruins of the ancient castle and took the air of a perfect September evening. Nearby, a number of Mexicans walked around on the grass, admired the view and made an examination of the Sebastopol cannon. Cameras were produced but the Indians beat a retreat as soon as an attempt was made to take their pictures. In contrast, the Mexicans proved more amenable and co-operated with the amateur photographers.

As regards the policing arrangements, Chief Constable Mair, assisted by Superintendent D. Cameron, acquitted himself admirably and the pair came in for honourable mention in the local paper.[13] These gentlemen had taken the wise precaution of placarding the town with 'beware of pickpockets' notices and these appear to have had the desired effect since no significant losses were reported.

When the hour of departure came, each of the trains was drawn out of the GNSR sidings in turn and transferred on to the Highland Railway for the journey to Inverness. Mr Drummond, locomotive superintendent, and T. Macewan, traffic superintendent, both of them officials of the Highland Railway Company, had been present in Elgin on the previous evening, with a view to making the necessary arrangements.

The Public Park appears on the Ordnance Survey map for 1905 as part of the Borough Briggs and is located to the west of Cooper

Park and the Lossie Green. The area has undergone considerable development but what remains is still used as a showground.

Almost eighteen years later, on the 6th of July 1922, 'Broncho Bill's Wild West and Circus' performed on Elgin's Lossie Green. This show was one of the many pale imitations that continued to appear in Great Britain for several decades after the final departure of Buffalo Bill.

Another of the odder legacies of the visit emerged in 2002, with the appearance of press reports that the genealogical research company, Scottish Roots, had received a commission from a lady seeking confirmation of the story that her grandmother had had an illegitimate child by Buffalo Bill following his visit to Elgin.[14] Further enquiries revealed that a closer approximation of the truth was that the grandmother had been inspired by the Wild West's visit to the Cathedral City to travel to the United States. She eventually returned home heavily pregnant and, for reasons that were probably unclear even then, Colonel Cody personally attracted the blame for her condition. A somewhat nebulous family tradition concerning the supposed descent from Buffalo Bill of a sixteen-year-old pupil at Kingussie High School in Newtonmore, named William Cody Winter, has also received media attention in recent years.[15]

Inverness (and John O'Groats)

According to remarks attributed to John M. Burke by *The Highland News*, Inverness was not merely the turning point on the itinerary but also the most northerly location at which the show had yet appeared or was expected to again.[16]

On arrival in the 'Highland Capital', the entourage proceeded from Inverness Station, on the other side of town, to a field on Dalneigh Farm, near Bruce Gardens. *The Inverness Courier and General Advertiser* advertised the venue as 'Cemetery Road'.[17] The performances took place there over two days, Friday the 2nd and Saturday the 3rd of September. The advanceman's log places the site, for which David A. Fraser received £20 for the two days' rental, opposite Victoria Park, apparently in the vicinity of the present Laurel Avenue. The entire area, including the park, has been swallowed up by a housing estate but the name of Dalneigh is still encountered in a few street names.

Interviewed by *The Highland News*, Colonel Cody waxed lyrical when asked for his assessment of the Highlands in general, and of the Valley of the Ness in particular:

With the exception of my own country, of course, I consider the Highlands of Scotland the finest country I ever visited. My only regret is that I am unable to see very much of it in consequence of being so much engaged during the day, and having to do my travelling by night. But,' continued Colonel Cody, as he stepped out a couple of yards from the tent door and pointed towards the Leachkin to the cottages that stud the face of the hill, 'that I consider is the finest bit of scenery I have ever seen, and if I had time I should certainly visit it. To-morrow I intend driving up to Tomnahurich, where I understand a delightful view of the town can be had.[18]

A range of Wild West souvenir postcards was on sale at Miss Johnstone's stationery shop in Bridge Street and these, no doubt, proved a great attraction to the immense crowds streaming over the Ness Bridge.

The Indian contingent, however, fell short of its usual complement. Apart from the unfortunate Little Bear, who was still convalescing in Fraserburgh, Chief Iron Tail and Philip Blue Shield were absent on Saturday the 3rd.

A photograph of a group of eleven Indians, which included Iron Tail and Lone Bear, had been taken at Land's End on the 29th of May so Colonel Cody deemed it fitting that Indians should also be photographed at John O'Groats, the most northerly settlement on the British mainland. Iron Tail and Blue Shield were dispatched by train to Wick – a rail service had been inaugurated in 1874 – travelling in the company of Mr Small. According to Griffin, Mr Small wore kilts on the Scottish leg of the tour and personally acted as the photographer.

The excursion appears to have been inspired by Major Burke. Buffalo Bill's press bureau then consisted of three members, of whom Charles Wells travelled in advance, with Burke following later and Small accompanying the show. Burke made a point of venturing as far afield as John O'Groats, arriving on the 25th of August. He managed to get himself on the guest list when Sergeant Douglas, a Highland soldier recently returned from India, married a girl from Wick at the hotel and was even moved to write a poem about the occasion. He also found the time to send Small a picture postcard bearing the humorous inscription 'From John O'Groats, John M. greets'.[19]

Small and the two Indians partook of luncheon in Randall's Station Hotel, Wick. (Located on the north side of the Bridge of Wick, this establishment is now the Riverside Nursing Home.) They next set out on the remaining eighteen miles or so of their journey to John O'Groats in a carriage hired for the purpose from George Nicol, operating from 5, River Street. A large crowd assembled in front of the hotel to speed the visitors on their way.

A reporter from the *Northern Ensign* was on hand to record his impressions of the two Indians:

> 'Iron Tail,' the older of the two, is chief of what was once the great and formidable Sioux Nation; and the younger man, 'Blue Shield,' quite a massive giant, is a chief of lower rank. They were dressed in their native garb, clean shaven, and wearing straight, long hair. Blue Shield was decorated with feathers, but no 'war paint' was visible. He was correctly described by Mr Small as 'an absolutely perfect specimen of manhood.'[20]

Nonetheless, *The People's Journal* adds the detail that certain onlookers, claiming to have seen the show at Inverness, insisted that the Indians were women, on account of their long hair and smooth faces, and that Mr Small, not for the only time in his career, was mistaken for Buffalo Bill.[21]

Once again, the enigmatic and incongruous motif of Indians gazing out to sea was favoured. Buffalo Bill's 1908 programme provides the detail that, while at Land's End the Indians had been posed looking towards their far distant home, at John O'Groats they faced east. The Land's End image, which was widely sold as a souvenir item, both in the form of a black-and-white photograph and a colour postcard, is still preserved in a number of archives. However, the photograph taken at John O'Groats has descended into relative obscurity. It is also referred to in Griffin's memoirs – in which it is implied that more than one photograph was taken – but copies of an actual print have proven highly elusive. A photograph surfaced shortly thereafter in the *Ardrossan and Saltcoats Herald*, but, in stark contrast to its Cornish counterpart, it is not otherwise known. It was captioned:

CHIEF IRON TAIL (Head Chief of the Sioux Indians of North America), and SUB-CHIEF PHILIP BLUE SHIELD of the Sioux.[22]

However, as on past occasions, it is quite certain that the validity of this statement never extended beyond the roles respectively ascribed to them in the show.

Back in Inverness, around the same hour as the photograph was being taken at John O'Groats, Colonel Cody, entertained at a cake-and-wine banquet held in the Palace Hotel by Primo Roderick Mackenzie and around forty members of the 'Clan Ord Lodge of the Royal Antediluvian Order of Buffaloes', was receiving one of the many honours accorded to him on his travels. He was affiliated to the Lodge and presented with a morocco-encased affiliation card. Responding graciously, the Colonel proposed a toast to the Mother Country. The affiliation card, which discloses the information that he was already a member of the 'Col. Cody' Lodge at Rhyl, is presently held at the Buffalo Bill Historical Center in Wyoming.

The Burgh Police controlled the massive crowds by enforcing a circular route to and from the show and it was to this prudent intervention that the *Inverness Courier & General Advertiser* attributed the absence of accidents.[23]

Spectators converged on Inverness from an immense surrounding area and Alan Gallop supplies the detail that almost five hundred spectators came from the northern isles of Orkney and Shetland and that considerable numbers also travelled from the Isle of Skye.[24] Over the two days, more than 46,000 people attended the show.

The *Inverness Courier* article continued: 'The pressure at the railway station was tremendous, especially before the departure of the special trains at night, and one cannot understand how the railway officials were able to cope with it.' But cope they did and the local station staff received the thanks and hearty congratulations of Mr Whitelaw, their chairman, for the efficient manner in which they had dealt with the unprecedented pressure experienced at the station and on the line. Special mention was made of Mr Macewan, the traffic manager (presumably the same gentleman already noted in connection with Elgin), W. MacIntyre, his chief assistant, and Colin Mackay, the station superintendent.

Notes

1 *Huntly Express*, 12 August 1904
2 *Huntly Express*, 2 September 1904
3 Ibid.
4 Ibid.
5 1 September 1904
6 2 September 1904
7 Ibid.
8 Ibid.
9 19 March 1986
10 *Elgin Courant & Courier*, 2 September 1904
11 3 September 1904
12 2 September 1904
13 *Northern Scot and Moray & Nairn Express*, 3 September 1904
14 For example, *The Herald*, 19 January 2002
15 *Sunday Express*, 2 June 2002
16 27 August 1904

17 2 September 1904
18 3 September 1904
19 *Evening Express*, 27 August 1904
20 6 September 1904
21 10 September 1904
22 16 September 1904
23 6 September 1904
24 *Buffalo Bill's British Wild West*, p. 240. His source is not known, but the presence of unspecified numbers from Orkney and Skye is referred to by *The Northern Chronicle*, 7 September 1904.

22

PERTH, STIRLING AND THE BIRTH OF CINEMA

```
ARCADE HALL,
TO-DAY AT 2.          TO-NIGHT AT 8.

         CALDER'S
     CINEMATOGRAPH.

           JUST ADDED,
     BUFFALO BILL'S
            WILD WEST SHOW.
        MUST BE SEEN TO BE BELIEVED.

   THE GREATEST AND MOST LIFE-LIKE ANIMATED PICTURE
                 EVER SHOWN.
     Along with a Host of others.   Absolutely Unrivalled.

       PRICES—Reserved Seats, 2s ;  Unreserved, 1s 6d, 1s, and 6d.
   Tickets for Reserved Seats to be had from Mr C. P. STEVENSON, Musicseller, Arcade.
```

PERTH

On Saturday, the 3rd of September, large quantities of fodder were unloaded on to the South Inch public park. From six thirty onwards on the following morning, Sunday the 4th, the trains arrived in the sidings of the Caledonian Railway goods yard, issuing forth a continuous stream of horsemen and wagons. These proceeded to break the Sabbath calm, as they tramped and rumbled their way through the streets to South Inch, the same venue as had been favoured by Barnum & Bailey in 1899. In addition to the crowds of locals who turned out to witness the detraining operation, others – many of them aroused from their slumbers by the clattering hoof beats and roll of heavy wheels – watched spellbound as they followed the progress of the strangers in their midst, from the vantage of the opened windows of the tenement dwellings lining the way.

The venue was specified in the advanceman's log as 'Eastern Division of South Inch, belonging to the City' and it was rented, at a cost of £14, from Robert Reay, the City Chamberlain.

Crowds were continuously present from first light onwards and no attempt was made to prevent them from strolling around the encampment and indulging their curiosity to its fullest satisfaction. The Indian village, roped off at the south-east corner of the park, once again proved to be the leading attraction:

> Within the allotted space little Indians – bright lively little fellows all – danced about in great glee, disregardful of the many eager eyes that watched their gambols. The laughing face of a squaw shows itself in the doorway and soon disappears.[1]

High winds prevailed overnight but no damage was done to the stables, marquee or to the great mess tent, so securely were these constructions fastened. This was thanks, no doubt, to the efficiency of the man in charge of the chain and stake wagons. The most aptly named Arthur Horseman was, as the *Perthshire Courier* proudly observed,[2] a native of Perth, who had begun his career in the printing trade as an apprentice in the *Courier* office. After a time working in Lancashire, ill health had obliged him to seek a change of direction in life – one providing a more generous supply of fresh air. He found employment in a variety of touring theatrical companies and circuses, latterly Barnum & Bailey, with whom he toured Scotland, England and the Continent. Horseman was subsequently transferred to Cody's outfit, with whom he travelled thereafter.

Street Parades

On the day of the shows, *The Perthshire Advertiser & Strathmore Journal* reported that:

> To-day, many of the braves, oblivious to the consternation that their presence evoked, paraded the streets, just as in the old days of their tribal glory they would stalk through the Prairies with the dignity begot of a consciousness that all they set eyes upon was theirs.

While this is open to misconstruction as referring to a street cavalcade, the truth of the matter is that Indians and other performers, as at the other venues, were actively encouraged to stroll through the streets in full costume, as one of the foremost means of promoting the show.

A cavalcade through the principal thoroughfares, on the morning of the opening performance at a new stand and duly advertised in advance, had featured regularly during the earlier history of the Wild West. Such parades were a standard circus practice which, by 1904, had fallen out of favour. It was particularly untenable now that an overwhelming majority of stands were for one day only.

Something of the philosophy was explained in the (Indiana) *Nuncie Evening Press*:

> A good many people came up town this morning, to see the parade but there was none, Buffalo Bill having discontinued parades in order that the time in the morning that is usually devoted to the parade may be used in perfecting arrangements for the afternoon exhibition.[3]

Increasing volumes of street traffic represented a further factor. The organisational effort involved, entailing the need for a police presence, was considerable. Informal perambulations were adopted as an alternative and far more cost-effective option which secured essentially the same purpose.

Charles Eldridge Griffin recalled that, in the whole of the 1903 season, only seven parades had been given and even then, in most cases, only as a protective measure in towns where direct competition from circuses was encountered.[4]

Insofar as can be determined, there is no record in connection with Buffalo Bill's show of any street parades whatsoever in Scotland during the course of the 1904 season nor, indeed, in 1891–92.

Buffalo Bill made an instant impression upon the Fair City, as the erecting of the tents did not, for once, go entirely to plan. On the morning of Monday the 5th, a few hours before the afternoon show commenced, a letter from Mr Lambert, Electric Engineer, was read out at the Town Council's Electric Committee, stating that a spike had accidentally been driven through an electric cable. The city's electricity supply was interfered with for about two and a half hours, before the connection could be restored.

The meeting decided upon remedial action and resolved that a chart indicating the location of the cables would be prepared for future reference. It was also agreed that the City Chamberlain should be instructed to warn future occupiers of the potential danger posed by the presence of the cables. Domestic electricity was still in its infancy during the years in which Buffalo Bill appeared in Scotland. Some towns and cities had a supply, others had yet to follow.

All of Perth's public schools closed during the Monday forenoon, in order to give the pupils the opportunity to visit the show.

The *Perthshire Constitutional & Journal* reported that the seating accommodation at both performances was fully occupied.[5] This is questionable, however, and conflicts with the account given in the *Perthshire Courier*, which related that, at the afternoon performance, 'the huge temporary enclosure on South Inch contained eight or ten thousand persons, though its capacity was far from being taxed'.[6]

The same source records that many of those who were present at the afternoon show were so impressed with what they saw that they returned in the evening. The enclosure was packed, with the exception of a small corner near the main entrance, and hundreds were turned away.

With one hour remaining before the start of the evening performance, all approaches to the South Inch were thronged with pedestrians. A crowd at the main entrance was described by the *Perthshire Courier* as 'something unprecedented'[7] but this was relieved to a considerable extent by the intervention of the police under Chief Constable Garrow, who kept the people moving in regular rotation.

As ever, people coming to the show utilised a variety of modes of transport. The *Perthshire Courier* contained the information that: 'There are 53 motor cycles and 37 motor cars registered in the county.'[8] Motor cars remained the preserve of the very wealthy. Those arriving for each show were probably only ever counted in dozens at most and, since the 'horseless carriage' was still a relative novelty, its appearance no doubt added to the excitement of the occasion.

The *Perthshire Courier* leaves us a graphic description of the spectacle that night:

> The evening was indeed the time to see the Show at its best; for then the interior was brilliantly illuminated by electric light, which, reflected on the green grass, with the sea of faces ranged on three sides of the enclosures, had a picturesque and taking effect begetting a feeling of being in wonderland.[9]

The South Inch still endures today and, in its present condition as a vast expanse of flat parkland, it has probably not changed markedly in over a hundred years. It continues to accommodate periodical shows and exhibitions.

Stirling

The show arrived on the early morning of Tuesday the 6th, at the Caledonian Railway loading bank sidings next to the Shore Road, on the north-west bank of the Forth, in the Riverside area.

The venue was a field on Raploch Farm which, at that time, was tenanted by Mr McKerracher. The advanceman's log identifies the lessors as McKerracher & Son, who had business premises at 7, Thistle Street. Rental for the one day was £18.

The field lay on the present site of the Raploch council housing estate, in the immediate environs of Woodlands Road. More specifically, Mr McKerracher's farmhouse lay just behind the old church buildings, on the east side of what is now Menzies Drive, themselves located behind the modern St Mark's Parish Church half way along Drip Road. The field extended from a little to the west of the farmhouse to the immediate east of the Combination Hospital, established the previous year and now known as Kildean Hospital. In common with the field itself, the farm buildings have disappeared without trace.

The site of the canvas arena can thus be located within the shadow of the rock on which Stirling's ancient and historical castle rises; no doubt a fair view of the day's proceedings was also to be had from the top of the Wallace Monument.

One myth that persists locally is that the show appeared in King's Park. The confusion obviously arises from the name 'King's Field', as it was referred to in the publicity materials. According to the *Stirling Journal and Advertiser*, King's Park, still the occasional venue for circuses, was Cody's preferred venue and it appears that the Town Council's objections were to blame for his failure to secure it.[10]

A certain measure of concern, and even paranoia, certainly seems to have attended the possible selection of King's Park. This was a legacy of the visit of Barnum & Bailey five years previously. An entry in the *Royal Burgh of Stirling Council Minutes 1903-04*, ran as follows: 'Buffalo Bill's Show. – The Clerk was instructed to communicate with Mr Stafford Howard and Messrs Dewar, asking that if an application is made for the use of King's Park for the show, the Town Council be consulted.'[11]

The opinion was expressed by the *Stirling Observer* that not only was 'King's Field' rather out of the way, its definite unsuitability for the purpose was evidenced by the dreadful underfoot conditions resulting from the heavy rain that fell at intervals in the evening.[12] However, owing to the uncommon size of the exhibition, it was undeniable that no ordinary field would suffice.

'King's Field' appears to have been an ad hoc designation only and, according to the *Stirling Sentinel*,[13] the reasons for this name were very far from clear, even at the time. It may have been chosen out of a sense of rivalry with King's Park or else it could have been intended as a tribute to the then Dean of Guild, Mr King. No doubt, like the 'Noon Stage', they had to call it something.

Councillor Bayne, together with several other local gentlemen, was accorded the privilege of having dinner with the staff and performers in the huge dining marquee. He had probably been involved in the negotiations with the show's management, in which connection the advanceman's log contains an interesting entry regarding the arrangements for the water supply: 'No contract made. Mr Morris the Town Clerk would not sign the contract saying he would have to put the matter before the Council, but he thought it would be £1.'

On hearing that the show was coming, the shop assistants in Aberfoyle launched a campaign to have the shops closed on the day of the show. Holidays there were few and far between and, now that the busiest part of the tourist season was at an end, the sales staff held high hopes that their employers would accede to their petition and permit them to attend the show. It might well be that they won the day for it was recorded that the majority of the villages around Stirling elected to mark the occasion with a holiday.[14]

The *Stirling Observer*, in those more class-conscious times, also remarked upon the difference to be discerned between the afternoon and evening attendances.[15] The matinee audience was composed mostly of country people, with the gentry and residents of the suburbs much in evidence. The evening audience was made up more of the townspeople and 'working classes'. No doubt a similar dichotomy manifested itself in the other towns and cities on the itinerary.

A familiar theme reprised in Stirling was that of the size of the crowds swelling through the streets, the *Stirling Observer* remarking: 'The aspects of the streets from the Station to the Drip Road was reminiscent of the scenes at Bridge of Allan Games.'[16]

A large number of stalls selling refreshments and other items took up strategic positions along the way, while the highways were also lined with 'the halt, the blind, and the lame',[17] commending themselves to the public sympathy.

The Burgh Police came out in force and were augmented by several members of the County forces. The precise arrangements are preserved by the Stirling Police Museum in the still-extant Chief Constable's Standing Orders for Stirling Police Burgh, dated the 5th of September 1904 and signed by Chief Constable Ferguson:

Inspector Young and Constables Bean and Dewar will take duty at the Show-yard from 6 to 11 a.m. and Constable Kennedy at the Caledonian Railway goods yard from 6 to 8 a.m.

Constable Forbes of Stirling Burgh Police, Constables Adam Ross Dunblane and James Crerar Doune, of the Perthshire Police, and Constables Smith, Stirling, Stormont Bridge of Allan, Dunbar Bannockburn, Crichton Whins of Milton, and Somerville, Cowie, of Stirlingshire Police will take duty at the Show Yard Drip Road from 11 a.m. to 11 p.m.

The 8 Constables last named will report themselves at the Show Yard about 10.30 a.m. when they will be posted by Inspector Young under the direction of the manager in charge.

Inspector Young, Constables Bean and Dewar will be relieved at 11 a.m. and they will then get dinner and resume street duty at 1 p.m.

Inspector Jenkins will remain on duty until 8 a.m. when he will be relieved by Sergeant Coutts.

Inspector Young, Constables Bean and Dewar will be allowed half an hour for tea from 4.30 to 5 p.m.

Special trains brought sightseers from a twenty-mile radius, and return tickets were issued for the price of a single. Two such special excursions came in from the 'Hillfoots' district of the nearby 'Wee County', Clackmannanshire.

In those days, the Forth and Clyde line brought people into Stirling from the west, a fact attested by the lone signal box still standing in the hamlet of Kippen Station. The traffic seen on the line that day was the heaviest since the visit of Barnum & Bailey. The train arriving in Stirling at 12.19 brought passengers from Balfron and Buchlyvie. In days gone by, Kippen had been the scene of a desperate showdown with Rob Roy McGregor but that could have been nothing compared to the melee that ensued when Buffalo Bill Cody hit town. The train, being of ordinary length, was already packed close to capacity when it reached Kippen. The waiting passengers stormed the train and crammed themselves into the carriages and even the guard's van. Twenty people piled into carriages meant for ten. Even so, on arrival at Stirling, the train was obliged to return to Kippen for those who had been left behind. Clearly, the lessons of five years before had not been learned.

In common with several other venues, the show's visit coincided more or less precisely with the appearance of General Booth, of Salvation Army fame, who was, at the time, engaged in a lecture tour by motor car. The public popularity of the general's mission to the lapsed masses had risen to unprecedented heights after he was invited to call upon King Edward VII. Even then, there was really no competition as to which was the more popular entertainment and the *Alloa Journal* drew some unkind comparisons.[18] Although two special trains had been required to transport local people to Buffalo Bill's show, the railway company's normal arrangements were found perfectly adequate for those desirous of seeing General Booth.

The evening performance was blighted by wet weather and took place in a deluge of rain so that the turnout was not as great as for the afternoon show, for which the weather had been fine. Some of the show's wagons stuck fast, their wheels sinking deep into the mire, and upwards of two dozen draught horses were yoked up to pull them out.

The arc lamps, as ever, illuminated the showground but there was no such arrangement for the roadway, which was congested with vehicles. As had happened in the afternoon, there was a crush at the exit gates and some people were pushed against a hedge. Once again, it was attributed to sheer good fortune that no accident resulted.

The misery of the spectators was compounded by the omission of the local pubs and hotels to apply for special licences to go on serving beyond 10 p.m. As a result, after the show ended at nine-forty, there was a scramble for the public houses in the immediate vicinity, which, of course, were unable to meet the demand. Others headed for the town centre and reached the licensed establishments before the clocks struck the fatal hour of ten but many with trains to catch to the outlying areas were obliged to forgo refreshments.

Various 'souvenirs' were discovered amidst the debris on the following morning. Among these were several ladies' shoes which had lodged in the mud and which their owners had been obliged to leave behind.

The total gate amounted to £1,200, a considerable sum for those days, leaving a clear profit margin over the estimated daily running cost of £1,100 advanced by the *Stirling Observer*.[19]

The Birth of Cinema

For those who, for one reason or another, had missed the show, there was one final chance to savour something of the occasion. Calder's Cinematograph paid a visit to the Arcade Hall on Saturday the 10th, where an excellent evening's entertainment was held in prospect. Of the many new films, there was one, newly added, featuring Buffalo Bill's show. The age of the cinema was just around the corner. The ad in the *Bridge of Allan Gazette and Visitor's List* said it all:

> MUST BE SEEN TO BE BELIEVED.
> THE GREATEST AND MOST LIFE-LIKE
> ANIMATED PICTURE EVER SHOWN.[20]

A similar entertainment, with full supporting programme, was held at Edinburgh's Operetta House the following spring.[21]

Coverage of the Russo-Japanese war then in progress, as highlighted by Buffalo Bill, provided one of the staples of Walker & Company's Royal Cinematograph, which came to Stirling's Albert Hall on the 31st of August 1904.

The first-ever Western movie, *The Great Train Robbery*, had been made in 1903 and was already doing the rounds. The death knell of the Wild West show was sounding loud and clear.

Frank Sherman adorns the walls of his barber's shop in the town's Lower Bridge Street with a collection of vintage photographs. One of these depicts a procession of horsemen riding along Port Street, led by a detachment of men in slouch hats. It was previously understood to depict the Wild West's visit but, since Buffalo Bill's men rode from the Shore Road to a location half way along Drip Road and must be taken to have passed in full view of that section of Stirling Rock which accommodates the beheading stone, it is far from obvious why they would have been proceeding down Port Street in the direction of Bannockburn. It can only be concluded that the photograph is of some other concern entirely and the most likely candidate is Barnum & Bailey's street procession, known to have passed that way in 1899.

Notes

1. *Perthshire Advertiser & Strathmore Journal,* 5 September 1904
2. 6 September 1904
3. 27 August 1907
4. *Four Years in Europe with Buffalo Bill,* p. 31
5. 7 September 1904
6. 6 September 1904
7. Ibid.
8. 30 August 1904
9. 6 September 1904
10. 19 August 1904
11. Minute number 997, meeting of Provost's Committee Stirling, 2 August 1904, p. 208
12. 7 September 1904
13. 13 September 1904
14. *Stirling Observer,* 7 September 1904
15. Ibid.
16. Ibid.
17. Ibid.
18. Cited by the *Stirling Sentinel* of 13 September 1904
19. 7 September 1904
20. 10 September 1904
21. As advertised by the *Scotsman,* 8 March 1905

23

RENFREWSHIRE

Paisley

On Wednesday the 7th of September, the show pulled into Paisley's Greenlaw sidings shortly after five in the morning. Many slumbering locals were roused to consciousness at this unusual hour as the procession rumbled its way along the streets forming the route from the station to the advertised venue. This was, in the words of the advert appearing in the *Paisley & Renfrewshire Gazette*, 'The Show Ground', located in a field off the Greenock Road, at the northern extremity of the town.[1]

More specifically, the location can be identified as the 'Clayholes'. As the name implies, the site had once been used for mining clay for the manufacture of bricks. The abandoned pits soon filled with water and, by around 1870, this activity had resulted in an entire tract of land on the north side of Paisley, extending for about a mile from the foot of Love Street westwards, being reduced to a surreal landscape pocked with a great number of deeply scored lagoons. These were fringed with reeds and were inhabited by pond life in abundance. All too often, they provided the setting for rafting expeditions by local boys, broadly similar in concept to the ill-conceived boating adventures from the eastern bank of the Mississippi, graphically recalled by Buffalo Bill in the opening pages of his autobiography.

The process of reclamation was begun and, by the time that Buffalo Bill hit town, the Clayholes existed only in name. Tenements and factories now stood where minnows, frogs and newts had sported amidst aquatic weeds. The title, however, continued to attach itself to the piece of vacant ground, above the junction with Caledonia Street, which the Town Council had agreed, on the 12th of June 1888, to lease for the accommodation of travelling fairs.

A little further to the north lies Saint James's Park, a large expanse of flat land now adjacent to Glasgow Airport but occupied, in those days, by a racecourse. It was by association with this facility that the Clayholes had come to provide the focus for sideshows and other itinerant public entertainments of the kind.

The Clayholes proper proved insufficient in size to accommodate the show in its entirety so only a portion of the canvas city was erected there. This consisted of the dining tent, the stabling facilities for the dray horses, the sideshow tent and several subsidiary structures. An adjacent field to the immediate north was also secured, the total rental of £8 being paid to Robert Thompson, acting on behalf of the Town Council. The advanceman's log notes that the field was normally under the occupation of Mr Lang, a local butcher.

The arena was put up on the adjoining field, at the rear of Buchanan Terrace, a name which appears to be no longer in use but refers to the block of tenements on the west side of the Greenock Road, immediately below the present junction with McFarlane Street. This location also contained the stables for the performing horses and a number of smaller tents, as well as the Indian encampment, occupying a well-frequented corner of the showground, lying directly across the road from the racecourse.

Among all the usual commercial arrangements, a handwritten note scrawled on the entry in the advanceman's log indicates that four sacks of flour were purchased from Duncan McNair & Son for the sum of two pounds and twelve shillings. Additional livery was hired from the local office of the Glasgow Tramway and Omnibus Company and accommodation at the Globe Hotel was provided by George Gwynne. Water was obtained from the Paisley Water Company for £1 10/-.

A report in the *Paisley Daily Express* indicates that the vital question of whether or not the schools should be conceded a holiday in honour of the occasion hung precariously in the balance.[2] At certain other venues, there were those who advocated meekly bowing to the inevitable but, in Paisley, the educational authorities were made of sterner stuff. The proposal that the Board Schools should be accorded a half holiday on the afternoon of the show received some discussion but the view prevailed that the concession was unnecessary. The schools were to be opened as usual, on the grounds that those parents who felt so inclined had the option of taking their children along to the evening performance.

The big day was favoured by excellent weather and among those who augmented the generous crowds of local people attending at both performances were the merchants of the Renfrewshire village of Lochwinnoch, whose monthly holiday, by a happy coincidence, fell on the day of the show. The operatives in the various works, incidentally, had their autumn holidays on Monday the 12th and, once again, Buffalo Bill – by this time in Ayr – provided the big attraction. Meanwhile, a pair of Lochwinnoch laddies perpetrated an outrage involving an air gun and a stairheid beacon, which was generally understood as being in homage to Buffalo Bill.

In the course of the morning, a party of Indians, luridly conspicuous in all the glory of their traditional costumes and warpaint, did the rounds of the shops on Paisley's High Street, exhibiting much curiosity over the items on sale and indulging their predilection for all things colourful and gaudy. Their impromptu appearance naturally occasioned high anxiety among the timid young ladies who made up the greater part of the serving staff in these establishments. Their gentle and sensitive hearts must have quivered at hastily recalled impressions of the wicked and blood-thirsty dispositions popularly bruited of the American Indian race but, on the evidence of the

'Town Talk' column of the *Paisley & Renfrewshire Gazette*, the strange visitors conducted themselves with impeccable propriety and their conduct gave not the slightest cause for complaint.

Exhibiting a rare degree of insight for 1904 and anticipating *Dances with Wolves* by eighty-six years, the columnist concluded:

> Everyone's ideas, I fancy, must have been modified of the Indian, and perhaps it is for the better, for truly those blood and thunder stories of our boyhood were awful things for perverting the truth – and I think the Red Indian suffered thereby.[3]

Back in 1891, a journalist[4] had recorded that young Johnny Burke No Neck knew well enough the value of an English sixpence and it would seem that, thirteen years on, tipping an Indian child a coin of this precise denomination remained a common enough impulse. In the course of one of the performances, a gentleman in the audience found himself near to a small Indian boy, who with a painted but expressionless countenance stood watching the other Indians dancing. The gentleman handed the child a sixpence, which was gravely accepted but without the slightest indication of whether its recipient was pleased or otherwise by the gesture. This incident illustrated the inscrutability that was so often remarked upon as a racial characteristic and a Yankee who chanced to be at hand commented, by way of explanation, that 'them kids neither laugh nor cry'.

Once again, we are indebted to the 'Town Talk' columnist of the *Paisley & Renfrewshire Gazette* for having preserved a record of this encounter. His closing words on the subject were, 'And as I looked at this marvel of Indian stolidity I passed a mental wish that some Paisley kids were constructed that very way.'[5]

As soon as the final performance was over, a permanent staff of 175 men set to work on dismantling the arena. In point of fact, the removal began even before the evening show had commenced. Just as the personnel and items of equipment arrived at a new venue in the order in which they were required, precisely the same principle applied in reverse on departure. Immediately a tent or other object was no longer required it was taken down and packed away. No sooner had Carter executed his daring leap than the operation to dismantle his chute was underway. And while the strains of 'God Save the King' rang out around the arena, the first of the wagons were already making their way back to the station.

The *Paisley & Renfrewshire Gazette* provides a lively account of Buffalo Bill's departure from Paisley and doubtless contains a great deal of insight into the procedures which were habitually followed:

In the rear of the amphitheatre where the performance was given, the horses were stabled in a tent. Ere the audience had left the shelter of the large tent, the canvas for the horses was cleared away, and the horsemen, just as they came out of the arena with their quaint and curious dresses and ornaments, waited close by for the orders to go to the railway station. 'Buffalo Bill' drove off in a neat little trap drawn by two grey horses, and then the others filed themselves into twos and formed a long procession 'en route' for Greenlaw siding. The sight was most picturesque, and those who missed seeing the show may have been rewarded by the sight of this procession of horsemen. The motley company was followed by a large crowd along the entire route. Once inside the station the work of entraining went forward with methodical precision. The large waggons specially built for the purpose were filled to the utmost by the horses. Each rider made for a waggon known to himself, dismounted, unharnessed his horse, and led it into the van. There was not the semblance of disorder in it at all; everything was prearranged and well conducted. A certain order was followed by the horses in going into the vans, so that some of them followed each other, without being led, and were quietly tied up for the night. A busy scene was witnessed at the Showground by an interested company of spectators until a late hour. The show left Greenlaw Station about 1 a.m. on Thursday for Greenock.[6]

GREENOCK

The *Greenock Herald*'s 'What The Folks Are Saying' column observed that the 8th of September was destined to be a big day in the town.[7] Not only was Buffalo Bill coming but the new minister was to be inducted at the West Parish Church. The column went on to surmise, somewhat mischievously though beyond the range of serious dispute, that the former was likely to prove the greater attraction.

When the great day came, the trains made the short journey from Paisley, arriving at the terminus in Gourock, the main port for Dunoon and the Western Isles. *The Greenock Telegraph & Clyde Shipping Gazette* recorded that: 'Unfortunately, the weather had broken completely down during the night, and the show's first glimpse of Greenock and Gourock was through a morning about as dark and dirty as could be imagined.'[8]

Greenock itself was the principal port from which countless thousands of Scots had sailed to a new life in the Americas and through which immense cargoes of cotton, tobacco and sugar were imported into Scotland.

Cody's entourage was greeted at the station by a small body of about forty ardent souls who had stayed up and about into the wee sma' hours, intent on missing nothing of the day's events. The performers and other personnel then made their way in seemingly endless procession to Fort Matilda and pitched camp in Battery Park.

This venue was rented from James McLaughlin, of Drum Farm, for £8, payable on the day of the show. The agreement further provided that the straw and litter were to be left on the ground. The water supply was obtained for £1 from James Brown of what the advanceman's log termed the 'Corporation water co.'. A pair of country teams and one town wagon was hired from P. B. Wright and Son of West Blackhall Street, telephone Greenock 60. Accommodation was provided by Jessie Matheson, of the Royal Hotel, at 1/6d for meals and the same sum for beds. A total bill of £3 13/6d was incurred. The billposter engaged was Matthew McMillan, whose head office was at 21 & 23, Cathcart Road, telephone 296. Mr McMillan's business must have been substantial, as he also took care of arrangements for the following day in Saltcoats and his Motherwell branch, it will be recalled, had been engaged in connection with the visit to the steel town.

Beyond lay the broad Clyde estuary, with the beginnings of the Highland line on the other side. From Kilcreggan Fort, not far from Helensburgh on the northern bank, a searchlight had shone from an early hour, focusing upon the park and on Low Gourock Road.

First upon the scene came a party of surveyors in a buggy, who proceeded to disperse in sections and commenced to lay out the foundations for the canvas city. Another of the earliest arrivals was a wagon carrying several ranges and, taking up position near to Paul Jones and Son's boatyard, the fires were lit within five minutes. The dining tent and the kitchen equipment were always amongst the first of the items to arrive and the arrangements for an extremely substantial breakfast began without delay. The vegetables were cooked by steam from a boiler constructed on the fire engine principle and with a forced draught which was capable of generating the required level of heat within five minutes. Tubes from the same boiler also fed the tea and coffee urns.

Wherever the show was appearing, the meat generally came each day from Birkenhead since only the large cities could meet the demand. Notice the statement in connection with the visit to Aberdeen that: 'Mr Thomas Tune, the advance contractor, made purchases of 1000 lbs of meat and some tons of vegetables of the best Aberdeen growth.'[9]

Milk and eggs in prodigious quantities were also supplied under contract. The bread and the vegetables, as we have seen, were obtained locally.

As soon as the dining tent was in place, a detachment of men moved in with seats and tables, followed by another with the plates and a third with cutlery.

The various parties of riders, all in high spirits despite the miserable weather, chaffed and vied with one another in friendly rivalry. They dismounted on arrival and secured their horses in the shelter of the canvas stable.

The tipis were also among the first arrivals, enabling the Indians to pitch their encampment on the easterly side of the park. One woman played with her child over a bale of straw but, as soon as the tipis were erected, the Indians immediately took shelter inside. Before long, bluish wreaths of smoke were issuing from the air vents at the summits.

One regularly reported theme was the astonishment expressed by onlookers at the speed with which the various tents composing the 'canvas city' sprang up like mushrooms. Once again, system and method provided the key to this rapid transformation. Even the tent pegs were hammered in according to a definite plan, with each man adhering rigidly to his own allotted role. A company of between eight and twelve powerfully built men would stand around a tent peg in a circle and at the word of command, the first gave the peg a gentle tap. The next struck a blow, followed by the others in turn, and then a second volley drove the peg three feet into the ground in less time than it takes to tell. The gang then moved on to the next peg and the same rhythmic procedure was followed again. Up in Elgin, this process had elicited a spontaneous round of applause, and a farmer who chanced to be present was heard to remark that he would be glad to give these men a job the next time he wanted to put up a fence.

The tent skeletons were next raised by means of a special mechanical device. The show carried 1,200 tent pegs, varying from two to five feet apiece, depending on the weight they had to support. 4,000 poles were secured with twenty-two miles of rope and over the poles were draped 23,000 square yards of heavy canvas. 2,000 planks served as seats, and an equal number of trestles were also in use.

As the first breakfast party took their places in the dining tent, the labourers continued in the work of erecting the covered seats around the arena. Each race sat at a table of its own but the fare provided was exactly the same for all.

Special trains were laid on from Port Glasgow to Fort Matilda, and the tramway company had extra cars on standby, ready to be brought into service as required. For the convenience of people from the coast, arrangements were made to run steamers at ten thirty from Princes Pier and Gourock to most of the Clyde resorts.

The flat expanse of Battery Park, standing on the lower bank of the Clyde, remains a familiar landmark today and, more than a century on from the visit of Buffalo Bill, is still the regular haunt of circuses and other travelling shows.

Notes

1. 3 September 1904
2. 6 September 1904
3. 10 September 1904
4. *Sheffield & Rotherham Independent*, 10 August 1891
5. 10 September 1904
6. Ibid.
7. 27 August 1904
8. 8 September 1904
9. *Aberdeen Free Press*, 26 August 1904

24

AYRSHIRE

Cavalry Drill

Saltcoats

Continuing down the west coast, the show appeared in Saltcoats Public Park on Friday the 9th of September. The advanceman's log specifies 'Lower half of Public Park, belonging to the city'. Rental of £10 was payable on the day of the show to D. Robertson, the Burgh Surveyor.

The Burgh of Saltcoats Town Council minutes confirm the above particulars. At a committee meeting on the 9th of April 1904, the surveyor was instructed to lease the ground to 'Barnum & Baillie (*sic*) for "Buffalo Bill's Wild West Show"'. Two weeks later, it was agreed to place advertisements inviting applications from football and cricket clubs interested in renting pitches. On the 16th of May, in the absence of any satisfactory applications, it was resolved that the lower field should be re-let to William Wyllie, of Border Farm, at £10 for the year's grazing, under reservation of the right to grant the use of the field on six occasions and of the let already concluded with Barnum & Bailey.

The water supply was by arrangement with David M. Scott, of the Irvine and District Water Board, at a cost of £1.

A week in advance of the big day, several local papers helped to fire the growing sense of anticipation and paid homage to the Cody legend. The *Dalry & Kilbirnie Herald*, the *Kilwinning Chronicle*, the *Irvine Herald* and the *Stevenston Gazette* all carried a quite extraordinary and implausible story about how the future Buffalo Bill, at the tender age of nine, had single-handedly held a band of desperados at bay with a pistol, after shooting their leader through the heart, while a companion ran to summon help.[1] This heroic endeavour is not known from any of Cody's numerous biographies and so we might reasonably assume that it owes a great deal to the limitless creative talents of Major Burke.

The Ardrossan Board Schools were given the day off, with the intention that it would take the place of the annual September holiday, normally set aside for bramble picking. This break with time-hallowed tradition did not, however, meet with general assent and on Wednesday the 14th the absentee list was considerable.

Special trains were run from Largs, where an entry in the parish school log sadly records: '9th September 1904: Attendance not so good today. Some of the children took a holiday to go and see "Buffalo Bill"!'

The weather was so wet and windy that Saltcoats was probably as close as any venue on the 1904 tour came to a cancellation. Colonel Cody's legions, however, were undaunted as ever and north Ayrshire was not to be disappointed. The storm reached a furious climax during the afternoon performance. The park was quickly reduced to a quagmire and many of the spectators went home as 'muddied oafs'.[2] No doubt some old body was on hand to recall the occasion when, sixty-five years before, the grand Eglinton jousting tournament had descended into farce under similarly miserable conditions.

The prevailing atmosphere appears to have been one of deep gloom and disappointment and an item in the 'Threshings' column preserves something of the mood of despondency:

> 'Buffalo Bill's Day' will long be remembered to their cost by many who ploughed into and through the mud of Saltcoats Public Park,

where the big show was situated on Friday last. Loud and deep are the grumblings over spoiled boots and damaged clothes, and condemnation of the authorities responsible for the want of properly prepared ground for the big crowd on a wet day.[3]

The general sense of desolation was compounded by the activities of a number of pickpockets, who took advantage of the crush in the evening. The police received several complaints concerning missing purses and one Glaswegian miscreant was apprehended at the railway station. He was later liberated on a bail of £5 and bound to appear at Saltcoats Burgh Court on the Monday morning.

There have been many wet weekends in Saltcoats before and since but never one quite like this!

Saltcoats Public Park no longer exists as such but an apparently nameless area of recreational open ground in the middle of a council estate still marks its former heart. The site is now partially built over around its periphery. Millar Road marks its former northern boundary and Kinnier Road its east. Kerr Avenue lies a little to the north of the park's southern limit. The show may be taken to have arrived in Saltcoats by means of the Lanarkshire and Ayrshire Railway line, either at the former station just off the Caledonia Road or else at sidings a little further down. The railway line too has gone though its route is traced by a recreational walkway.

A photocopy of the 'Rough Rider', one of the several publications produced for the show, is preserved at the Museum of North Ayrshire in Saltcoats. Priced sixpence, the front cover bore the overprint 'Saltcoats'.

The museum also contains exhibits betokening other transatlantic connections. These include a section commemorating the local roots of American writer Edgar Allan Poe, as well as a gold-topped cane, bearing the proud inscription:

Presented to
Arthur Guthrie Esq.
    Editor of the Ardrossan & Saltcoats Herald by friends in New

York in token of their appreciation of his words of cheer and encouraging defence of the Union cause as opposed to the slaveholders' rebellion.

New York March 4th 1865

KILMARNOCK

The crowds witnessed in Kilmarnock on Saturday the 10th were widely reported as the largest in the town's history, enticed by Buffalo Bill's saturation advertising campaign, both in Kilmarnock itself and in the surrounding towns and villages.

The show found itself in direct competition with another grand attraction for Harry Lauder was appearing at the Corn Exchange theatre, performing his latest hit song, 'The Saftest o' the Family'. Also on the bill was 'Ko-Ko, the Juggling Jap'. Whether this gentleman had the opportunity to meet up with his compatriots from the Imperial Japanese Cavalry is unfortunately not recorded.

Buffalo Bill's show appeared at Beansburn, on a six-acre lot on the west side of the main road northwards, a little below the point at which it becomes Glasgow Road. The advanceman's log records that it was secured for a rental of £10, payable on the day of the show, from 'Wulliam Cleland' of Wardneuk Farm. Once again, no doubt, the advanceman was faithfully recording what he heard in the gentleman's Scottish accent and this factor may be taken as fully accounting for the unorthodox rendering of his Christian name.

The field at Beansburn, which is commemorated by the stretch of road bearing the same name and extends roughly opposite the present site of Dean Park, has since been developed so that the former open space is now occupied by a complex of streets, in the vicinity of Campbelltown Drive and Innellan Drive. According to local lore, the name of Beansburn derives from 'a tragic tale of a hapless maiden', known as Beanie, who, at some unspecified time long past even in 1904, had drowned herself in one of its pools.[4] The *Kilmarnock Standard* on the day of the show encapsulated the sense of excitement and occasion on that Saturday afternoon and evening:

> Of course you're going – we're all going Beansburn way to-day. Not since it rose out of the silence and the mists of time will so many visitors have wended their way to the little village and taken the north road, as to-day.[5]

Regarding the suitability of the venue, one journalist was moved to regret that tramcars had not yet arrived in the town:

> The location of the Show at Beansburn is excellent, though a year hence, when the cars are running, it would have been super-excellent. Ample facilities will be provided for those who prefer a 'bus to Shanks-his-naigie.[6]

Heavily laden trains poured into Kilmarnock from the surrounding districts throughout the day and, during the morning, a large number of people presented themselves at the showground for an early look at the attractions.

Once again, several performers went abroad during the early part of the day so that, whether you went to the show or not, as observed by the *Ardrossan & Saltcoats Herald*, a glimpse of the various exotic specimens of humanity was to be had, as they walked the streets and did their shopping.[7] The *Kilmarnock Herald* recorded:

> The members of 'Buffalo Bill's' remarkable company of rough riders, including cowboys, Redskins, Cossacks, and Japanese, excited great interest as they strolled through the town, the Red Indians being followed with open-mouthed curiosity, not unmixed with awe, by the small boys who are in the habit of feasting their imagination on the 'blood and thunder' literature which deals with the Wild West.[8]

'Brothers of the Mystic Tie'

The show's one-day visit to Kilmarnock prompted ceremonials among the town's Masonic fraternities. The Moira Union Royal Arch Chapter No. 249 convened a meeting at five in the afternoon at the Oddfellows' Hall in John Finnie Street, at which twenty-four men were exalted. Of these, four were local men, with no apparent connection to the show, but the remaining twenty were employees of Buffalo Bill Cody.

Following the Chapter meeting, the Lodge was adjourned and opened in the Degree of Mark Masonry. Four of the twenty Cody employees were given its secrets.

That same evening, at 10 p.m., a Knights Templar Encampment met at the Masonic Hall, also on John Finnie Street. A body of men from the show, who had attained the requisite qualifications, had this additional and higher Degree conferred upon them by M. E. C. Wiseman.

Of the twenty Wild West Show employees who became Chapter members that day, eighteen were entered as belonging to Lodge Renfrew County Kilwinning 370 in Paisley. The other two were affiliated to Lodges in the USA.

Previously, on the 4th of August, while the show was in Glasgow, seventeen of those eighteen and four other members of Buffalo Bill's company had been initiated into the first Degree of Freemasonry in Paisley. On the 19th August, by arrangement with Lodge 370, the twenty-one Entered Apprentices were passed to the second, Fellowcraft, Degree at the Lodge Ancient Dundee, No. 49. They were raised to the third and Sublime Degree of Master Masons by their joining Lodge, 370, on the 7th of September, when the show members returned to Paisley, three days before their visit to Kilmarnock.

The *Ardrossan & Saltcoats Herald* offered the broad assessment that the men concerned 'were chiefly Cowboys',[9] which was probably prompted by the fact that all or almost all of them were white Americans. However, in addition to such performers as cowboys, rough riders and at least one member of the Cowboy Band, there were others, engaged in diverse aspects of running the show. The most notable among them were: 'Johnnie' Baker (real name Lewis Henry Baker junior), 'Manager'; his brother William Dietrich Baker, a rough rider; Edward Ackerman Totten, the show's Orator; Joseph Esquivel, the chief of the cowboys, here designated as Riding Stock Superintendent; and John Francis Burke, the driver of the Deadwood Stage.

The initial contact with Lodge 370 Paisley had been made five years before, when a number of employees joined during Barnum & Bailey's 1899 tour. Dewitt Ballard, who travelled with both entourages, appears to have been a key figure. The twenty-one Wild West initiates in 1904 were introduced by two returning members.

So why would these Americans want to join a Masonic Lodge in Paisley? The inclusion of 'Kilwinning' in the title was probably part of the attraction since that not especially picturesque north Ayrshire town is at least noteworthy as the location of Lodge Mother Kilwinning No. 0, the home of Scottish Freemasonry. Lodge membership proved invaluable in establishing networks for men who were perpetually on the move and, since Colonel Cody himself was certificated as a Mason of the 'Ancient Accepted Scottish Rite', it was probably also a matter of keeping in with the gaffer.

The Human Pincushion and Other Wonders

The *Kilmarnock Herald*'s 'What The People Are Saying' column recorded another equally unusual, and largely unexplained, occurrence:

> That Barnum's 'Human Pincushion' found refuge in the Police Office the other night.
> That he can stick a pennyworth of pins into his body without drawing blood.
> That for doing this every night he received the handsome salary of £1 per week.[10]

It is known that 'Tomasso, the human pin-cushion' had toured with Barnum & Bailey five years earlier, in 1899, but how exactly he came to be in Kilmarnock in 1904 is unfortunately not recorded and nor is the immediate reason for him seeking asylum in the Police Office. The most obvious explanation is that he was now employed by Buffalo Bill in the sideshow, although his presence is not mentioned in the official programme and nor is it otherwise known.

The crowds were generally very well behaved and the Burgh Police came in for an honourable mention from the *Kilmarnock Herald* for the capable manner in which they dealt with the huge volumes of vehicular and pedestrian traffic without outside assistance.[11]

However, proceedings at Kilmarnock's Burgh Police Court on the morning of Monday the 12th of September were dominated by the cases of two pickpockets, who had come to town in order to prey on the crowds going to the show.

The afternoon performance had been attended by the Rev. James Armstrong, the popular and respected minister of the town's St Marnock's Church. At about four on Saturday afternoon, Mr Armstrong found himself part of a large crowd that was leaving the arena at the end of the afternoon performance. It occurred to him to take out his watch to look at the time but, on placing his hand in his pocket, he was somewhat disturbed to find another hand already there, as a pickpocket struggled to detach it from its chain. The minister seized hold of his assailant, who then struggled to get away. Fortunately, the police were on hand and the would-be thief was taken into custody. On Monday morning, the accused, John Graham, describing himself as a clerk, residing at Arthur Street, Greenock, pled guilty before Bailie Pearson, who imposed a sentence of sixty days' imprisonment.

The account of the incident given in the *Kilmarnock Herald* concluded: 'The accused was evidently delighted to get off with this sentence, for he smiled as if quite well pleased, and exclaimed: "Thank you, sir. God bless you!"'[12]

Thomas Shaw, a commission agent from Sheffield, also received sixty days' imprisonment at the same session of the Burgh Police Court for having stolen a purse containing thirty shillings from the pocket of an elderly man named John Morgan, who had just arrived at Kilmarnock Railway Station at about 10 p.m. with his daughter and had found himself caught up in the crowds. Shaw was apprehended by Sergeant Martin and Constable McPhee, who had been posted at the station in plain clothes and was taken from a railway carriage, just before the train left town. He was immediately identified by Mr Morgan and his daughter and the missing purse and its contents were found in the carriage.

William Cleland's farmhouse was situated near the top of Glasgow Road, on what is now Grougar Drive, and is likewise now a memory. However, its name lives on, as the northernmost district of Kilmarnock is still known as Wardneuk.

Ayr

The show arrived in the sleeping county town – 'Auld Ayr, wham ne'er a town surpasses, For honest men, and bonie lasses'[13] – bright and early on the morning of Sunday the 11th, just in time for the start of the town's carnival week. It was a lively time indeed for the seaside town, as Buffalo Bill's coming also coincided with the start of the week-long Western Meeting – all this and the Ayr races too!

In years past, the town's annual visitors, the showmen, had set up their stalls on the quayside but this time, to the accompaniment of a certain measure of nostalgic regret, they were directed to Newton Public Park, under reservation of a site for Buffalo Bill. Hence the assessment of the *Ayrshire Post*:

> And in any case Buffalo Bill was but an incident in a crowded week; a showman among showmen, a traveller among travellers; a giant in his own way among the pigmies but of the very same sort and variety as they.[14]

'YOUR FATHERS THE GHOSTS'

The company spent their day of rest on the Ayrshire coast, prior to performances on the following day, and the *Ayrshire Post*, with fitting Sabbatarian sensibilities, appealed to the local people to allow the visitors their leisure and to refrain from mobbing round their dwellings.[15] Predictably, this admonition appears to have taken no effect whatsoever for, all day long, the showground was crowded with visitors. The day was fine and the performers, for their part, took a wander around the seaside town and, at every turn, their strange faces and even stranger costumes met with much attention.

On the great day itself, thousands from along the Ayrshire coast took advantage of the Glasgow and South Western Railway Company's cheap day returns.

Ayr had stolen something of a march on Kilmarnock in the matter of public transport for the county town had tramcars and Kilmarnock hadn't. For folk going to the show, express tramcars thundered all the way from the Town Hall right to the foot of Northfield Park Road, at just a penny a fare.

The joyous news in the Prestwick High School logbook reads, under the entry dated Monday, 12th September 1904, 'Half holiday given today for Buffalo Bill's Wild West Show (at Ayr).'[16]

Sadly, the weather was once again a source of disappointment. Particularly during the evening performance, cold and stormy conditions prevailed. The stands were swept by gusts of wind that made the experience an uncomfortable one for many. This factor, together with the general feeling that the electric lighting was defective, probably goes some way to explaining why the *Ayrshire Post* reported that many people, having built up rather over-exalted expectations, went away at the end nursing a definite sense of disappointment.[17]

Notes

1 All 2 September 1904
2 *Ardrossan and Saltcoats Herald*, 16 September 1904
3 Ibid.
4 *Kilmarnock Standard*, 10 September 1904

5 Ibid.
6 *Kilmarnock Standard*, 3 September 1904
7 16 September 1904
8 Same date
9 Same date
10 Same date
11 Same date
12 Same date
13 Robert Burns, *The Complete Illustrated Poems, Songs and Ballads of Robert Burns*, p. 242
14 16 September 1904
15 9 September 1904
16 Quoted by Norman Dunsmore, in *Put It in the Log, Scottish Memories*, June 2001
17 16 September 1904

25

GALLOWAY, DUMFRIES AND THE GREAT TRAIN HOLD-UP

BUFFALO BILL
(from the painting by
Rosa Bonheur)

STRANRAER

On Tuesday the 13th of September, the show rolled into Stranraer, the seaport for Ireland at the south-west corner of Scotland. Of the old railway station little now remains, beyond a reminder of its former site in the name of Station Street.

Rephad Park, otherwise the Agricultural Show Field opposite Rephad House, on the north side of London Road, a short distance to the east of Stair Park, was rented from James Thorburn of Bellevilla Saw Mills for the sum of £25. The location is now occupied by sports fields. 'Rephad' derives from two Celtic words – reidh, 'a plain or level piece of ground', and fada, signifying 'long', and it is therefore perhaps not surprising that the tract's eventual destiny was to receive a visit from Buffalo Bill.

A billboard was erected on the corner of Edinburgh Road and Station Street, on a site provided by William McCormack, of Station Street, for £1. The George Hotel, then in the hands of W. T. Wheatley, provided accommodation and additional livery. The water supply was obtained for £1 from John Douglas, the Inspector of Water for the Burgh of Stranraer.

The *Wigtown Free Press* commented:

> Fully an hour and a half before the time at which the afternoon performance was advertised to start the people began to flock in their hundreds in the direction of Rephad Park, and as 2 o'clock approached the scene in London Road was one of extraordinary bustle and excitement.[1]

London Road was lined by 'vendors of beads and other articles', a 'swarthy astrologer, wearing student's cap and gown' and a number of 'maimed mendicants', who did a roaring trade.[2] This latter aspect was in all likelihood a universal experience for, as the *Dunfermline Journal* had observed: 'Distributed along the way to the field were also the usual concomitant of all great gatherings – the professional mendicant who, minus either upper or lower limbs, sought to excite pity and extort charity.'[3]

Similar scenes were also recorded at Stirling. In 1909, pensions were introduced for those aged seventy and over and national insurance followed in 1911. But, back in 1904, the welfare state still lay in the future and the poorhouse remained a routine feature on contemporary maps.

As people thronged into Stranraer from the surrounding Galloway countryside, crowded trains were augmented by a large contingent of arrivals on the midday steamer from 'the good old Ulster shore'.

Hartmann, a leading postcard publisher, issued a card depicting 'George Street, Stranraer' around this time. A poster on a gable wall, depicting a cowboy on a bucking bronco, was included in the scene. It would appear that its inclusion was more or less fortuitous – it just chanced to be there when the photograph was taken!

The Great Train Hold-up

Well, to be perfectly honest, there wasn't a bandit in sight but Buffalo Bill got his trains held up good and proper just the same. The first one didn't arrive at Dumfries until six thirty in the morning, two and three-quarter hours behind schedule.

The essential cause of the difficulty was the high viaduct of twenty arches, spanning the River Fleet between Dromore station and the Skerrow siding. Since the brick tops of the arches had become insecure, work was in progress to replace them with cement blocks. All vehicles were therefore required to make the approach to the viaduct very slowly. The first show train was travelling at just four miles per hour when it was approached by the watchman, who displayed his red lamp and insisted that the speed be reduced even further and its momentum was lost. Owing to the steep gradient after passing the bridge, combined with the train's great weight – a total of 430 tons – the engine was unable to get up speed again, despite being one of the most powerful in the service of the Caledonian company.[4]

James F. McEwan, contributing to *The True Line, Caledonian Railway Journal*, cited anecdotal evidence to conclude: 'The poor watchman got a severe ticking off from Stranraer headquarters.'[5]

Dumfries

The first train finally arrived at the Caledonian Railway Company goods station on Wednesday the 14th. It consisted of a complex of sidings, sheds and loading banks to the east of the Glasgow and South Western, which survives today as Dumfries's one remaining railway station. The process of unloading was effected in double quick time. One train was drawn into the siding adjoining the coal depots, while the others berthed on the siding flanked by the goods shed and loading bank. A large crowd of local people assembled at the gates of the yard and passengers were witnessed through open windows and partially drawn blinds, still sleeping and undisturbed by all the bustle and commotion.

Followed by large crowds, the entourage next headed for Cresswell Park, approaching by the long avenue to Cresswell House, and pitched camp in two adjoining fields. An unresolved difficulty relates to the precise point of entry. The OS map for 1900 shows the avenue running past a lodge house from the Brooms Road, while the *Dumfries & Galloway Courier & Herald* states that 'between seven o'clock and half-past nine there was an almost continuous procession to the Glebe Street entrance to Cresswell'.[6]

This site was obtained for £35 from Miss Jeanie Murphie, the proprietrix, who operated from a butcher and game dealer's shop at 4, English Street. The water supply was obtained from Nigel B. Watson, of the Dumfries and Maxwelltown Water Commissioners, charged at £1 5/-.

Cresswell House stood in fields to the south-east of the town centre. It has long since been demolished and a council housing estate was built on the fields c. 1931, bounded by Brooms Road, Eastfield Road, Rosevale Street, Aldermanhill Road and Glebe Street. Cresswell House and its immediate precincts lay within the square now formed by Barrie, Grierson, McKie and Martin Avenues. Cresswell Park had previously been the home of Queen of the South Wanderers, a Dumfries football club which had gone defunct. The precise site on which the Wanderers played from 1887 until 1892 was later occupied by Dumfries Fire Station.

Specials ran from Sanquar in the afternoon and from Moffat and Kircudbright in the evening, all calling at intermediate stations. There were also special returning trains for these towns and for Annan. The Glasgow and South Western and Caledonian Railway Companies issued return tickets to Dumfries for the price of a single, from all stations within a thirty-mile radius.

Buffalo Bill had received no official recognition of any kind during his Scottish sojourn and, particularly since Dumfries was the last town on the itinerary, it was deemed appropriate to raise a subscription for a presentation that might serve as a lasting reminder of his visit. A meeting for all interested parties was held in John Raphael's Coffee House Hotel at 110, High Street, on the evening of Tuesday the 30th of August.[7]

Sufficient funds were generated to commission a gold medal, of which a detailed description was given in the *Dumfries & Galloway Courier & Herald*:

> The medal, which is a really handsome article, is of beautiful design and artistic workmanship. It is emblazoned with laurel leaves, the crescent and shield, and is surrounded by a crown. On the shield in front are the Masonic emblems, the square and compass – the Colonel being a member of the brotherhood – and underneath inscribed along the crescent are the words – 'From friends in Bonnie Scotland.' On the shield on the other side is engraved the Scottish thistle – the emblem of the land of the brave and the free, and also the inscription – 'Presented at Dumfries on 14th Sept, 1904 to Colonel W.F. Cody.' The badge, which was supplied by Mr Theodore Thompson, jeweller, Dumfries, is enclosed in a handsome morocco leather case, lined with beautiful silk plush.[8]

The performances were graced by splendid harvest weather. In the afternoon, Colonel Cody, riding a spirited black charger and flanked as ever by riders proudly bearing the Union flag and the Stars and Stripes, took up his customary position at the head of the company and raised his hat to the audience amidst a tumult of deafening applause.

Provost Joseph Johnstone Glover, a painter and decorator to trade and Dumfries's energetic and popular Chief Magistrate, interrupted the accustomed order of proceedings by stepping forward from a reserved box, accompanied by the members of the presentation committee.

Provost Glover, who rendered sterling service to the people of Dumfries in this capacity for twelve years from 1896 until shortly before his untimely death in 1908, next demonstrated his universally acknowledged flair for oratory in a brief speech:

> Ladies and gentlemen – I have a very pleasant duty to discharge to-day. On behalf of a number of my fellow-citizens I have to present

Colonel Cody with a very handsome gold medal as a souvenir of his visit to the Queen of the South, and to express our warmest good wishes to a man who has done signal service to the honour and glory of his own country – (loud applause) – and, so far as I can learn, who enjoys the esteem and affection of his own people. (Applause.) It demonstrates that the scenes he has passed through have rather softened than hardened his heart, and I am proud to be the medium of asking his acceptance of this token of admiration, and of expressing our warmest good wishes towards him, with the hope that he may be spared to revisit the Queen of the South. (Loud and prolonged applause.)[9]

Colonel Cody, 'speaking with a voice which showed how much he appreciated the kindly feelings entertained towards him',[10] delivered a gracious speech of acceptance:

I would be devoid of all the finer feelings if I were not greatly touched and flattered by your kindness on an occasion such as this. This souvenir will be treasured for ever as a Cody heirloom. (Applause.) I am proud to be here in this ancient and historic city of Dumfries. When I was a younger man the greater part of my life was spent on the borderland between the Red Indian territory and civilization. (Applause.) Long ago, Dumfries stood as the border city between England and Scotland – in the days of the Bruce, when wars ravaged the country – and I feel that I have met the descendants of a people who, like mine, were in the thickest of the fray. (Applause.) As regards my visit to Scotland, it has been one of the greatest pleasures, and one of the happiest tours of my life. (Loud applause.) In your Robert Burns who made the whole world kin – (hear, hear) – is another link between civilization the world over, and between America and Scotland – (applause) – he was the world's poet, and America claims its share. (Loud applause.) Again, too, Dumfries, being our last place of visit in Scotland, will always be the first to be recalled to memory, and this souvenir will be a remembrance, not only to your descendants but to mine, and perhaps when we are no more they will meet, and, because of this souvenir, they may become the friends that I feel we have become. (Loud applause.) Gentlemen, I thank you. (Loud and continued cheering, during which the gallant Colonel and his congress of Rough Riders retired from the arena.)[11]

The medal now graces the collection of the Buffalo Bill Historical Center, where I had the singular pleasure and good fortune of finding it on public display during October 2002.

Colonel Cody afterwards reciprocated this kindness by inviting Provost Glover, Mrs Glover and the members of the presentation committee to a champagne banquet in his quarters. The committee consisted of: Harry Adams, bandmaster and chairman of the committee; W. G. Hay, hatter, secretary; J. Raphael, treasurer; J. J. Clark, auctioneer; Mr Maxwell, hairdresser; H. Tait, commercial traveller, from Edinburgh; Mr Francis, picture dealer; Mr Mill (or Mills), formerly of the White Swan Inn; John Glover, painter (probably Provost Glover's son of that name); John Currie, steward of the Working Men's Club; and Lawrence Hutchison, shop manager. They were afterwards accorded a guided tour of the encampment. Amidst an atmosphere of general good feeling, a further presentation was made, on this occasion by Mr Adams. Frank Small, Colonel Cody's press agent, was made the proud recipient of a handsome silk umbrella, bearing the inscription 'Mind Dumfries. F. Small, 1904.' Mr Small 'feelingly acknowledged' this kindly gesture.[12]

Dumfries was the home of Robert Burns from 1791 until his death in 1796, a fact of which today's visitor is appropriately reminded by the 'Welcome to Dumfries' signs on driving into town. Perhaps some members of the entourage chanced to admire the famous statue of the poet in the town's centre, unveiled in 1882. Buffalo Bill was certainly fully cognisant of the Burns connection, as evidenced in his speech and also by a further noteworthy incident.

The collection of the Buffalo Bill Museum and Grave at Golden, Colorado, includes a set of three photographs depicting a group of figures at the poet's mausoleum in the graveyard of Saint Michael's Church. The first of these bears an inscription:

Sioux Indian with Buffalo Bill Show, placing Wreath on Robert Burns Tomb Ayre Scotland 1904

It is not known when exactly this inscription was appended but 'Ayre' is certainly erroneous, on two separate counts. Firstly, 'Ayr' has no 'e' at the end when referring to the Scottish town and, more fundamentally, the locus is undoubtedly Dumfries. The other two photographs show the structure from different angles and distances. Two of those present are an unidentified Lakota man and a boy of the same race. Among the several white people, one man is instantly recognisable as Johnnie Baker. Others are probably local people, perhaps members of the presentation committee or else of the local Burns Club. (It can be conclusively stated, however, that Provost Glover was *not* among the persons present.)

No reference to the photographs can be found in any of the contemporary press reports. Some light is however shed by an article in the *Dumfries & Galloway Courier & Herald*, which reproduced the visitors' book to the Burns' House and Mausoleum for the previous fortnight. Among the names listed are Mr and Mrs Johnny Baker, USA, and Mr and Mrs M. B. Bailey, Chicago, USA. (Michael B. Bailey had charge of the show's electrical plant.) The article concludes: 'An interesting ceremony took place at the Mausoleum during the visit of Buffalo Bill's Wild West, one of the Indians placing a wreath of evergreen leaves upon the poet's tomb.'[13]

It is regrettable that the Indian is not identified by name. It is suggested that, on a balance of probabilities, the mausoleum visit was at some time between the afternoon and evening shows.

A photograph, broadly similar in composition, dating to the 25th of January, earlier in the same year, captures Provost Glover laying a wreath at the tomb. In paying its own tribute to the memory of Robert Burns, the Wild West party was simply accommodating itself to an existing local custom, by which, more than one hundred years later, the poet's birthday is still annually observed.

According to the *Dumfries & Galloway Saturday Standard*, several changes were made to the advertised programme for the evening performance.[14] It is unclear what these were since the only additional item specifically referred to was the fighting of a prairie fire – the inspiration for which may have arisen at Dundee!

A large crowd gathered once more at the Caledonian station to speed the visitors on their way. The 1904 tour's momentous Scottish leg was over. In a few hours more, the company would be over the border in Carlisle, where the daily routine was commenced once more.

Sadly, Provost Glover followed Burns to Saint Michael's churchyard less than four years after the visit of Buffalo Bill. He died on the 12th of April 1908, aged just fifty-five, suffering from cirrhosis of the kidney, with complications. His elaborate headstone is liberally inscribed with Masonic symbols, the compass and set square motif among them and this association no doubt helps to explain the use of such symbolism on Colonel Cody's medal.

Postcards

Surviving examples of contemporary postcards are an important part of the pictorial record of the 1904 tour.

Since the picture postcard fad came into vogue in the years immediately following the turn of the century, the Wild West show's tours had been accompanied by these colourful items wherever it went.

An August edition of the *People's Journal* carried the Postmaster General's report, issued three days earlier, which had highlighted the 35% increase in the number of picture postcards passing through the postal system in Scotland in the course of the previous year. This higher-than-average success was attributed to the outstanding scenic beauty of the country. The 'official' postcard was in danger of extinction and the Postmaster General was quoted as saying that the picture postcard 'shows a tendency to displace letters as well'.[15]

While some cards were produced locally by private manufacturers, the Wild West offered its own official range of picture postcards as colourful souvenirs of the show. William Dickson had packets of these mementoes on sale in his tobacconist and newsagent's shop at 41, English Street. They were also advertised in the official programme as available from the attendants at the shows.

Colonel Cody was presumably fully aware of their advertising potential, as visitors to the show sent cards to friends and relatives in areas where it was yet to appear.

One set of six colour postcards, copyrighted to Barnum & Bailey Ltd., depicted American Indians who had been prominent in the previous season, and were supplied in an envelope inscribed:

Souvenir of Buffalo Bill's Wild West: Six Handsome INDIAN POST CARDS Original Copyrighted Designs. Price Sixpence.

These designs were line drawings, based on real photographs. Two of the images also appeared as vignettes, used as illustrations for newspaper articles and advertisements. Five depicted individuals, one of them a young warrior on a galloping horse – probably one of the riders in the bareback race. The sixth depicts an Indian attack on the Deadwood Stage.

A similar card was based on a publicity poster, the mounted figure of Buffalo Bill as its central motif, with both horse and rider taking a bow, the Union flag and the Stars and Stripes in the background and the words 'BUFFALO BILL'S WILD WEST' in big letters.

There are also numerous examples of cards depicting the sideshow acts.

Some specimens of these postcards exist in used condition and bear handwritten inscriptions, personal messages coming to us across the decades, offering tantalising glimpses of a unique and quite unsurpassed event, now lost to the living memory, and permit the departed witnesses to speak for themselves. For instance:

This is one of the freaks we saw last night at the Show. We enjoyed it very much indeed but oh the crowd. (Postmarked Glasgow, but apparently referring to the final Edinburgh performance.)

Was at B.B.'s W.W. last night. Only paid 1/-. Really worth ten of them. Whom (*sic*) do you think was the best? Guess? The Cossacks. This is also Robert's opinion but does not mean that it's everybody's. By the papers B.B. does an awful lot though in reality he does nothing much. (Edinburgh)

Finishing up our holidays with a visit to Buffaloe's (*sic*) Bill's Show. Wish you could only see it. (Dundee)

The show is, I think, simply splendid. (Aberdeen)

Postscripts

On the 29th of September, the *Wigtown Free Press* carried a report headed 'Buffalo Bill's Show – A Sequel', relating to proceedings at a special sitting of the Stranraer Sheriff Court, on Friday the 23rd of September, ten days after the day of the shows, by which time the entourage was in Lancaster.

A sixteen-year-old youth named John Frazer was brought from Wigtown Prison to appear before the honorary Sheriff-Substitute Watson, charged that, on the day of the show, he had broken into the house of Michael Ravertie at the farm of Lower Barbeth. Once inside, he had forced open two locked drawers and stolen twelve shillings sevenpence-halfpenny in cash, as well as a ring. It was a deliberately planned crime although the efficiency of its execution appears to have left a great deal to be desired. The motive was clear – the boy was short of money and wanted to raise the price of admission to Buffalo Bill's show.

Frazer was apprehended on the day following the shows and he was held on remand for nine days. At the time of his arrest, he was found to have spent all of his ill-gotten gains during his visit to

Stranraer. He made no attempt to deny the charges. Sheriff-Substitute Watson, taking into account the prisoner's youth, limited his sentence to a further twenty days' incarceration.

Buffalo Bill's great show had come and gone and, despite the earnest hopes expressed by Provost Glover in Dumfries, the last of the great scouts would never more return.

After Dumfries, one month and seven days remained of the 1904 tour, directing the grand exhibition southward through Cumberland, Lancashire, Yorkshire, Cheshire and Staffordshire and culminating in Buffalo Bill's last-ever British engagement at Hanley on the 21st of October 1904. The next day, Cody and the greater part of his entourage set sail from Liverpool on board the *Campania*, arriving at New York on the 28th.

The annual general meeting of Barnum & Bailey Ltd was held on the 12th of December 1904 in the Winchester Hotel, London. George Oscar Starr chaired the meeting, in the absence of Mr Bailey. A healthy profit for the year was announced despite adverse trading conditions and a six per cent dividend was declared. It was specifically stated that:

> The Buffalo Bill Wild West Show had an admirable season in Great Britain so far as weather was concerned, not a single performance being lost, and had the patronage bestowed upon it throughout the tour been equal to that in Scotland and some of the cities in Wales, the result would have been much more satisfactory.[16]

Let us allow Charles Eldridge Griffin the final word: 'We put in two months in Scotland, and our business was immense throughout the Scottish tour.'[17]

Notes

1   15 September 1904
2   Ibid.
3   20 August 1904

4 The incident came in for some learned and highly technical discussion in issues 23, 25, and 28 of *The True Line, Caledonian Railway Journal*. The topic was opened by a letter from Mike Williams, in issue no. 23, in which he cited a reference to the incident in A. B. McLeod's work *The McIntosh Locomotives of the Caledonian Railway*.
5 No. 28, March 1990
6 14 September 1904
7 John Raphael proved a remarkably prominent local figure in Buffalo Bill's visit. His Coffee House Hotel also provided accommodation for members of Cody's staff, on top of which, John Raphael & Son, of 60 Queensberry Street, landed the billposting contract.
8 17 September 1904
9 *Dumfries & Galloway Courier & Herald, Dumfries & Galloway Saturday Standard*, both 17 September 1904
10 *Dumfries & Galloway Courier & Herald*, 17 September 1904
11 Ibid.
12 Ibid.
13 24 September 1904
14 17 September 1904
15 *People's Journal*, 20 August 1904
16 *The Scotsman*, 13 December 1904
17 *Four Years in Europe With Buffalo Bill*, p. 46

26

FALSE TRAILS

On the 3rd of July 1889, the *Greenock Telegraph and Clyde Shipping Gazette* reported on the annual Greenock Fair:

> Among the shows Clark's famous ghost illusion, stands out conspicuous, and there are also Buffalo Bill's Wild West Show, a theatre of varieties, a nautical exhibition which should prove attractive in a town like Greenock, and other exhibitions.

The same paper, on the 2nd of July 1890, reported that, amongst other attractions, the 'Buffalo Bill exhibition' was once again in town.

Whoever or whatever lay behind the enigma of these phantom Scottish venues, it is a matter of record that, on the first of these dates, Buffalo Bill's Wild West was in the midst of a lengthy season in Paris and, on the second, it was on tour in Germany.

The Scottish public at this time held a general awareness of Buffalo Bill's 1887–88 season in London but relatively few would actually have witnessed it. During this critical period leading up to the advent of the real Buffalo Bill in 1891, a particular opportunity for such calculated deceptions obviously existed.

Buff Bill

On the 1st of February 2007, the *Press and Journal* reported the sale of a watercolour painting by Forfar-born artist James Watterston Herald. The work of art, stated to depict 'legendary American frontiersman Buffalo Bill, otherwise known as William Cody, on stage at Arbroath in 1904', had confounded a pre-sale estimate of four to five thousand pounds, by realising £24,000 at Taylor's Auction Rooms in Montrose.

The painting clearly depicts a fairground barker, in a red gown and large black hat and sporting a goatee beard, together with other outlandish figures milling about on a walk-up stage of the type in common use around the turn of the twentieth century. A bass drum, standing alone, dominates the far side of the stage. A modest audience looks on, all of them standing in what has every appearance of a town square.

The central figure admittedly bears a superficial resemblance to Buffalo Bill but anyone who has followed my text thus far will also wonder how anyone with even an approximate understanding of the subject matter could possibly identify the painting as a representation of the Wild West show.

The *Press and Journal* published my misgivings in a follow-up article two days later. I was permitted to assert that I could relate nothing in the painting to anything I had encountered in my detailed study of Buffalo Bill's establishment. I also provisionally identified the true subject as an obscure small-time fairground operator of the period who went by the name of *Buff* Bill.

Referring to a series of paintings by Herald all capturing similar scenes, Jonathan Taylor, the auctioneer, was quoted as professing himself 'satisfied' with the watercolours' authenticity, adding that 'it's widely accepted they show Buffalo Bill'. He also adduced the (uncontested) fact that adverts for Buffalo Bill's show had appeared in the *Arbroath Herald* in 1904 — as if this were the winning argument.

The media circus which predictably ensued reached a dramatic climax on the 17th of February when the *Press and Journal* published comments received from Lynn Houze from the Buffalo Bill Historical Center, emphatically endorsing my position. Ms Houze very relevantly highlighted the glaring discrepancy between, on the one hand, the Wild West, of such staggering dimensions that it required ten acres of land and boasted 800 personnel and 500 horses, and, on the other, an unimpressive stage presentation. Notice, of course, that Buffalo Bill's show was a massive equestrian spectacular. Only a couple of horses appear in the painting sold by Mr Taylor – and those are in the audience!

The *Sunday Post* picked up on the story on the 25th of February. Mr Taylor, clearly close to exasperation, remained 'adamant' and was quoted in the following terms:

> This painting has always been deemed to be of Buffalo Bill. Anyone in the art world will say that it is him. Herald may well have used some artistic licence but it is Buffalo Bill, that is a fact of life. We are happy and the buyer is happy. Everyone is happy except Mr Cunningham.

A solid and long-standing consensus of the 'blind leading the blind' variety has indeed established itself in the art world. One of Herald's paintings was used as the accompanying illustration for the *When Annie Brought Her Gun to Arbroath* retrospective feature in 1951.[1]

Another painting in the series was sold by Lindsay Burns Auctioneers of Perth on the 23rd of September 1999, on which occasion the following comments were attributed to Mr Burns: 'Due to the American association it may well push the price up in excess of the estimate of £4,000 to £6,000.'[2] Mr Burns was right in his valuation at least for £12,000 was realised. My already well-formed doubts on the subject received a premature public airing some months later when remarks made in private correspondence were passed to the *Dundee Courier* by John Watt, of 'Heroes' fame.[3]

A similar transaction was conducted by Sotheby's, Gleneagles, on the 28th of August 2002.

I can only suggest that the art world now questions its assumptions and considers whether it has anything more compelling than Mr Taylor's personal fiat to offer by way of evidence. I would be extremely interested to learn which particular aspect of Buffalo Bill's show I am supposed to be looking at. The entrance to the sideshows and the concert after the show remain hypothetical possibilities but even these appear to be excluded by the available evidence. Can the location even be verified as Arbroath? And – I ask because I genuinely do not know – can it be substantiated that Herald ever claimed that his paintings were of Buffalo Bill?

Perhaps it is all a question of the immortal quote from the film, *The Man Who Shot Liberty Valance*: 'This is the West, Sir. When the legend becomes fact, print the legend.'

In point of fact, a rival showman, calling himself 'Buff Bill', was one of many lesser luminaries who made a living out of riding upon the coat-tails of Colonel Cody's success. On each occasion on which I have found a record of him, there has been evidence of confusion with his more famous contemporary.

An article appeared in the *Kilmarnock Standard* on the 5th of August 1893, relating to a lion which had escaped from its cage in the town, and it was indexed by Dick Institute staff under 'Buffalo Bill'.

In 1896, a lioness gave birth to three cubs at Hawick. As a further highlight of this visit, the show's general manager, William Pattison, donated a dozen python eggs to the local museum. The *Hawick Express*, on the 5th and 19th of June respectively (correctly) attributed these events to 'Buff Bill'. However, when the story was resurrected in 1946 for the *Hawick and the Borders 50 Years Ago* feature, 'Buff Bill' was mistakenly transcribed as 'Buffalo Bill', presumably having been taken for an abbreviation.[4] Almost undoubtedly, this is what Buff Bill intended his paying customers to think and people are still falling for it today.

It is clearly established that Buffalo Bill's Wild West did *not* visit Scotland at any time between 1892 and 1904. It is humbly submitted, therefore, that the misidentification of J. Watterston

Herald's paintings as depicting Buffalo Bill Cody is a further and spectacular instance of precisely the same error.

John A. Hammerton, incidentally, places 'Buff Bill's Wild West', billed as 'the same show that has caused such great excitement in London' and complete with lions, wolves and snakes, at Glasgow's Vinegar Hill showground in 1893.[5]

The waters are further clouded by the fact that several itinerant showmen apparently used the name 'Buff Bill'. It is believed that the central figure in the Herald paintings is in fact Peebles-born William Kayes but even this cannot be stated with certainty.

Crucially, at least two photos of Buff Bill's show survive. The key elements – the audience standing in front of a stage on which surreal figures perform, a frontman bearing a passing resemblance to Buffalo Bill and a bass drum to the edge of the stage – are unmistakably similar and almost beyond a shadow of doubt disclose the definitive solution to the mystery.

Grey Owl

One of the most audacious hoaxes of its genre was perpetrated by the writer and conservationist 'Grey Owl' who, between the wars, carved a niche for himself in the Canadian wilds and passed himself off for years as the intercultural product of an Apache mother and a Scottish father. Shortly after his death in 1938, it emerged that his real name was Archibald Stansfeld Belaney and he had been born in Hastings, Sussex, in 1888, where Buffalo Bill's show had greatly impressed him in 1903. He emigrated to Canada in 1906. He complemented his activities as a writer with lecture tours of Great Britain during the 1930s, appearing before captivated audiences in braids and full Native American costume. In one of his fraudulent press releases, he claimed that he had first come to England as a knife-throwing act with Buffalo Bill![6]

Chief Red Fox

The Memoirs of Chief Red Fox, published in 1971, purports to be a factual account of the life and times of an extremely elderly Sioux chief but was quickly discounted by responsible scholarship as bearing all the hallmarks of deliberate fabrication.[7]

Red Fox claims, somewhat implausibly, to have been born on the 11th of June 1870, implying that he was ninety-eight when the book was written, 101 when it was published and 106 when he died in 1976. Everyone he claimed to have met or been associated with and who might have contradicted the statements made in his narrative was therefore conveniently dead by the time that it was finally brought to the public attention. Significantly, he also claimed to be a first cousin of Crazy Horse.

Of most immediate relevance, Red Fox asserts that he was a performer and Indian interpreter with Buffalo Bill's show from 1893 until 1898 and again from 1903 to 1908. Ominously, no mention of him can be found anywhere in the show's surviving records.

The book contains what superficially appears to be a great deal of specific and detailed information about the show but there is little that can be reconciled with even the broad outlines of the historical record. His account of Cody's tour of Great Britain and Europe, which, in his version, took place between late 1904 and February 1908, is a litany of wild misstatements and his descriptions of the show are so odd that one has to question whether he even saw it, never mind appeared in it. The dates and venues which he advances appear in particular to be a work of the unaided imagination. He offers the following pronouncement:

> We traveled across the United States and Canada that summer and fall of 1904 and holed up in winter quarters in late October. Buffalo Bill was planning to take the show to Europe the next spring, and asked me to help in the preparations.[8]

The chief objection to this, of course, is that the summer and fall of 1904 was precisely the time when the Wild West toured Scotland!

I do not doubt that the man who called himself 'Chief Red Fox' lived a very full and interesting existence but his 'memoirs' are a transparent work of fiction. On sober analysis, Red Fox's magnum opus emerges as a contribution to an already substantial body of mythology and little else.

REACH FOR THE SKY – THE LEGACY OF 'COLONEL' SAMUEL FRANKLIN CODY

When the Wild West returned to Glasgow in 1904, many locals were no doubt baffled by a spectacular instance of apparent bi-location for, during the very week when Buffalo Bill was performing elsewhere on the south side, 'the Famous S. F. Cody'[9] was announced to perform at the Royal Princess's Theatre, in a blood-and-thunder Western drama entitled *The Klondyke Nugget*.

Stranger still, on the day after Buffalo Bill's visit to the town, the *Dunfermline Citizen & West of Fife Mail* reported an incident at the Bradford Exhibition, on Saturday the 6th, when a young engineer named Baker had 'made an ascent in one of Colonel Cody's war kites'.[10] At an altitude of 1,500 feet, the kite was seized and tossed violently around by the wind and almost wrecked. It was only with considerably difficulty that the attendants succeeded in lowering the craft, enabling its terrified passenger to alight on to the roof of a nearby house.

Samuel Franklin Cody, the subject of these reports, was born in Davenport, Iowa, in 1867. Recent scholarship reveals that his real name wasn't Cody at all but Cowdery.[11] He even carefully modelled his appearance upon that of his more famous namesake and 'Colonel' was a rank to which he held no formal entitlement.

After several seasons working the Western ranges, he and his first wife came to England as a trick-shooting double act in 1890. Buffalo Bill's legal representatives soon had the couple in their sights when, at a hearing before the Chancery Division of the High Court, on the 3rd of July 1891, an injunction was (unsuccessfully) sought to restrain an entertainment held at the Half Moon grounds, Putney. The show was entitled 'Capt. Cody, son of the great Buffalo Bill, and his charming sister, Miss Cody: with portions of the great drama, the "Wild West"'.[12]

For a number of years thereafter, S. F. Cody carried on his theatrical activities in tandem with forays into the nascent science of aviation. He experimented with huge man-carrying kites, which were seriously believed to have a potential military application. On the 18th of June 1902, crowds of passers-by stood on Trongate and Stockwell Street, Glasgow, gazing mystified into the skies, as he flew massive bat-like figures from the roof of the Metropole Theatre between performances during an engagement there.

It is unsurprising that S. F. Cody's exploits are routinely attributed to Buffalo Bill.[13] There was clearly a degree of confusion even at the time, as exemplified by the occasion on which he shattered his arm in North Shields, after it became entangled in the winching gear of one of his kites. The *Shields Daily News* reported the accident as having befallen 'Colonel W. F. Cody'.[14]

Samuel Franklin Cody's metamorphosis was complete in 1905, when he abandoned the theatre entirely on his appointment as a civilian employee of the British Army and devoted himself to a series of projects at the Balloon Factory, Farnborough, including the development of a Zeppelin-style airship – the *Nulli Secundus* – and finally bona fide aeroplanes.

On the 16th of October 1908, he became the first man to achieve powered flight in Great Britain, in – what made the distinction all the more remarkable – a machine of his own design and construction.

In 1909, he was naturalised as a British subject and in 1910 he appeared at an air show on Lanark Racecourse. Such events ushered in a new form of mass popular entertainment, fanatically followed by many and worthy successors all but eclipsing the Wild West shows of recent memory. In the summer of 1911, he participated in – and completed – the 'Circuit of Britain' race, landing at control points in Edinburgh, Stirling and Paisley. This event was sponsored by Lord Northcliffe, proprietor of the *Daily Mail*, with a prize of

£10,000 for the winner. The culmination of Cody's career came in 1912, when his entry took first prize in military trials held on Salisbury Plain.

The aviator's life was brought to an abrupt close, at the age of just forty-six, when he was killed in a flying accident near Farnborough on the 7th of August 1913. For reasons which remain largely a matter for conjecture, his aeroplane suddenly disintegrated in mid air, causing him and his army officer passenger to plunge to their doom several hundred feet below.

Four days later, he was buried with the fullest military honours, in the presence of thousands of mourners.

On the day following the accident, *The Scotsman* ran an obituary, referring to, inter alia, 'the misapprehension regarding his relationship to Buffalo Bill' and correctly stating that the two men were not related in any manner whatsoever.[15]

This lesson had clearly been forgotten thirty years later, when the same publication reported Pilot Officer Cecil Kingsborough Cody, who had recently been presented to the King and Queen, to be 'a relative of the famous Colonel William Cody – "Buffalo Bill" – who was killed in 1913'.[16]

During the opening phases of my research into the more farcical aspects of his early career, my first impression of Samuel Franklin Cody was of a crankish nonentity but, on subsequent proper enquiry, I came to appreciate his accomplishments in his principal field of excellence as something truly astounding. It is no exaggeration whatsoever to consider him the founding father of British aeronautics. In his time, Samuel Franklin Cody's fearless and peerless exploits, combined with a resolute and ever-ready theatrical flair, brought him more or less continuous press coverage, together with what at least approached mass adulation. In the final analysis, the most startling aspect of his life story is that he is not more widely and accurately remembered than he is today.

The supreme irony is that he is now recalled, when at all, as merely an obscure footnote in someone else's legend. The meticulously counterfeited connection to 'the other Cody' was his launching pad but in the longer run served only to cast the shadow of obscurity upon the personal fame of a man who, for his genius, material contribution to the direction of the historical process and sheer personal flamboyance, is richly entitled to the status of a first-rank figure in his own right.

BUFFALO BILL IS ALIVE AND WELL AND LIVING IN LEITH

In a letter dated the 12th of February 1990, David Gardner, responding to the 'Anyone Know a Navajo?' article, appearing in the *Evening Times* five days previously, upbraided the contributor for having failed to mention the showman's performances at the Govan Lyceum between 1910 and 1912.

> My mother, (now deceased) came to Govan in 1910, and I as a young boy can remember her recounting witnessing Buffalo Bill & his Indian on the stage of the Lyceum, with wigwams, dancing, smoking and cursing and swearing etc. shooting off their guns etc.[17]

Mr Gardner concluded with an arresting afterthought – 'PS I don't know of <u>any</u> real Indians in Govan.'

According to ninety-seven-year-old Jock Wilson, interviewed for 'Simon Pia's Diary' in *The Scotsman*, similar visits were received at The Gaiety theatre in the Kirkgate, Leith, c. 1910.[18] Buffalo Bill's sole Indian companion on that occasion earned the local nickname of 'Big Chief Willie Woodbine' from the fact that a cigarette was never absent from his mouth. For good measure, Jock assures us that the Western icon was a Hibernian supporter, who regularly attended Easter Road around this time.

In an appropriately erudite article, 'Scottish Studies Flourishing at Gilmorehill', in Glasgow University's *Avenue* magazine, Lesley Duncan cites Douglas Gifford, Professor of Scottish Literature, as referring to 'appearances by Buffalo Bill' as a featured attraction at Glasgow's 'Empire Exhibition' (apparently a reference to the Scottish

Exhibition of National History, Art and Industry held at Kelvingrove) in 1911.[19]

It seems fatuous to ask whether this could possibly have been the *real* Buffalo Bill and any enquiry into the true nature of the impostor is superfluous. In the course of his visits, Cody had created a sufficient reservoir of goodwill and affection in the hearts and minds of the Scottish public to be providing the basis of a generous living for at least one minor music hall turn – or, more probably, several. The phantom venues of Buffalo Bill were clearly still doing brisk business. 'Bjorn Again', the 'Australian Doors' et al. would do well to note that tribute acts – and identity theft – are nothing new!

After the conclusion of his epic British tours in the autumn of 1904, Buffalo Bill had continued to pursue an equally ambitious itinerary in Continental Europe during the 1905 and 1906 seasons. Thereafter, his activities as a showman were wholly confined to North America and a protracted decline began.

At one time, performers dishonestly passing themselves off as the blood relatives of Buffalo Bill were cropping up everywhere and his legal team had trained an ever-vigilant eye upon such encroachments but, once his glory days were behind him, the most shameful of impostures were allowed to pass with impunity. Events in Scotland were now particularly remote from the focus of the showman's business concerns.

As early as the Glasgow season of 1891–92, Cody had been proclaiming his imminent intention of retiring from the entertainment business but a series of overreaching financial investments ensured that this remained a perpetually unattainable goal. Long since reduced to a phantasmal parody of his former self, Buffalo Bill Cody's final professional engagement was fulfilled at Portsmouth, Virginia, on the 11th of November 1916. Less than two months later, on the 10th of January 1917, the frontier legend passed away in Denver, Colorado.

The 'Deadwood Stage' made a belated curtain call at the 1938 Empire Exhibition in Bellahouston Park, Glasgow, forming part of a procession made up of seventy performers from the Bertram Mills International Circus and headed by a band.

The *Govan Press* assumed that this was the actual vehicle that 'Buffalo Bill brought to Glasgow forty years ago',[20] which seems questionable in the extreme, but at least the echoes from a glorious memory of a generation or more before were resonating with the powerful appeal that, even twenty-one years after his death, Cody continued to exert upon the public imagination. The major themes and elements in the legend of Buffalo Bill were still in common currency. The older folks who remembered doubtless had their stories to tell but some at least of their youthful relatives must have paused to wonder whether any of it was true.

In 1945, if an advert appearing in *The Scotsman* was to be believed, Buffalo Bill was alive and well and appearing in the Pilrig Park, off Leith Walk, Edinburgh. To forestall any doubts that this was *the* Buffalo Bill, the advertisement specified:

>   ROYAL GEORGE VICTORY CIRCUS
>   WORLD FAMOUS
>   BUFFALO BILL
>   IN WILD WEST SHOW.
>   Thrills of the Prairie . . .[21]

By now, Buffalo Bill Cody was, like Santa Claus, a universally recognisable symbol, capable of manifesting himself at almost any time and in almost any place – even in several different locations simultaneously. The fact of his bodily survival or otherwise barely seemed to enter into the equation.

Viewed in hindsight, Buffalo Bill Cody's primary historical significance was not as an army scout and Indian fighter during a relatively transient period in his long career but that his, almost more than anyone's, was the directing spirit suffusing practically every strand of the frenetic activity occupying the temporal midway lying intermediately between the concluding phase of Columbia's epic westward sweep and modernity.

His was the finger on the trigger that discharged shock waves of creative imagination, surpassing even the professional mendacity of the showman in both extravagance and intensity.

Buffalo Bill's heyday came in a golden age, in which the overwhelming majority experienced the realities of armed conflict only vicariously and war was reduced to the status of a mere memory, re-enacted in pageant before a myriad dreams of a bright new tomorrow faded into shadows, merging as the universal nightmare of World War I.

As the world awaited the emergence of powerful new media of communication, Buffalo Bill laid the groundwork for one of the foremost genres of the mass entertainment industry that would shortly burst into prominence as the imaginative reflex of the industrial age.

Dance of the Ghosts

Buffalo Bill, his Indians and other performers, along with the countless thousands of individuals upon whose everyday existences they impacted, belong to an age that has only in recent decades slipped almost unnoticed across the twilight threshold of living consciousness. They inhabit that stark and rugged landscape known to us only as history, a dance of the ghosts, to whom we are shackled by the unbroken permanence of death and the passing time.

In the shadow of our dreams and imaginings, their spirits rise and waver formlessly before us and, by the historian's unholy work of general resurrection, the shroud of oblivion is lifted and we hear their voices still.

Notes

1 *Arbroath Herald,* 13 April 1951
2 *Dundee Courier,* 24 July 1999
3 21 February 2001
4 On the 5th and 12th of June 1946

5 In *Sketches From Glasgow*, p. 171
6 See, for example, *Cotswold Journal, 50 years ago*, 13 February 1986
7 An accompanying article, entitled 'I was with Buffalo Bill', by Chief Red Fox and Lenore Sherman, *Real West*, April 1968, vol. XI, pp 26–28, 64–65, appeared in the April 1968 edition of the *Real West* magazine, three years in advance of the book's publication.
8 p. 138
9 *Evening Times*, 1 August 1904
10 17 August 1904
11 Garry Jenkins, *'Colonel' Cody and the Flying Cathedral*, p. 8
12 *Evening Express*, 4 July 1891
13 See, for example, 'What a Silly Billy!' by Mike Amos, *The Northern Echo*, 17 February 2000
14 10 July 1902
15 8 August 1913
16 29 January 1943
17 Letter from David Gardner to Barrie Cox, 12 February 1990
18 30 June 2000
19 No. 29, January 2001, p. 12
20 3 September 1938
21 25 June 1945

BIBLIOGRAPHY

Abbreviations
BBHC – Buffalo Bill Historical Center, Cody, Wyoming
BBM&G – Buffalo Bill Museum & Grave, Golden, Colorado
SNBBA – Scottish National Buffalo Bill Archive

Books

Ambrose, Stephen E., *Crazy Horse and Custer* (London: Simon & Schuster UK Ltd, 2003)

Baird, George F., *Edinburgh Theatres, Cinemas and Circuses 1820–1963* (Edinburgh: George Baird, July 2000) (3 Volumes, Edinburgh Room YPN 2605)

Blackstone, Sarah J., *Buckskins, Bullets and Business – A History of Buffalo Bill's Wild West* (New York: Greenwood Press, 1986)

Blackstone, Sarah J., *The Business of Being Buffalo Bill – Selected Letters of William F. Cody, 1879–1917* (New York: Praeger, 1988)

Brash, Ronald W., *Glasgow in the Tramway Age* (London: Longman Group Ltd, 1971)

Bridger, Bobby, *Inventing the Wild West* (Austin: University of Texas Press, 2002)

Broomfield, G. A., *Pioneer of the Air, The Life and Times of Colonel S. F. Cody* (Aldershot: Gale and Polden Ltd, 1953)

Brown, Dee, *Bury My Heart at Wounded Knee* (London: Arrow Books Ltd, 1990)

Buchan, Jim, *Bygone Buchan* (Peterhead: Buchan Field Club, 1987)

Burke, John M., *"Buffalo Bill" from Prairie to Palace – An Authentic History of the Wild West* (Chicago and New York: Rand, McNally & Company, 1893)

Burns, Robert, *The Complete Illustrated Poems, Songs and Ballads of Robert Burns* (London: Lomond Books, 1990)

Cant, Malcolm, *Gorgie and Dalry* (Edinburgh: Malcolm Cant Publications, 1995)

Carter, Robert A., *Buffalo Bill Cody – The Man Behind the Legend* (New York: John Wiley & Sons Inc., 2000)

Daiches, David, *Glasgow* (London: Grafton Books, 1982)

Eunson, Eric, and Bill Early, *Old Dundee* (Ochiltree: Stenlake Publishing, 2002)

Fisher, Joe, *The Glasgow Encyclopaedia* (Edinburgh: Mainstream Publishing, 1994)

Foote, Stella, *Letters from "Buffalo Bill"* (El Segundo, Ca: Upton & Sons, 1990)

Foreman, Carol, *Did You Know?* (Glasgow: Glasgow City Libraries and Archives, 1996)

Gallop, Alan, *Buffalo Bill's British Wild West* (Stroud: Sutton Publishing Ltd, 2001)

Griffin, Charles Eldridge, *Four Years in Europe with Buffalo Bill* (Albia, Iowa: Stage Publishing Co., 1908)

Hammerton, J. A., *Sketches From Glasgow* (Glasgow and Edinburgh: John Menzies & Co., 1893)

Havighurst, Walter, *Annie Oakley of the Wild West* (London: Robert Hale Ltd, 1955)

Havighurst, Walter, *Buffalo Bill's Great Wild West Show*, (New York: Random House, 1957)

Horan, James David, *The Pinkertons: The Detective Dynasty That*

Made History (New York: Bonanza Books, a division of Crown Publishers, Inc., 1967)

Jack, Walter, *In Days Gone By: A Collection of Short Stories* (Lossiemouth: Lossie Printers, 1993)

Jenkins, Garry, *'Colonel' Cody and the Flying Cathedral* (London: Simon & Schuster Ltd, 1999)

King, Elspeth, *The People's Palace and Glasgow Green* (Edinburgh: Chambers Harrap Ltd, 1995)

Leonard, Gary, *Black Twin – Dark Lord of the Oglala* (London: Westerners Publications Ltd, 2005)

Lewis, Jon E., *The West – The Making of the American West* (Bristol: Siena, 1998)

McDonald, Charles, *Old Parkhead* (Ochiltree: Stenlake Publishing, 1996)

Mackay, James, *Allan Pinkerton – The Eye Who Never Slept* (Edinburgh: Mainstream Publishing, 1996)

McLaughlin, James, *My Friend the Indian* (Boston and New York: Houghton Mifflin Company, 1926)

Maddra, Sam, 'Glasgow's Ghost Shirt' (Glasgow: Glasgow Museums, 1999)

Maddra, Sam, *Hostiles? The Lakota Ghost Dance and Buffalo Bill's Wild West* (Norman: University of Oklahoma Press, 2006)

Makharadze, Irakli and Akaki Chkhaidze, *Wild West Georgians* (Tblisi: New Media, 2002)

Mortimer, Peter, *Camlachie – The Forgotten Village* (Glasgow: Garlyn Books, 1998)

Moses, L. G., *Wild West Shows and the Images of American Indians 1883–1933* (Albuquerque: University of New Mexico Press, 1996)

Murray, David, *Memories of the Old College of Glasgow* (Glasgow: Jackson Wylie and Co., 1927)

Neihardt, John G., *Black Elk Speaks* (Lincoln and London: University of Nebraska Press, 1995)

Noble, James, *Around the Coast with Buffalo Bill* (Beverley: Hutton Press, 1999)

Parker, Lew, *Odd People I Have Met* (publication details not given)

Posey, Jake, *Last of the Forty-Horse Drivers – The Autobiography of Jake Posey* (New York: Vantage Press Inc., 1959)

Red Fox, William, *The Memoirs of Chief Red Fox* (New York: McGraw-Hill, 1971)

Rennert, Jack, *100 Posters of Buffalo Bill's Wild West* (New York: Darien House, 1976)

Ricker, Eli S., *The Indian Interviews of Eli S. Ricker, 1903–1919 – Voices of the American West, Volume 1* (Lincoln and London: University of Nebraska Press, 2005)

Rosa, Joseph G. and Robin May, *Buffalo Bill & His Wild West – A Pictorial Biography*, (University Press of Kansas: Lawrence, 1989)

Rowand, David, *Pictorial History of Paisley* (Darvel: Alloway Publishing Ltd., 1993)

Russell, Don, *The Lives and Legends of Buffalo Bill* (Norman: University of Oklahoma Press, 1960)

Sayers, Isabelle S., *Annie Oakley and Buffalo Bill's Wild West* (London: Constable, 1981)

Smith, Robert, *Grampian Curiosities*, (Edinburgh: Birlinn Ltd, 2005)

Standing Bear, Luther, *Land of the Spotted Eagle* (Lincoln and London: University of Nebraska Press, 1978)

Standing Bear, Luther, *My People, the Sioux* (Lincoln and London: University of Nebraska Press, 1975)

Stewart, Alexander M., *Chronicles of the Stickleback Club* (Paisley: Alexander Gardner Ltd., 1930)

Stoker, Bram, *Dracula* (Barcelona: MDS Books, 2003)

Sutherland, Halliday, *A Time to Keep* (London: Geoffrey Bles, 1934 and 1936)

Stuart, Andrew, *Old Dennistoun* (Catrine: Stenlake Publishing, 1995)

Szasz, Ferenc Morton, *Scots in the North American West, 1790–1917* (Norman: University of Oklahoma Press, 2000)

Taylor, Colin F. (ed.), *The Native Americans – The Indigenous People of North America* (London: Salamander Books Ltd, 1991)

Twydell, Dave, *Rejected FC of Scotland, Vol. 2 Glasgow & District*, (Harefield: Yore Publications, 1993)

Urie, John, *Reminiscences of Eighty Years* (Paisley: Alexander Gardner, 1908)

Utley, Robert M., *The Last Days of the Sioux Nation* (New Haven and London: Yale University Press, 1963)

Utley, Robert M., *The Lance and the Shield – The Life and Times of Sitting Bull* (New York: Ballantine Books, 1993)

Vestal, Stanley, *Warpath – The True Story of the Fighting Sioux, Told in a Biography of Chief White Bull*, (Lincoln and London: University of Nebraska Press, 1984)

Warren, Louis S., *Buffalo Bill's America: William Cody and the Wild West Show* (New York: Alfred A. Knopf, 2005)

Wetmore, Helen Cody, *Buffalo Bill – Last of the Great Scouts – The Life Story of Colonel William F. Cody* (Lincoln and London: University of Nebraska Press, 1965)

Weybright, Victor and Henry Sell, *Buffalo Bill and the Wild West* (London: Hamish Hamilton, 1956)

Wojtowicz, James W., *The W. F. Cody Buffalo Bill Collector's Guide with Values* (Paducan, Kentucky: Collector Books, 1998)

Wright, Ronald, *Stolen Continents – The Indian Story* (London: Pimlico, 1992)

The Good News Bible (Glasgow: Harper Collins, 1976)

Unpublished Manuscripts

As Narrated by Short Bull (BBM&G, 1891)

Black, James and Hamish Whyte, *Dennistoun – A Brief History* (Mitchell Library, Glasgow, call number G941 435 DA, 1973)

Robeson, Robert, *Life Story of Montana Bill* (Bailey family collection)

Buffalo Bill's Wild West Publications

'Official Programme, 1891' (tour of England and Wales)
'Official Programme, 1891–92' (Glasgow winter season)
'Official Programme, 1893'
'Buffalo Bill's Wild West Route Book, Season of 1896'
'Buffalo Bill's Wild West Route Book, Season of 1902'

'Official Programme, 1903'
'Official Programme, 1904'
'The Rough Rider, 1904'
'Official Programme, 1908'
'Official Programme, 1910 (Buffalo Bill Bids You Good-Bye)'

Official Records
Census Records 1891
Thomas Edgar and family, 110, Duke Street, Glasgow – Volume 664/5, Enumeration District 46, Page 8, Schedule 43

Rev. David Lowe and family, 1, Whitehill Gardens, Glasgow – Volume 644/3, Enumeration District 35, Page 8, Schedule 41

John F. Sutherland and family, 2, Cathedral Square, Glasgow – Volume 664/5, Enumeration District 14, Page 27, Schedule 128

Mr and Mrs Joseph Shelley, Kent Street, Jarrow – Class RG 12; Piece 4165; Page 10; Folio 96 – Civil Parish Hedworth, Monckton, Jarrow; Town Jarrow; Eccles. Parish St Paul

Circus on Pit Heap – Class RG12; Piece 4166; Page 36; Folio 99 – Civil Parish Hedworth, Monckton, Jarrow; Town Jarrow; Parish St Peter

Census Records 1901
Mr and Mrs Joseph Shelley, 16, Caledonian Road, Jarrow – Class RG13; Piece 4743; Folio 114; Page 22. Civil Parish Jarrow Eccles. Parish Jarrow Grange

Postal Directories
Norwich City Directory, No 31, 1891, Otis Library, Norwich, Connecticut

Post Office Glasgow Directory, 1891–92

Edinburgh and Leith Postal Directory, 1904–05

Prison Registers
West Register House, Edinburgh: Duke Street Prison Register 1891–92 (HH21/32/119)

West Register House, Edinburgh: Barlinnie Prison Register 1891–92 (HH21/70/010)

Council Minutes
Glasgow Town Council Minutes, 1892
Minutes of Galashiels Burgh Council, 1904
Minutes of Dundee Town Council and of Dundee Water and Gas Commissioners 1903–1904
Royal Burgh of Stirling Council Minutes 1903–1904
Burgh of Saltcoats Town Council Minutes, September 1901–October 1904

Passenger Lists
City of Chester, arriving at New York from Liverpool, 21 July 1873, National Archives, Waltham, Massachusetts
Switzerland, sailing from Philadelphia to Antwerp, 1 April 1891, Crager Scrapbook, BBHC
Ancoria, arriving at New York from Glasgow, 3 February 1892; *Umbria*, arriving at New York from Liverpool, 8 February 1892; *State of California*, arriving at New York from Glasgow, 11 February 1892; *Teutonic*, arriving at New York from Liverpool, 9 March 1892; *Corean*, arriving at New York from Glasgow, 18 March 1892; *Mohawk*, arriving at New York from London, 27 October 1892; *New York*, arriving at New York from Southampton, 7 of July 1894; *Campania*, arriving at New York from Liverpool, 28 October 1904, all Ellis Island Museum – website http://www.ellisisland.org/
Lucania, arriving at Liverpool from New York, 16 April 1904; *Umbria*, arriving at Liverpool from New York, April 1904; *Campania*, sailing from Liverpool to New York, 22 October 1904, all National Archives, Kew, BT 26 and 27

Miscellaneous Official Records
Architectural plans for the conversion of the East End Exhibition Buildings, 1891, Dean of Guild file 1/1570, Mitchell Library, Glasgow

Glasgow Museums Accession Register, 1892, Glasgow Museums Resource Centre

Chief Constable's Standing Orders for Stirling Police Burgh, 1904, Stirling Police Museum

Largs Parish School Log, National Archives of Scotland

Certificates of Birth, Death and Marriage

Birth

William Kayes, 1856 768/00 22 Peebles
Henry Livingston, 1865 644/3 196 Bridgeton, Glasgow
David Livingstone, 1869 644/3 1626 Bridgeton, Glasgow
Halliday Gibson Sutherland, 1882 644/3 1124 Dennistoun, Glasgow
Hasonega Olympia Jefferson, 1892 644/8 183 Milton, Glasgow

Death

Paul Eagle Star, 1891, Registration District of Sheffield, sub-district of North Sheffield, No. 55
Gavin Ralston, 1894, 623 2 Biggar
John Fraser, 1904 282/1 317 St Peter, Dundee
Joseph Johnstone Glover, 1908 882 34 Troqueer
Michael Bow, 1911 644/4 195 Dennistoun, Glasgow
David Bow, 1958 644/2 126 Bridgeton, Glasgow

Marriage

William Kayes and Harriet Reader, 1882 685/3 34 Canongate, Edinburgh
Black Heart and Calls the Name, 1891, Parish of St Bride's, Stretford, No. 90
William Kayes and Elizabeth Prigg, 1899 647 299 Hamilton
John Shangrau and Lillie Orr, 1892 644/3 23 Dennistoun, Glasgow
David Bow and Martha Young, 1908 644/2 50 Camlachie, Glasgow
Robert Bailey Robeson and Agnes Wilson, 1897 644/7 776 Blythswood, Glasgow
Robert Bailey Robeson and Alice Harrold, 1919 644/3 889 Calton, Glasgow

Masonic Records
St Mark's Masonic Lodge, Archives and Special Collections, the Mitchell Library, Glasgow, TD 1449

Lodge Renfrew County Kilwinning, The Grand Lodge of Antient Free and Accepted Masons of Scotland, Lodge Minutes 1904; Grand Lodge of Scotland Museum and Library, Edinburgh, and Lodge Renfrew County Kilwinning No. 370

Moira Union Royal Arch Chapter No 249, Lodge Minutes 1904

Letters
BBHC
J. R. Brennan to Department of the Interior, United States Indian Service, 9 April 1904

Glasgow Museums Resource Centre
George C. Crager to James Paton, 17 December 1891

Whitehill Secondary School
Charging Crow to Kathleen Lowe, 1 November 1892

Steven P. Isaacson collection, Oregon
Letter from Col. Cody to Messrs Watson & Wilson, on 'Grand Hotel, Charing Cross' headed notepaper, 31 December (1891)

SNBBA
Thomas McAllister to Barry Dubber, 4 April 1990

Alex Sutherland to Barry Dubber, 2 May, year not given but probably 1990

Sheena Crook to Barry Dubber, 21 September 1990

Christine Carse to Barry Dubber, undated but circa 1990

Robert Porterfield to John Whelan, undated but circa 1990

David C. Gardner to Barrie Cox, 12 February 1990

National Archives and Records Administration, Kansas City, Box V.10, Record Group 75
Captain Charles G. Penney, Acting Indian Agent at Pine Ridge to Hon T. J. Morgan, 26 March 1891
Captain Charles G. Penney to Colonel W. F. Cody, 30 July, 4 August, 22 August (x 2), 4 September, all 1891
Colonel W. F. Cody to Captain Charles G. Penney, 30 September 1891
Colonel W. F. Cody to Acting Indian Agent at Pine Ridge, 1 December 1891, 16 January 1892
George C. Crager to Captain Charles G. Penney, Acting Indian Agent at Pine Ridge, 2 May 1891 and 11 January, 12 January, both 1892

National Archives and Records Administration, Washington D.C., Box 56, Record Group 94
Nate Salsbury to General Miles, 29 February 1892

Miscellaneous Primary Sources

Agreement with the Sioux of various tribes, 1882–83, reproduced at http://www.sioux.org/agreement_of_1883.html
SS *State of Nebraska* charter contract, 24 February 1887, Maritime Museum, Irvine
Glasgow Art Club, *Special Guest Books*, Volume One, (1891–1901), pp. 32 and 33
Pen and Pencil Club, Archives and Special Collections, the Mitchell Library, Minute Book No. 4, Record Reference 424588–94
John Shangrau's business card, Negative 12148, Wyoming State Archives
George C. Crager Scrapbook, BBHC
Annie Oakley Scrapbook, BBHC
William F. Cody Scrapbook, Colorado State Historical Society, Mss 126
Montana Bill's headed notepaper, Bailey family collection
Mexican Joe, handbill, John Johnson Collection, Bodleian Library, Oxford University

Standard billposting contract, 1893, Gérard Crouzier collection, France

Eleanor Hinman interviews, Nebraska State Historical Society, Lincoln

Advanceman's Log 1904, BBHC, MS VI

Notice posted by J. R. Brennan, Indian Agent, Pine Ridge, dated 4 April 1904, Document J. R. B. (L), BBHC

Newspapers

Aberdeen Daily Journal; Aberdeen Free Press; Airdrie Advertiser & Linlithgowshire Standard; Airdrie & Coatbridge Advertiser; Arbroath Guide; Arbroath Herald; Ardrossan and Saltcoats Herald; The Argus (Brighton); Army and Navy Gazette; Ayr Advertiser; Ayrshire Post; The Bailie; Banffshire Advertiser; Birmingham and Aston Chronicle; Birmingham Daily Mail; Birmingham Daily Post; Birmingham Weekly Mercury; (Aberdeen) Bon-Accord; Border Advertiser; Bridge of Allan Gazette and Visitor's List; Bristol Times and Mirror; Callander Advertiser; Coatbridge Express; Cotswold Journal; The Courier; Cowdenbeath & Kelty Echo; Croydon Advertiser; Daily Record and Mail; Dalry & Kilbirnie Herald; Dumbarton Herald; Dumfries & Galloway Courier & Herald; Dumfries and Galloway Saturday Standard; Dundee Advertiser; Dundee Courier; Dunfermline Citizen & West of Fife Mail; Dunfermline Express; Dunfermline Journal; Dunfermline Press; Eastern Bells; Edinburgh Evening Dispatch; Edinburgh Evening News; Elgin Courant; Elgin Courant and Courier; Evening Citizen; (Aberdeen) Evening Express; (Cardiff) Evening Express; (Edinburgh) Evening News; (Portsmouth) Evening News; (Sheffield) Evening Telegraph & Star; Evening Times; Falkirk Herald & Midland Counties Journal; Falkirk Mail; Fife Free Press; Fifeshire Advertiser; Forfar Herald & Kirriemuir Advertiser; Fraserburgh Advertiser; Fraserburgh Herald; Glasgow Evening News; Glasgow Herald; Glasgow Observer; Glasgow Weekly Mail; Govan Press; Greenock Herald; Greenock Telegraph and Clyde Shipping Gazette; Grimsby News; Hamilton Advertiser; Hamilton Herald & Lanarkshire Weekly News; Hawick Advertiser; Hawick Express; Hawick News; The Herald (Glasgow); The Herald (London); The Highland News; Huntly

Express; Inverness Courier and General Advertiser; Irvine Herald; Kilmarnock Herald; Kilmarnock Standard; Kilwinning Chronicle; Leeds Daily News; Leicester Advertiser; Leicester Daily Mercury; Lennox Herald; Liverpool Daily News; Liverpool Daily Post; Manchester Courier and Lancashire General Advertiser; Montrose, Arbroath and Brechin Review; Montrose Standard and Angus & Mearns Register; Motherwell Standard; Motherwell Times; New York Herald; New York Times; North British Daily Mail; The Northern Chronicle; Northern Ensign; Northern Scot; Northern Scot and Moray & Nairn Express; North-Western Daily Mail; Nottingham Daily Express; Nuncie Evening Press; Paisley Daily Express; Paisley & Renfrewshire Gazette; The People's Journal; The People's Journal for Inverness & Northern Counties; Perthshire Advertiser & Strathmore Journal; Perthshire Constitutional & Journal; Perthshire Courier; Peterhead Sentinel & Buchan Journal; Press and Journal; Quiz; Saturday Review; The Scotsman; Scottish Border Record; Scottish Leader; Scottish Sport; Scottish Referee; Sheffield and Rotherham Independent; Shields Daily News; Staffordshire Sentinel; Stevenston Gazette; Stirling Journal & Advertiser; Stirling Observer; Stirling Sentinel & County Advertiser; Sunday Post; Sussex Daily News; Wigtown Free Press

Retrospective Features

Amos, Mike, 'What a Silly Billy!', *The Northern Echo*, 17 February 2000

Baird FSA Scot, James, '"Sitting Bull's Folly" – Dennistoun Days of Noted Author', *Glasgow Eastern Standard*, 3 October 1936

Campbell, James, 'Day a legend of the West came to town', *The Press and Journal*, 20 March 1974

Duncan, Lesley, 'Scottish Studies Flourishing at Gilmorehill', *Avenue* (University of Glasgow), No. 29, January 2001

Dunsmore, Norman, 'Put It in the Log', *Scottish Memories*, June 2001

Felkin M.D., Robert W., 'The Emin Pasha Relief Expedition', *The Graphic*, 29 January 1887

Ferguson, Niall, 'The Wild West comes to Toon: Buffalo Bill Cody's Wild West Show's visits to Scotland', *Backtrack*, July 2005

House, Jack, 'Ask Jack', *Evening Times*, 21 January 1981
Jack, Walter, 'Buffalo Bill Brings the Wild West to Elgin', *Scottish Field*, September 1987
McDonald, Charles, 'Buffalo Bill Fae Vinegarhill!!', *Parkhead People's Press*, Issue 3, 1989
McLeish, Norman, 'Hawick Heritage – Buffallo (*sic*) Bill Comes To Town', *The Hawick Banner*, 2 November 1988
Maddra, Sam, 'Whose Ghost Dance Shirt Is This . . . Can Anyone Help?', *American Indian Review*, Twin Light Trail, Issue No. 15
Morrow, Bob, 'Cowboys, Indians and Glaswegians', *The Scots Magazine*, February 1997, New Series, Vol. 146, No. 2
Paul, Robert, 'Tracking Buffalo Bill all the way to Falkirk', *Falkirk Herald*, 12 September 2002
Chief Red Fox and Lenore Sherman, 'I was with Buffalo Bill', *Real West*, April 1968, vol. XI, pp. 26–28 and 64–65
Swanson, Brian, 'When the Wild West came to the East-End', *The Daily Express*, 14 July 1998
'Wagons Roll . . . it's off to Gorgie with Buffalo Bill', *Evening News*, 4 August 1984
'We 'Arra People! – Anyone know a Navajo?', *Evening Times*, 'Mr Glasgow', 7 February 1990
'Group Searches for lost Navajos in Scotland', *New Mexico Magazine*, November 1990
'How Buffalo Bill won the west (of Fife)', *Dunfermline Press and West of Fife Advertiser*, 25 February 2000
'My family ties with Buffalo Bill', *Sunday Express*, 2 June 2002
'Whitehill School Diamond Jubilee School Magazine'
'The True Line', *Caledonian Railway Journal*, issues 23, 25 and 28
Letter from Joseph Mitchell, *The Scots Magazine*, May 1997
Letter from Ronald Watt, 'Buffalo Bill and the Shetland Pony', *Dunfermline Press*, 3 March 2000

Films

Costner, Kevin, *Dances with Wolves* (TIG Productions and Orion Pictures Corporation, 1990)

Ford, John, *The Man Who Shot Liberty Valance* (Paramount Pictures, 1962)
The Hughes Brothers, *From Hell* (Twentieth Century Fox Film Corporation, 2001)

CD

Watt, John, *Heroes* (The Tradition Bearers, 2000)

INDEX

A

Aberdeen 170, 245–51, 288, 312
Aberfoyle 277
Airdrie 83, 150, 208
Alchise, the Indian boy shot 123
Alexander, Bailie 239,
American Civil War 4, 58, 184, 237
American Horse, Thomas 199
Anderson, David 237
Anderson, Thomas 126
Annie Get Your Gun 240
Apache 30, 120, 122, 123, 128, 129, 319
Arapaho 18, 197, 227
Arapaho, David 201
Arbroath 237–41, 316–19
Arbroath Police Court 238
Ardrossan 292
Arlberger Singers 59, 149, 150, 153
Armstrong, Rev. James 298
Ayr 299, 300, 309

B

Bailey, James A. 160, 161, 167, 313
Bailey, Michael. B. 160, 309
Baker, Johnnie xiii, 5, 11
Baker, William Dietrich 297
Balaclava 21, 136, 185
Ballard, Dewitt 297
Banff 170
Barlinnie Prison, Glasgow 32, 33, 97, 99–101, 105
Barnum, Phineas T. 160
Barnum & Bailey 160, 161–65, 167, 170, 171, 188, 190, 206, 207, 215, 222, 240, 243, 251, 271, 272, 276, 278, 281, 291, 297, 298, 311, 313
Bear Growls 73
Bear Lies Down 151
Beatrice, Mlle 191
Bedouin Arabs 183, 247
Belaney, Archibald Stansfeld 319
Bellgrove Station, Glasgow 1, 11, 82, 83

Bertram Mills International Circus 326
Big Foot 5, 8, 9
Bilds, R. W. 85
Birnie, Sheriff 99, 126
Black Elk 7, 119
Black Heart 19, 21, 22, 24, 108,
Blue Shield, Philip 172, 196, 266–68
Bo'ness 82, 224
Bone Necklace 19, 72
Bonheur, Rosa 4, 44, 302
Boone, Daniel 12
Booth, General William 279
Bostock and Wombwell's menagerie 130, 141
Bostock Arena and Jungle, Glasgow 130
Bostock, E. H. 130
Bostock, Frank 130
Both Sides White 151
Bow, David 'Nav' 73–75
Bowman, Fred 142
Boyd and Lovely 191
Boys' House of Refuge, Glasgow 43, 78
Braes, Andrew Gardiner 4
Brandon Club, Glasgow 142
Brave 151
Brennan, a cowboy 188
Brennan, J. R. 195, 196
Bridgeton, Glasgow 12, 67, 116, 117
Brings the White 151
Brodie, Sir Thomas Dawson 220
Broncho Bill's Wild West and Circus 265
Broomielaw, Glasgow 35, 160
Bruce, Dr 126
Buchanhaven 252
Buff Bill 316–19
Buffalo Bill Historical Center vi, 268, 308, 317
Buffalo Bill Museum and Grave vi, 308
Bull Bear, David *see* Arapaho, David
Bull Stands Behind 22
Buntline, Ned 3
Burke, John Francis 297
Burke, John M. 4, 5, 8, 10, 15, 21, 24, 25, 52, 53, 95, 96, 136, 145, 147, 159, 167, 194, 212, 254, 265, 267, 292
Burmese elephants 136, 137, 139–41, 148
Burns, Robert 165, 307–310
Butler, Frank E. 85

C

Calder's Cinematograph 280
Caledonian Railway Company 29, 81, 82, 86, 171, 207, 211, 216, 224, 231, 232, 234, 241, 242, 271, 275, 278, 304, 305, 310
Calls the Name 21, 93, 99, 107, 108, 113
Calton Hill, Edinburgh 87
Cambuslang Football Club 49
Campania 198, 199, 201, 313
Canfield, Sherman 24
Carnegie, Andrew 226
Carter the Cowboy Cyclist *see* Davis, George C.
Celtic Football Club 46, 47, 49, 95, 96
Celtic Park, Glasgow 95, 96, 117, 142, 143
Central Station Hotel, Glasgow 86
Central Station, Glasgow 29, 36, 42, 104
Chalmers, James 43
Charging Crow 117, 159
Charging Hawk 199
Charging Thunder 78, 96–107, 123, 125, 126, 148, 151

INDEX

Cheyenne 3, 19, 109, 138, 197, 227
Cheyenne River reservation 5, 112
Clarence and Avondale, Duke of 133
Clark and Gold 191
Clayholes showground, Paisley 159, 282, 283
Clemmons, Viola 24, 37, 73, 150
Clifford, H. M. 18, 56
Close To Home 134
Clyde, River 4, 11, 27, 30, 33, 35, 46, 161, 205, 209, 288, 290
Clyde Football Club 49
Clyndon, Carl 123
Coatbridge 83, 149, 150, 208, 209
Cody, Samuel Franklin 321–24
Comes Last 196
Comes Out Holy 134
Coming Grunt 25
Cook, Rev. Charles 110
Corean 149, 151
Cossacks 135, 157, 158, 183, 184, 188, 189, 207, 222, 236, 237, 246, 253, 263, 264, 295, 312
County Buildings, Glasgow 99, 126
Court of Session, Edinburgh 87, 210
Cowboy Band 12, 17, 18, 21, 55, 65, 88, 135, 137, 142, 145, 149, 150, 177, 182, 190, 296
Cowdenbeath 227
Cox, Barrie 74
Coyle, Mike 234
Crager, Cuno 21, 134
Crager, George C. xiii, 10, 11, 15, 16, 21, 22, 25, 43, 86, 93, 97, 98, 100, 102, 103, 106, 108, 110–15, 134, 146, 147, 151, 201
Crager, Julia 21, 134
Crager, Minna 21, 134
Crager, Winifred, 134

Cranston, Lord Provost Sir Robert 219
Crawford, Arthur William 91, 92
Crazy Horse 5, 109, 320
Crockett, Davy 12
Crook, General 194
Crouch's Waxworks, Glasgow 162
Cuban patriots 166, 183
Custer, George Armstrong 17, 61–64, 110, 114, 187, 199, 200
Custer's Last Stand *see* Little Bighorn, Battle of
Cut-off 19, 56
Cuts, Ellis 196

D

Dalmuir Iron Works 42
Daly, Claude Lorraine xiii, 11, 18, 59, 60
Daulton, H. J. 4
Davidson, Detective Inspector Alexander 225
Davis, George C. 189, 190, 210, 212, 232, 233, 261, 286
Davis, Ovinius 222
Deadwood 64, 65, 152
Deadwood Stage 1, 18, 65, 189, 219, 223, 249, 297, 311, 325
Delphi, Miss 163
Dennistoun Village, Glasgow xii
Dennistoun, Glasgow xii, xiii, 2, 32, 55, 69, 76, 80, 81, 88, 116, 141, 155, 159
Dennistoun, Sir Alexander 32
Diamond, Charles 191
Diamond, Professor and Madame 180
Donnelly, W. A. 48
Duke Street Prison, Glasgow 33, 98–100, 104
Dumbarton 164, 209, 210
Dumbarton Football Club 49, 95, 96

Dumfries 82, 162, 304–11, 313
Dundee 82, 150, 170, 194, 200, 231–36, 239, 250, 296, 310, 312
Dunfermline 165, 226–28, 303, 321

E
Eagle Star, Paul 21–23, 72, 256
East End Exhibition Buildings, Glasgow xiii, 2, 35, 78, 100, 108, 111, 213
East End Industrial Exhibition xiii, 35, 41, 78, 100, 103, 108
Eastern Division Police Station and Court, Glasgow 91, 92, 96–99
Edgar, Annie 67–69
Edgar, Thomas and family 67–69
Edinburgh 37, 53, 82, 83, 87, 120, 122, 162, 164, 170, 176, 200, 214, 216–22, 224, 225, 280, 308, 312, 322, 326
Edinburgh and Glasgow Railway Company 29
Edinburgh Castle 87
Edinburgh Police Bazaar 42, 51
Edison, Thomas Alva 159, 160
Elgin 262–65, 269, 289
Elliot, James 172
Ellis Island 127, 128
Emin Pasha 136
Empire Exhibition 1938 325
English Lancers 21, 140, 157, 183, 185
Esquivel, Antonio 19
Esquivel, Joseph 183, 297
Etruria 161, 170
Etruria 170

F
Falkirk 164, 191, 201, 220, 222–25
Falkirk Burgh Police Court 223

Fife Pottery 229
Flynn, John A. 142
Forfar 241, 242, 316
Forfar Athletic Football Club 242
Fort Robinson, Nebraska 109,
Fort Sheridan, Illinois 8, 14, 15, 151
Forth and Clyde Railway 165, 278
Fortune, Dr 36
Frame, Flint 88
Fraser, John 232
Fraserburgh 180, 253, 254–57, 259, 266
Frazer, John 312, 313
Freemasons 142, 149, 296, 297, 306, 310
Furniss, Harry 84

G
Galashiels 162, 192, 193, 203, 209
Galloway, John 86
George Square, Glasgow 28, 52, 86
Georgians 158, 236, 237
Ghost Dog, Willie 202
Gilbert & Sullivan 150
Gingras, Andrew 108
Giovanni, G. A. 180
Glasgow v, xi–xiii, 1, 2, 4, 6, 9, 11, 12, 24, 26, 27–35 and generally chapters 4–12; 157, 158, 159, 160, 161, 162, 164, 166, 170, 209, 211–16, 218, 219, 220, 234, 296, 312, 317, 321, 322, 324, 325, 326
Glasgow and Greenock Railway 29
Glasgow and South Western Railway Company 29, 81, 300, 304, 305
Glasgow Art Club 52, 53
Glasgow Athenaeum Dramatic Club 46
Glover, Joseph Johnstone 306, 308, 309, 310, 313

INDEX

Glover, William 42, 44, 105
Good Crow 196
Good Crow, Abraham 196
Gordon Castle 264
Gordon, General 62
Gorgie, Edinburgh 216–19
Govan 33, 149, 324, 325, 326
Graham, John 298
Grand Hotel, Charing Cross, Glasgow 86–88
Great American Company 36–39, 152–54
Great North of Scotland Railway Company 171, 249, 250, 251, 258, 264
Great Western Road, Glasgow 32, 127
Greatest Show on Earth, The *see* Barnum & Bailey
Greenock 29, 30, 83, 149, 286, 287–90, 298, 315
Grey Owl *see* Belaney, Archibald Stansfeld
Griffin, Charles Eldridge 173, 174, 180, 209, 210, 219, 266, 268, 273, 313
Guilford, William 88
Guthrie, Arthur 293, 294
Guthrie, Bailie 48, 91
Guthrie, Oklahoma 153, 154

H

Hamad, Ameen Abou 247
Hamilton 83, 149, 205, 206
Hamilton, Robert 206
Hart, Joseph H. 149, 150
Hartley, Elizabeth Grame 209
Has No Horses 151
Hawick 171–76, 177, 209, 318
Healy, Tim 95
Heart of Midlothian Football Club 216

Hengler's Circus, Glasgow 133
Her Blanket 151
Herald, James Watterston 316–19
Hibernian Football Club 324
High Bear 25, 73
High Court of Justiciary 102, 239
High Eagle 151
Highland Railway Company 264
Holy Bird 151
Horn Point Eagle 72
Horseman, Arthur 272
House, Jack 70
Houze, Lynn vi, 317
Huntly 198, 258–62
Hutchinson, Fred B. 234

I

Ibrox Park, Glasgow 32, 46–49, 50, 95, 143
Ice 134
Ice, Mrs 134
Imperial Japanese Cavalry 183, 207, 212, 236, 261, 263, 294, 295
Indian Territory 58, 154
Inverness 82, 170, 264, 265–69
Iron Tail 172, 196, 199, 200, 212, 218, 233, 266–68
Iron Tail, Philip 196
Irving, Broncho Bill 138
Irving, Henry 24, 46, 53, 83, 84, 87

J

Jack the Ripper 133
Jack, Walter 262
James, Henry 142
Jefferson, Charles 122, 123, 125, 129
Jefferson, Hasonega Olympia 125, 129
Jefferson, Nana 122, 125, 129

John O'Groats 172, 266–68
Johnstone 213

K
Kadjaia, David 237
Kansas Pacific Railroad 2
Kayes, William 319
Keen, Jule 58, 142
Keith, John 257
Keith, Merrill 257
Kelty 227
Kelvingrove Museum, Glasgow 102, 110–15
Khusania 163
Kicking Bear xi, xiii, 5–8, 14–16, 19, 22, 25, 56, 71, 86, 114, 116, 117, 129, 137–39, 145–48, 151, 154, 155, 194
Kills Ahead 196
Kills Crow 151
Kills Deer 201
Kilmarnock 164, 294–300, 318
Kilmarnock Burgh Police Court 298
Kinnaird Head 256
Kinnaird Head Preserve Works 256
Kirkcaldy 228, 229
Knights Templar 296
Knows His Voice 151

L
Ladyhill, Elgin 264
Lalla and Lallo, Siamese twins 163
Lanark Racecourse 322
Land's End, Cornwall 201, 266, 268
Langan, William 91, 142, 149
Largs 292
Lauder, Harry 227, 243, 294
Leachkin, Inverness 266
Leith 120, 127, 324
Leith Industrial School 120

Leonard, John A. 142
Lincoln 20, 71
Lindsay Burns, Auctioneers 317
Lindsay, Thomas v, 212
Link, Barney 142
Linthouse Football Club 49
Little Bear 256, 266
Little Bighorn, Battle of 5, 38, 61–64, 114, 186, 187, 199, 200, 202, 246
Livingstone, David 12
Livingston, Harry 12
Lochgelly United Football Club 229
Lochwinnoch 284
Lockhart, Sam 136, 139
Lodge Renfrew County Kilwinning 370 296
Lodge St Mark, Glasgow 142
Lone Bear, Samuel 199, 200, 213, 218, 266
Lone Bull 19, 22, 24, 25, 86, 113, 115
Long Wolf 19, 72
Long Wolf, Mrs 71
Lossie Green, Elgin 265
Lossie, River 263
Lowe, Kathleen 117, 159
Lowe, Rev. David 116, 117
Lowe, Theodore D. 116, 117
Lozano, Roman 238, 239
Lucania 198, 199, 202

M
Mackaye, Steele 3
Maddra, Sam 112, 114, 116, 146, 257
Makharadze, 'Prince' Ivan 157
Makharadze, Pavle 222
Mavisbank Quay, Glasgow 148
McIntyre, 'Tuck' 142
McLaughlin, James (Standing Rock) 8
McLaughlin, James (Greenock) 287

McMillan, Matthew 206, 207, 287, 288
McNairn, John 172, 176
Medicine Horse 151
Merrick, John 162
Mexican Joe see Shelley, Joseph
Mexicans xii, 11, 17, 18, 19, 53, 134, 135, 137, 158, 183, 184, 186, 188, 238, 264
Midland Railway 1
Miles, General Nelson A. 8, 110
Miller, Edward 243
Miller, James 130
Minor, a cowboy 188
Mitchell Library, Glasgow 44, 60, 155
Mitchell, Jim 18, 19
Mohawk 158
Moira Union Royal Arch Chapter No. 249 297
Molendinar burn, Glasgow 27, 34, 35
Montana Bill see Robeson, Robert
Montrose 164, 165, 242, 243, 316
Montrose Police Court 243
Moody, Dwight Lyman 92
Mooney, James 96
Moore, Aaron 180
Morgan, John 299
Morgan, Matt 42
Motherwell 205–209, 288
Motherwell Football Club 96
Muir, Lord Provost John 54, 89, 90
Murphy, Christopher C. 214, 215, 223
Murphy, Thomas V. 142
Murray, Private William 175
Murvanidze, Aleksandre 222
Mustard, James Bell 238–40

N

Navajo 74, 114, 324
Nelson, Jim 19, 71
Nelson, John 19, 71
New City Road, Glasgow 122, 123, 129, 141
New Mexico 74, 129, 167
New Olympia, Glasgow 119–30
Ninian, Bennett B. 142
No Neck 9, 10, 19, 21, 24, 25, 71, 86, 93, 99, 100, 108, 134, 138, 143
No Neck, Johnny Burke 9, 10, 24, 25, 71, 88, 134, 159, 285
Noordlund 15
North British Railway Company 32, 81, 192, 216, 217, 222, 224, 243
Northern Football Club 46, 49
Northern Police Court, Glasgow 123
Notman, William 3
Nouma Hawa, 'Princess' 180

O

O'Donnel, Patrick 203
O'Neill, Charles 214
Oakley, Annie xiii, 11, 17, 32, 43, 44, 54, 57, 58, 67, 85, 86, 90, 91, 103, 149, 159, 166, 167, 181, 186, 241
Oakley, Georgina 32
Octavia, Mlle 180
One Star 151
Oragvelidze, Simon 222
Orkney 269, 270
Oropeza, Vincente 183
Orr, Lillie 107, 159

P

Paisley 3, 122, 149, 159, 164, 176, 282–86, 287, 296, 297, 322
Palace of Holyroodhouse, Edinburgh 87
Parker, Lewis 35, 56, 59, 66, 136, 137, 138, 144
Paton, James 110, 111

Pattison, William 318
Pawnee 10, 153, 154, 227
Pearson, Bailie 298
People's Palace, Glasgow xiii, 35
Perth 82, 256, 271–75, 317
Peterhead 251–54
Pierre, the Elastic-Skin Man 123
Pilgrim Fathers 42, 57
Pine Ridge reservation 5, 8–10, 15, 71, 72, 73, 109, 110, 114, 117, 134, 148, 151, 195, 196, 197, 198, 199, 201
Pinkerton National Detective Agency 214, 215
Pinkerton, Allan 215
Plenty Blankets 151
Plenty Wolves 18, 71, 72, 113
Poe, Edgar Allan 293
Ponca, Minnie *see* White, Minnie
Pony Express 2, 17, 38, 65, 185
Prestwick 300
Primrose, Sir John Ure 48
Pulls Him Out 151

Q

Queen of the South Wanderers Football Club 305
Queen's Park Football Club 46–49, 142
Queen's Park Police Court, Glasgow 214

R

Rain in the Face 114, 128
Raith Rovers Football Club 229
Ralston, Gavin 105
Randall's Station Hotel, Wick 267
Rangers Football Club 32, 46–49, 96, 142, 237
Raphael, John 305, 308, 314
Red Cloud 108

Red Fox, 'Chief' William 320, 321
Regency Homes xii–xiv
Reid, Dr W. L. 60
Renshaw, W. R. 161
Revenge 16, 116, 151
Richardson, F. R. 99
Robertson, Patrick 83
Robeson, Robert 127, 128
Rocky Bear 138
Rocky Mountain Jack 126
Roosevelt's Rough Riders 166, 183
Royal Antediluvian Order of Buffaloes 268
Royal George Victory Circus 326
Royal Hotel, Edinburgh 164, 220
Royal Princess's Theatre, Glasgow 36, 39, 50, 152, 321
Run Along Side Of 72
Running Wolf *see* Jefferson, Charles
Rushville, Nebraska 8, 73, 195, 196
Russell, Bailie 223
Russell, Don 135, 139, 144, 173, 174, 226
Russell, Jack 15
Russo-Japanese War 236, 280

S

Sacketto, Professor 180, 181
Salsbury, Nate 4, 16, 24, 41, 71, 145, 146, 160, 169
Saltcoats 172, 268, 288, 291–94
Salvation Army 252, 279
Sankey, Ira David 92
Sano 183
Sawder, a cowboy 188
Scatter 16, 72, 79
Schensley, William Ferdinand 142
Schulis *see* Shulis
Scottish Society for the Prevention of Cruelty to Animals 174

INDEX

Scottish Zoo, Glasgow 130
Shangrau, John xiii, 10, 15, 21, 78, 86, 100, 102, 107–10, 159, 201
Shangrau, Jule and family 108
Shangrau, Louis 15
Shanton, Harry 21
Shaw, Thomas 299
Sheible, Albert E. 142
Shelley, Joseph 37, 119–31
Shetland 269
Shetland pony 226
Shooting Star 151
Short Bear, Mrs 202
Short Bear, Laura 202
Short Bull xiii, 5–8, 15–17, 19, 24, 25, 71, 86, 93, 109, 112, 113, 115–17, 138, 147, 148, 151, 154
Short Man 151
Shulis 136–39, 141
Simmons, James 238, 239
Sitting Bull 3, 8, 11, 22, 62, 87, 101, 112–114, 147, 199, 220, 221, 257
Sitting Bull, William 199
Skye 269, 270
Slessor, Dr 256
Smith, George, the Gypsy King 123, 127
Smithhills showground, Paisley 122
Smoke 108
Snyder, Edward Yoder 142
Snyder, William Okey 142
Sorrel Horse 72
Sotheby's, Gleneagles 317
Spens, Sheriff 84, 107
Spotted Weasel 201
Spotted Weasel, Mrs 201
Spotted Weasel, Washington 202
St Enoch's Station, Glasgow 29, 34, 43, 82
St Mark's Masonic Lodge, Glasgow 142

Standing Bear (Brulé) 72
Standing Bear (Oglala) 151
Standing Bear (Ponca) 194, 204
Standing Bear, Alexandra 125, 169
Standing Bear, Laura 169
Standing Bear, Luther 169, 195, 196
Standing Rock reservation 8, 87
Stands Up 134
Stands, James 196
Stanley, Henry Morton 136, 144
Starr, George Oscar 313
State of California 134
State of Nebraska 3
Stephenson, Professor 246
Stewart, Alexander 48
Stirling 165, 242, 275–81, 303, 322
Stobs 172, 175
Stoker, Bram 46, 83, 84
Stone of Destiny 241
Stranraer 69, 302–304, 312, 313
Stranraer Sheriff Court 312, 313
Surrounded 23
Sutherland, Dr John Francis 103, 104
Sutherland, Halliday 85, 101–105
Sutherland, Major 191
Sweeney, William 12, 81, 142, 182
Switzerland 15, 16, 71, 73

T

Taggart, Bailie 214
Tall Holy 195, 196
Taylor, Jonathan 316–18
Terry, General 63
Theatre Royal, Glasgow 4, 51, 133
Third Lanarkshire Rifle Volunteers Football Club 211
Thomas Walker Hospital, Fraserburgh 256

Tobago Street Police Station and Court, Glasgow *see* Eastern Division Police Station and Court
Tomasso, the Human Pincushion 297, 298
Tomnahurich, Inverness 266
Toole, J. L. 87
Tora 183
Totten, Edward Ackerman 182, 297
Trossachs 105
Tune, Thomas 288
Two Bonnets 134
Two Elk 199
Two Strikes 10

U
Umbria 133, 198, 200
United States 10th Colored Cavalry 183, 185
United States 6th Cavalry 183, 189
United States 7th Cavalry 8, 10, 62, 109
United States 5th Artillery 184
United States Life Saving Service 184, 232

V
Vale of Leven 210
Valentine, J., and Son 235, 236
Victoria, Queen 33, 133, 157, 249
Vinegar Hill showground, Glasgow 74–79, 319

W
Walker's Cinematographic Company 243, 280
Walters, Captain Fred 180
Warner, Frank 122, 127, 129

Waterloo Rooms, Glasgow 149
Watson and Wilson, photographers, Glasgow 86, 91
Watson, Charles, P. 36
Watson, Sheriff-Substitute 312, 313
Watt, Gordon 226
Watt, John 226, 227, 317
Watt, Ronald 226
Wells, Charles 212, 267
Wetmore, Helen Cody 44–46
Whalen, Charles 191
Whirlwind Horse 199
White Cloud 25, 134
White Horse 151
White Spot *see* White, John
White, John 122, 129
White, Minnie 122, 129
Whitefield Football Club 49
Whitehill Public School, Glasgow xii, xiv, 44, 54, 55, 69, 70, 116, 117
Whiteside, Major 109
Wick 266–68
Wine Tower, Fraserburgh 256
Winnebago 127, 128
Wisconsin 127, 161
Wooden Face 134
World's Fair 135, 158, 159, 160, 214
Wounded Knee 8, 9, 10, 22, 62, 71, 109, 112, 113, 154, 159
Wounded with Many Arrows 151
Wovoka 6, 16, 96

Y
Yankton Charlie *see* Plenty Wolves
Yellow Hand 17, 62, 143
Yellow Horse *see* Nelson, Jim

Z
Zulus 136, 144